Care Proceedings
and Learning Disabled Parents

A Handbook for Family Lawyers

# Care Proceedings and Learning Disabled Parents

# A Handbook for Family Lawyers

**Abigail Bond**

With a Foreword by Mrs Justice Pauffley

**Family Law**

Published by Family Law
a publishing imprint of
Jordan Publishing Limited
21 St Thomas Street
Bristol BS1 6JS

Whilst the publishers and the author have taken every care in preparing the material included in this work, any statements made as to the legal or other implications of particular transactions are made in good faith purely for general guidance and cannot be regarded as a substitute for professional advice. Consequently, no liability can be accepted for loss or expense incurred as a result of relying in particular circumstances on statements made in this work.

© Jordan Publishing Ltd 2011

All rights reserved. No part of this publication may be reproduced, stored in a retrieval system, or transmitted in any way or by any means, including photocopying or recording, without the written permission of the copyright holder, application for which should be addressed to the publisher.

Crown Copyright material is reproduced with kind permission of the Controller of Her Majesty's Stationery Office.

British Library Cataloguing-in-Publication Data

A catalogue record for this book is available from the British Library.

ISBN 978 1 84661 178 0

Typeset by Letterpart Ltd, Reigate, Surrey

Printed in Great Britain by CPI Antony Rowe, Chippenham and Eastbourne

# FOREWORD

One of my most satisfying days as a family law advocate was when a local authority compromised its public law application in favour of my client, a 'learning disabled' mother. She and her son, who also had a learning disability, were to be supported and assisted by a carefully devised collection of measures, from a variety of agencies. I cannot now recall the form of order which resulted from the hearing. But what I shall never forget, as she left court, was the mother's radiant smile. It signified joy, unadulterated joy, that she and her son could look forward to life together. It was one of those memorable occasions when it felt that something priceless had been achieved and it was a privilege for me personally to have been involved.

Public law applications where the parents (or one of them) have a learning disability pose particular difficulties for judges, lawyers and the many professionals who work within the family justice system. Cases in this special branch of the law require and deserve sensitive handling on the basis of sound knowledge. They are amongst the most demanding for any family practitioner or judge.

This erudite, concise and immensely readable handbook, therefore, is a most welcome addition to the legal literature. Abigail Bond's lucid writing style enables the reader rapidly to develop an understanding of the development of policy relating to learning disabled parents. She provides a useful overview of the sociological, psychological and psychiatric research as well as an invaluable guide to procedure, including the appointment of a litigation friend.

Perhaps of most immediate interest to busy practitioners will be the chapter which analyses the various factors of importance relating to the threshold criteria and also the welfare principle. Special considerations most certainly apply where parents have a learning disability; and this book specifies how and why. The text is supported by a handy digest of the case-law and a full appendix including the 2007 Good Practice Guidelines.

In short, this succinct volume contains all of the required materials to litigate in this complex field. It is highly recommended reading for children law specialists.

Anna Pauffley
*March 2011*

# CONTENTS

| | |
|---|---|
| Foreword | v |
| Table of Cases | xi |
| Table of Statutes | xv |
| Table of Statutory Instruments | xvii |
| Table of Conventions | xix |
| List of Abbreviations | xxi |

**Chapter 1**
**Learning Disabled Parenting: An Introduction** 1
Learning disabilities or learning difficulties? 4
Defining learning disabilities 6
Discrimination against learning disabled parents and their children? 9
The research studies 11
Outline 14

**Chapter 2**
**Supporting Learning Disabled Parenting: The Policy and the Law** 17
Introduction 17
*Valuing People*, 2001 18
Supported parenting within adult social care 20
Supported parenting under the Children Act 1989 and the Children Act 2004 23
Good Practice Guidance on Working with Parents with a Learning Disability, Department of Health, 2007 26
   Promoting children's best interests 27
   Ensuring equitable treatment for parents with learning disabilities 28
Wales 31
Summary 32

**Chapter 3**
**Learning Disabled Parenting: The Research Base** 35
Introduction 35
The risk factors 37
   Choice of partner 37
   Parental childhood history 38
   Maternal stress 39
   Mental health 39
   Developmental delay 41

Implications 43
Appendix: Summary of research studies 46

**Chapter 4**
**The Threshold Test: Establishing 'Significant Harm' and the Need for Parenting Support** 55
Introduction 55
The threshold criteria 56
Objectivity or subjectivity? 60
Support under community care legislation 62
Unmet needs 69
Summary 70

**Chapter 5**
**Protected Parties and the Litigation Friend** 73
The common-law test of capacity 75
Capacity under the Mental Capacity Act 2005 77
Procedure 79
The appointment of the litigation friend 83
The role of the litigation friend 86
Adoption proceedings 88
Summary 88

**Chapter 6**
**Learning Disability: Case Summaries** 89
Discrimination and social engineering 89
    Re L (A Child) (Care: Threshold Criteria) [2006] EWCA Civ 1282, [2007] 1 FLR 2050 89
    Re S (A Child) [2008] EWCA Civ 1284 91
    Re D (A Child) (Care Order: Evidence) [2010] EWCA Civ 1000 92
    Re G and A (Care Order: Freeing Order: Parents with a Learning Disability) [2006] NI Fam 8 94
    A Local Authority v A [2010] EWHC 1549 96
The role of the Official Solicitor 98
    RP v Nottingham City Council [2008] EWCA Civ 462 98
    Re M (A Child) (Assessment: Official Solicitor) [2009] EWCA Civ 315 100
    Re B (Children) [2010] EWCA Civ 363 101
Procedural fairness and appropriate assessments 102
    Kutzner v Germany [2003] 1 FCR 249, (2002) 35 EHRR 25 102
    M v Neath Port Talbot CBC [2010] EWCA Civ 821 103
Litigation capacity 104
    Re W (Children) (Care Proceedings: Litigation Capacity) [2008] EWHC 1188 (Fam) 104

## Appendix 1
**National Health Service and Community Care Act 1990, ss 46, 47**    107

## Appendix 2
**Mental Capacity Act 2005, ss 1–3**    111

## Appendix 3
**Mental Capacity Act 2005 Code of Practice**    113
1. What is the Mental Capacity Act 2005?    113
2. What are the statutory principles and how should they be applied?    116
3. How should people be helped to make their own decisions?    123
4. How does the Act define a person's capacity to make a decision and how should capacity be assessed?    131

## Appendix 4
**Practice Note 2 April 2001**    153

## Appendix 5
**President's Joint Guidance December 2010**    157

## Appendix 6
**Letter to Independent Expert**    159
1. The parties and their representatives    159
2. Background    160
3. Legal framework    160
4. These proceedings    162
5. Documents    164
6. Contact with others    164
7. Factual issues and your report    165
8. Your instructions    165
9. Expert's duties    166
10. Timescale    166
11. Your fees    167

## Appendix 7
**Family Procedure Rules 2010, Pt 15**    169

## Appendix 8
**Learning Disability: Definitions and Contexts**    175
Introduction    175
Scope of the Current Guidelines    177

### Part 1: Defining 'Learning Disability'
1.1 Assessment of impairment of intellectual functioning    179
1.2 Impairment of adaptive/social functioning    180
1.3 Age of onset    182

1.4  Systems of sub-classification                                            183

**Part 2: Associated Contexts**
2.1  Mental health legislation                                                188
2.2  Criminal justice system                                                  193
2.3  Local government/benefits legislation                                    194
2.4  Miscellaneous                                                            195
2.5  'Gate-keeping' – access to services                                      195

**Part 3: Appendices**
Appendix I: Clinical definitions                                              196
Appendix II: Sample of related definitions                                    198
Appendix III: Confidence limits in psychometric assessment                    202
References                                                                    204
Afterword                                                                     206

**Appendix 9**
**Good Practice Guidance on Working with Parents with a Learning Disability**  **209**
Introduction and Executive Summary                                            209
Section 1   Key features of good practice                                     211
Section 2   Good practice where safeguarding procedures are necessary         229
Section 3   Good practice in commissioning                                    238
Appendix A   What do we know about the needs and circumstances of
             parents with learning disabilities?                              244
Appendix B   Policy and legislative framework                                 258
Appendix C   Resources                                                        269
Appendix D   Bibliography                                                     272

**Index**                                                                     **277**

# TABLE OF CASES

**References are to paragraph numbers.**

| | |
|---|---:|
| A (Mental Patient: Sterilisation), Re [2000] 1 FLR 549, [2000] 1 FCR 193, [2000] Lloyd's Rep Med 87, (2000) 53 BMLR 66, [2000] Fam Law 242, (2000) 97(2) LSG 30, (2000) *The Times*, March 15 | 6.5, A.3 |
| A Local Authority v A [2010] EWHC 1549 (Fam), [2011] 1 FLR 26, (2010) 13 CCL Rep 536, [2010] Fam Law 928 | 5.23, 5.25, 6.5 |
| AK (Adult Patient) (Medical Treatment: Consent), Re [2001] 1 FLR 129, [2001] 2 FCR 35, (2001) 58 BMLR 151, [2000] Fam Law 885 | A.3 |
| Associated Provincial Picture Houses Ltd v Wednesbury Corp [1948] 1 KB 223, [1947] 2 All ER 680, (1947) 63 TLR 623, (1948) 112 JP 55, 45 LGR 635, [1948] LJR 190, (1947) 177 LT 641, (1948) 92 SJ 26 | 4.27 |
| B (A Child) (Residence: Second Appeal), Re [2009] UKSC 5, [2009] 1 WLR 2496, [2010] 1 All ER 223, [2010] 1 FLR 551, [2010] 1 FCR 1, [2010] Fam Law 143, (2009) 106(46) LSG 18, (2009) *The Times*, November 23 | 4.10 |
| B (A Minor) (Wardship: Sterilisation), Re [1988] AC 199, [1987] 2 WLR 1213, [1987] 2 All ER 206, [1987] 2 FLR 314, 86 LGR 417, [1987] Fam Law 419, (1987) 151 LG Rev 650, (1987) 84 LSG 1410, (1987) 137 NLJ 432, (1987) 131 SJ 625 | 6.5 |
| B (Children), Re [2010] EWCA Civ 363 | 5.27, 6.8 |
| Banks v Goodfellow (Costs) (1870-71) LR 11 Eq 472 | A.3 |
| Beaney (Deceased), Re [1978] 1 WLR 770, [1978] 2 All ER 595, (1977) 121 SJ 832 | A.3 |
| Boughton v Knight (1872-75) LR 3 P & D 64 | A.3 |
| D (A Child) (Care Order: Evidence), Re [2010] EWCA Civ 1000, [2011] 1 FLR 447, [2010] 3 FCR 244, [2010] Fam Law 1166 | 4.12, 6.3, 6.4 |
| D (A Minor) (Wardship: Sterilisation), Re [1976] Fam 185, [1976] 2 WLR 279, [1976] 1 All ER 326, (1975) 119 SJ 696 | 6.5 |
| Dundee City Council v McL [2005] Scot SC 34 | 3.2, 3.3 |
| F (Sterilisation: Mental Patient), Re [1989] 2 FLR 376, *sub nom* F v West Berkshire HA [1990] 2 AC 1, [1989] 2 WLR 1025, [1989] 2 All ER 545, (1989) 139 NLJ 789, (1989) 133 SJ 785 | 6.5 |
| Folks v Faizey [2006] EWCA Civ 381, [2006] CP Rep 30, [2006] MHLR 239, (2006) *The Independent*, April 12 | 5.2, 5.20 |
| G and A (Care Order: Freeing Order: Parents with a Learning Disability), Re [2006] NI Fam 8 | 4.14, 6.4 |
| H (Child) (Care Proceedings: Intervener), Re [2000] 1 FLR 775, [2000] 2 FCR 53, [2000] Fam Law 464, (2000) 164 JPN 606, (2000) *The Times*, March 22 | A.4 |
| H (Local Authority) v KJ [2007] EWHC 2798 (Fam) | 4.13, 4.14 |

H (Minors) (Sexual Abuse: Standard of Proof), Re [1996] AC 563, [1996] 2
   WLR 8, [1996] 1 All ER 1, [1996] 1 FLR 80, [1996] 1 FCR 509,
   [1996] Fam Law 74, (1995) 145 NLJ 1887, (1996) 140 SJLB 24,
   (1995) *The Times*, December 15, (1996) *The Independent*, January 17  4.6
Humberside CC v B [1993] 1 FLR 257, [1993] Fam Law 61  4.6

K, Re [2005] EWHC 2956 (Fam), [2007] 1 FLR 399, [2007] Fam Law 298,
   [2007] Fam Law 211  4.11, 4.12
KD (A Minor) (Ward: Termination of Access), Re [1988] AC 806, [1988] 2
   WLR 398, [1988] 1 All ER 577, [1988] 2 FLR 139, [1988] FCR 657,
   [1988] Fam Law 288, (1988) 152 JPN 558, (1988) 132 SJ 301, (1988)
   *The Times*, February 19, (1988) *The Independent*, February 19  4.8
Kenward v Adams (1975) *The Times*, November 29  A.3
Kutzner v Germany (46544/99) [2003] 1 FCR 249, (2002) 35 EHRR 25  1.5, 4.15, 6.9

L (Children) (Care Proceedings: Threshold Criteria), Re [2006] EWCA Civ
   1282, [2007] 1 FLR 1068, [2006] 3 FCR 301, [2007] Fam Law 17,
   (2006) 103(36) LSG 36, (2006) 150 SJLB 1152; L (A Child) (Care:
   Threshold Criteria), Re [2007] 1 FLR 2050, [2007] Fam Law 297  1.2, 1.4, 3.13, 4.6, 4.8,
   4.9, 6.1, 6.5
LC (Medical Treatment: Sterilisation), Re [1997] 2 FLR 258, [1997] Fam
   Law 604  6.5
Local Authority X v M [2007] EWHC 2003 (Fam), [2009] 1 FLR 443, [2008]
   3 FCR 788, (2008) 11 CCL Rep 119, [2008] Fam Law 213  5.5, 5.26

M (A Child) (Assessment: Official Solicitor), Re [2009] EWCA Civ 315,
   [2009] 2 FLR 950, [2009] Fam Law 570  5.27, 6.7, 6.8
M (Wardship: Sterilisation), Re [1988] 2 FLR 497, [1988] Fam Law 434  6.5
M v Neath Port Talbot CBC [2010] EWCA Civ 821, [2010] 2 FLR 1827,
   [2010] 3 FCR 100, [2010] Fam Law 1051  1.9, 6.10
MA (Children) (Care Threshold), Re [2009] EWCA Civ 853, [2010] 1 FLR
   431, [2010] 1 FCR 456, [2009] Fam Law 1026  4.7, 4.10
Masterman-Lister v Jewell; Masterman-Lister v Brutton & Co [2002]
   EWCA Civ 1889, [2003] 1 WLR 1511, [2003] 3 All ER 162, [2003] CP
   Rep 29, (2004) 7 CCL Rep 5, [2003] PIQR P20, [2003] Lloyd's Rep
   Med 244, (2003) 73 BMLR 1, [2003] MHLR 166, [2003] WTLR 259,
   (2003) 147 SJLB 60, (2002) *The Times*, December 28  5.2, 5.6–5.8, 5.14, 5.20, A.3
MB (Caesarean Section), Re [1997] 2 FLR 426, [1997] 2 FCR 541, [1997] 8
   Med LR 217, (1997) 38 BMLR 175, [1997] Fam Law 542, (1997) 147
   NLJ 600, (1997) *The Times*, April 18, (1997) *The Independent*, April 8  A.3

P (A Minor) (Wardship: Sterilisation), Re [1989] 1 FLR 182, [1989] Fam
   Law 102  6.5

R (on the application of Chavda) v Harrow LBC [2007] EWHC 3064
   (Admin), [2008] BLGR 657, (2008) 11 CCL Rep 187, [2008] LS Law
   Medical 127, (2008) 100 BMLR 27, [2008] ACD 31, (2008) 105(3)
   LSG 29  4.27
R (on the application of Dudley) v East Sussex CC [2003] EWHC 1093
   (Admin), [2003] ACD 86  4.28
R (on the application of F) v Wirral BC [2009] EWHC 1626 (Admin),
   [2009] BLGR 905, (2009) 12 CCL Rep 452  4.28
R (on the application of G) v Barnet LBC [2003] UKHL 57, [2004] 2 AC
   208, [2003] 3 WLR 1194, [2004] 1 All ER 97, [2004] 1 FLR 454,
   [2003] 3 FCR 419, [2004] HRLR 4, [2004] HLR 10, [2003] BLGR
   569, (2003) 6 CCL Rep 500, [2004] Fam Law 21, (2003) 100(45) LSG
   29, [2003] NPC 123, (2003) *The Times*, October 24, (2003) *The
   Independent*, October 29  2.10

| | |
|---|---|
| R (on the application of Ireneschild) v Lambeth LBC [2007] EWCA Civ 234, [2007] HLR 34, [2007] BLGR 619, (2007) 10 CCL Rep 243, [2007] NPC 31 | 4.28 |
| R (on the application of JL (A Child)) v Islington LBC [2009] EWHC 458 (Admin), [2009] 2 FLR 515, (2009) 12 CCL Rep 322, [2009] Fam Law 485 | 4.25 |
| R (on the application of McDonald) v Kensington and Chelsea RLBC [2010] EWCA Civ 1109, (2010) 13 CCL Rep 664 | 4.25 |
| R (on the application of S) v Plymouth City Council [2002] EWCA Civ 388, [2002] 1 WLR 2583, [2002] 1 FLR 1177, [2002] BLGR 565, (2002) 5 CCL Rep 560, (2002) 5 CCL Rep 251, [2002] MHLR 118, [2002] Fam Law 513, (2002) 146 SJLB 115, (2002) *The Daily Telegraph*, May 13 | A.3 |
| R (on the application of Spink) v Wandsworth LBC [2005] EWCA Civ 302, [2005] 1 WLR 2884, [2005] 2 All ER 954, [2005] 1 FCR 608, [2005] HLR 41, [2005] BLGR 561, (2005) 8 CCL Rep 272, (2005) 84 BMLR 169, (2005) 102(19) LSG 34, (2005) 149 SJLB 390, (2005) *The Times*, April 5, (2005) *The Independent*, March 23 | 4.25 |
| R v Collins ex parte Ian Stewart Brady [2000] Lloyd's Rep Med 355, (2001) 58 BMLR 173, [2000] MHLR 17 | A.3 |
| R v Gloucestershire CC ex parte Barry [1997] AC 584, [1997] 2 WLR 459, [1997] 2 All ER 1, (1997) 9 Admin LR 209, (1997-98) 1 CCL Rep 40, (1997) 36 BMLR 92, [1997] COD 304, (1997) 94(14) LSG 25, (1997) 147 NLJ 453, (1997) 141 SJLB 91, (1997) *The Times*, March 21, (1997) *The Independent*, April 9 | 4.25, 4.26 |
| R v Islington LBC ex parte Rixon [1997] ELR 66, (1997-98) 1 CCL Rep 119, (1996) 32 BMLR 136, (1996) *The Times*, April 17 | 2.7, 4.24 |
| Royal Bank of Scotland v Etridge (No 2) [2001] UKHL 44, [2002] 2 AC 773, [2001] 3 WLR 1021, [2001] 4 All ER 449, [2001] 2 All ER (Comm) 1061, [2002] 1 Lloyd's Rep 343, [2001] 2 FLR 1364, [2001] 3 FCR 481, [2002] HLR 4, [2001] Fam Law 880, [2001] 43 EG 184 (CS), (2001) 151 NLJ 1538, [2001] NPC 147, [2002] 1 P & CR DG14, (2001) *The Times*, October 17, (2001) *Daily Telegraph*, October 23 | A.3 |
| RP v Nottingham City Council [2008] EWCA Civ 462, *sub nom* P (A Child) (Care and Placement Order Proceedings: Mental Capacity of Parent), Re [2008] EWCA Civ 462, [2008] 2 FLR 1516, [2008] 3 FCR 243, [2009] BLGR 213, (2008) 11 CCL Rep 316, [2008] Fam Law 835, (2008) 105(20) LSG 24, (2008) 152(21) SJLB 31 (2008) *Times*, June 10 | 5.2, 5.5, 5.16, 5.18, 5.22, 5.26, 5.27, 6.6, 6.8 |
| S (A Child), Re [2008] EWCA Civ 1284 | 1.30, 6.2 |
| S (Adult Patient: Sterilisation: Patient's Best Interests), Re [2001] Fam 15, [2000] 3 WLR 1288, [2000] 2 FLR 389, [2000] 2 FCR 452, [2000] Lloyd's Rep Med 339, (2000) 55 BMLR 105, [2000] Fam Law 711, (2000) 97(24) LSG 40, (2000) *The Times*, May 26 | A.3 |
| SA (Vulnerable Adult with Capacity: Marriage), Re [2005] EWHC 2942 (Fam), [2006] 1 FLR 867, [2007] 2 FCR 563, (2007) 10 CCL Rep 193, [2006] Fam Law 268 | 5.1 |
| Saulle v Nouvet [2007] EWHC 2902 (QB), [2008] LS Law Medical 201, [2008] MHLR 59, [2008] WTLR 729 | 5.5 |
| Sheffield City Council v E [2004] EWHC 2808 (Fam), [2005] Fam 326, [2005] 2 WLR 953, [2005] 1 FLR 965, [2005] Lloyd's Rep Med 223, [2005] Fam Law 279, (2005) 102(9) LSG 30, (2005) *The Times*, January 20 | 5.8, 5.9, A.3 |

T (Adult: Refusal of Treatment), Re [1993] Fam 95, [1992] 3 WLR 782, [1992] 4 All ER 649, [1992] 2 FLR 458, [1992] 2 FCR 861, [1992] 3 Med LR 306, [1993] Fam Law 27, (1992) 142 NLJ 1125, (1992) *The Times*, August 21, (1992) *The Independent*, July 31, (1992) *The Guardian*, August 5 — A.3

W (An Adult: Mental Patient) (Sterilisation), Re [1993] 1 FLR 381, [1993] 2 FCR 187, [1993] Fam Law 208 — 6.5

W (Children) (Care Proceedings: Litigation Capacity), Re [2008] EWHC 1188 (Fam), [2010] 1 FLR 1176, [2010] Fam Law 15 — 5.1, 5.8, 6.11

W v Egdell [1990] Ch 359, [1990] 2 WLR 471, [1990] 1 All ER 835, (1990) 87(12) LSG 41, (1990) 134 SJ 286, (1989) *The Independent*, November 10 — A.3

Wyatt v Hillingdon LBC 76 LGR 727, (1978) 122 SJ 349, (1977) *The Times*, December 20 — 4.23

X (Adult Patient: Sterilisation), Re [1998] 2 FLR 1124, [1999] 3 FCR 426, [1998] Fam Law 737 — 6.5

# TABLE OF STATUTES

**References are to paragraph numbers.**

| | |
|---|---|
| Abolition of Domestic Rates (Scotland) Act 1987 | A.8 |
| Adoption Act 1976 | A.4 |
| Adoption and Children Act 2002 | |
| s 19 | 5.8, 5.28 |
| s 20 | 5.8, 5.28 |
| s 22(2) | A.6 |
| s 52 | 5.28 |
| Care Standards Act 2000 | A.3 |
| Carers (Recognition and Services) Act 1995 | |
| s 1(1) | A.9 |
| Carers and Disabled Children Act 2000 | |
| s 2(1) | 2.8 |
| Child Care Act 1980 | |
| s 1 | 2.11 |
| Childcare Act 2006 | A.9 |
| Children Act 1989 | 1.20, 2.1, 2.10–2.14, 4.5, 4.6, 4.8, 6.2, A.4, A.9 |
| Pt III | 2.11, 4.8, 4.9 |
| Pt IV | 4.4 |
| s 17 | 2.9, 2.12, 2.18, 4.15, 6.2, A.9 |
| s 17(1) | 2.10, 2.11, 4.3 |
| s 17A | 2.9, 2.12 |
| s 20 | 2.18, A.9 |
| s 31 | A.6 |
| s 31(2) | 4.3, 4.8, 6.3 |
| s 31(2)(b)(i) | 4.11 |
| s 31(9) | 4.5 |
| s 31(10) | 4.5 |
| s 38(6) | 6.7 |
| s 47 | A.9 |
| Sch 2 | 2.11 |
| Sch 2, para 1(2) | A.9 |
| Children Act 2004 | 2.11–2.14, 4.15, A.9 |
| s 10 | 2.14, A.9 |
| s 10(4) | 2.14 |
| s 11 | A.9 |
| s 12 | A.9 |
| s 53 | 2.18, A.9 |
| Children and Young Persons Act 1933 | |
| Sch 1 | 3.4 |
| Chronically Sick and Disabled Persons Act 1970 | A.9 |
| s 1(2) | A.9 |
| s 2 | 4.25 |
| s 2(1) | 4.20, 4.22, 4.23, 4.25, 4.26 |

| | |
|---|---|
| Chronically Sick and Disabled Persons Act 1970—*continued* | |
| s 29 | 4.22 |
| Criminal Justice (Scotland) Act 1980 | A.8 |
| Criminal Justice and Court Services Act 2000 | |
| s 12 | A.4 |
| Data Protection Act 1998 | A.3 |
| Disability Discrimination Act 1995 | 6.3, A.3, A.8, A.9 |
| Pt III | A.9 |
| s 49A | 4.27 |
| Disability Discrimination Act 2005 | 2.15, 4.12, A.9 |
| Disabled Persons (Employment) Act 1944 | 4.18 |
| Disabled Persons (Services, Consultation and Representation) Act 1986 | A.1 |
| s 3 | A.1 |
| s 4 | 4.22, A.1, A.9 |
| s 8 | 4.22 |
| Employment and Training Act 1973 | 4.18 |
| Equality Act 2010 | 1.17, 2.15 |
| s 6(1) | 1.17 |
| s 6(5) | 1.17 |
| s 19 | 1.17 |
| s 20 | 1.17 |
| s 20(6) | 1.17 |
| s 212 | 1.17 |
| Sch 1, para 4 | 1.17 |
| Family Law Act 1986 | A.4 |
| Pt III | A.4 |
| Family Law Act 1989 | A.4 |
| Family Law Act 1996 | |
| Pt IV | A.4 |
| s 43 | A.4 |
| Health Act 1999 | |
| s 31 | A.9 |
| Health and Social Care Act 2001 | |
| s 57 | 2.8 |
| s 57(1) | 2.8 |
| s 58 | 2.9, A.9 |
| s 58(2)(b) | 2.10 |

| | | | |
|---|---|---|---|
| Health Authorities Act 1995 | A.1 | Mental Health Act 1983—*continued* | |
| Health Services and Public Health Act 1968 | | s 117 | 4.16, 4.19, A.1 |
| | | s 135 | A.3 |
| s 45 | 4.16, 4.19, A.1 | Mental Health (Amendment) Act 1982 | A.8 |
| Homelessness Act 2002 | A.9 | Mental Health (Scotland) Act 1984 | A.8 |
| Housing Act 1985 | A.1 | s 106 | A.8 |
| Human Rights Act 1998 | A.3 | s 107 | A.8 |
| Human Tissue Act 2004 | A.3 | | |
| | | National Assistance Act 1948 | |
| Local Authority Social Services Act 1970 | | Pt III | 4.16, 4.17, 4.20, A.1 |
| | | s 21 | 4.17 |
| s 7 | 2.7, 2.8, 4.24 | s 29 | 4.17, 4.20, 4.22 |
| s 7(1) | 4.20 | s 29(1) | 4.18, 4.20 |
| s 7A | 4.20 | s 29(4) | 4.18 |
| Local Government (Wales) Act 1994 | A.1 | s 35(2) | 4.20 |
| Local Government Finance Act 1988 | A.8 | National Health Service Act 1977 | |
| Local Government Finance Act 1992 | A.8 | s 21 | 4.16, 4.19 |
| | | Sch 8 | 4.16, 4.19 |
| | | National Health Service Act 2006 | A.1 |
| Matrimonial Causes Act 1973 | A.4 | s 254 | A.1 |
| Mental Capacity Act 2005 | 1.18, 5.3, 5.5, 5.10, 5.13, 5.15, 5.29, 6.6, 6.11, A.3, A.5–A.7 | Sch 20 | A.1 |
| | | National Health Service (Consequential Provisions) Act 2006 | A.1 |
| s 1 | 5.10, A.2, A.3 | National Health Service (Wales) Act 2006 | A.1 |
| ss 1–3 | 5.17 | s 192 | A.1 |
| s 1(2) | 5.10, A.3 | Sch 15 | A.1 |
| s 1(3) | 5.10, A.3 | National Health Service and Community Care Act 1990 | 4.22, 5.27, A.3 |
| s 1(4) | 5.10, A.3 | | |
| s 1(5) | 5.10, A.3 | | |
| s 1(6) | 5.10, A.3 | | |
| s 2 | 5.11, 5.12, A.2, A.6 | s 46 | 2.8, A.1 |
| s 2(1) | A.3 | s 46(3) | 4.16 |
| s 2(2) | A.3 | s 47 | 2.7, 2.8, 2.12, 2.18, 4.16, 4.21, 4.23–4.26, 5.29, A.1 |
| s 2(3) | A.3 | | |
| s 2(4) | A.3 | s 47(1) | A.9 |
| s 3 | 5.12, A.2, A.3, A.6 | s 47(1)(a) | 4.23 |
| s 3(1) | 6.5, A.3 | s 47(1)(b) | 4.23 |
| s 3(2) | A.3 | s 47(2) | 4.22, 4.26 |
| s 3(3) | A.3 | s 47(2)(b) | 4.22 |
| s 3(4) | 6.5, A.3 | s 47(3) | A.9 |
| s 4 | A.3 | National Health Service Reform and Health Care Professions Act 2002 | A.1 |
| s 4(6) | 5.26 | | |
| s 4(7) | 5.26 | | |
| s 5(1) | A.3 | | |
| s 16(2)(b) | 5.19 | | |
| s 27 | A.3 | Offences Against the Person Act 1861 | |
| s 28 | A.3 | s 20 | 6.11 |
| s 42 | A.3 | | |
| s 42(4) | A.3 | | |
| s 42(5) | A.3 | Police and Criminal Evidence Act 1984 | A.8 |
| s 62 | A.3 | | |
| Sch 6 | A.3 | Registered Homes Act 1984 | A.8 |
| Sch 6, para 20 | A.3 | Road Traffic Act 1988 | A.8 |
| Mental Health Act 1959 | | | |
| s 128 | A.8 | Sexual Offences Act 1956 | A.8 |
| Mental Health Act 1983 | 5.6, A.3, A.8 | Sexual Offences Act 1967 | A.8 |
| Pt 4 | A.3 | Social Security Contributions and Benefits Act 1992 | |
| s 1(2) | A.8 | | |
| s 10 | A.8 | | |
| s 12 | 5.16 | s 73 | A.8 |

# TABLE OF STATUTORY INSTRUMENTS

**References are to paragraph numbers.**

| | |
|---|---|
| Allocation and Transfer of Proceedings Order 2008, SI 2008/2836 | |
| Sch 2, art 5 | 5.15 |
| | |
| Civil Procedure Rules, SI 1998/3132 | 5.7, 5.20 |
| r 21.1 | A.3 |
| r 21.6 | 5.20 |
| r 23.4(1) | 5.20 |
| r 23.11 | 5.20 |
| Community Care, Services for Carers and Children's Services (Direct Payments) (England) Regulations 2009, SI 2009/1887 | |
| reg 7 | 2.8 |
| Community Care, Services for Carers and Children's Services (Direct Payments) (Wales) Amendment Regulations 2006, SI 2006/2840 (W.256) | 2.8 |
| Community Care, Services for Carers and Children's Services (Direct Payments) (Wales) Regulations 2004, SI 2004/1748 (W.185) | |
| reg 5 | 2.8 |
| Court of Protection Rules 2007, SI 2007/1744 | A.5 |
| r 21 | A.5 |
| | |
| Family Procedure (Adoption) (Amendment) Rules 2007, SI 2007/2189 | 5.3 |
| Family Procedure (Adoption) Rules 2005, SI 2005/2795 | 5.3 |
| PD Pt 7, r 1 | 6.6 |
| Pt 7 | 5.1 |
| Family Procedure Rules 2010, SI 2010/2955 | 5.15, 5.16, 5.20 |
| PD 5A | 5.28 |
| PD 15A | 5.2, 5.20, A.5, A.7 |
| PD 15A, para 2.1 | 5.26, 6.6 |
| PD 15A, para 3.1 | 5.22 |
| PD 15A, para 3.1(a) | A.7 |
| PD 15A, para 3.1(b) | 5.22 |
| PD 15A, para 3.1(b)(iii) | A.7 |
| PD 15A, para 3.3 | 5.21, A.7 |
| PD 15A, para 4.2 | 5.20 |
| PD 15A, para 4.3 | A.7 |

| | |
|---|---|
| Family Procedure Rules 2010, SI 2010/2955—*continued* | |
| PD 15A, para 4.3(d) | A.7 |
| PD 15A, para 4.5 | 5.21 |
| PD 15A, para 9 | A.5 |
| Pt 15 | 5.2, 5.20, A.7 |
| Pt 18 | A.7 |
| r 2.3 | 5.3, 5.5, A.7 |
| r 6.28 | A.7 |
| r 14.10 | 5.28 |
| r 15.2 | 5.1, 5.3 |
| r 15.3 | 5.4 |
| r 15.3(2) | 5.4 |
| r 15.3(4) | 5.4, 5.14 |
| r 15.4 | 5.19 |
| r 15.4(2) | 5.19 |
| r 15.4(3) | 5.19, 5.20, 5.22, A.7 |
| r 15.4(4) | A.7 |
| r 15.5 | 5.22 |
| r 15.5(6) | 5.19 |
| r 15.6 | A.7 |
| r 15.6(2) | 5.20 |
| r 15.6(4) | 5.20 |
| r 15.7 | 5.22, A.7 |
| r 15.9(1) | A.7 |
| r 15.9(2) | A.7 |
| Family Proceedings (Amendment) (No 2) Rules 2007, SI 2007/2187 | 5.3 |
| Family Proceedings Courts (Children Act 1989) Rules 1991, SI 1991/1395 | 5.15, A.4 |
| Family Proceedings Rules 1991, SI 1991/1247 | 5.3 |
| Pt IX | 5.1, 5.15, A.4 |
| r 2.57 | A.4 |
| r 9.1 | A.4 |
| r 9.2 | A.4 |
| r 9.2A | A.4 |
| r 9.5 | A.4 |
| | |
| Mental Health (Northern Ireland) Order 1986, SI 1986/595 | A.8 |
| | |
| Police and Criminal Evidence (Northern Ireland) Order 1989, SI 1984/1341 | A.8 |
| | |
| Residential Care Homes Regulations 1984, SI 1984/1345 | A.8 |

Rules of the Supreme Court 1965,
SI 1965/1776
   Ord 80     5.20
      r 10     5.6

Social Security (Disability Living
Allowance) Regulations 1991,
SI 1991/2890     A.8
   reg 12(5)     A.8
   reg 12(6)     A.8

Social Security (Incapacity Benefit)
(Transitional) Regulations 1995,
SI 1995/310     A.8

Social Security (Incapacity for Work)
(General) Regulations 1995,
SI 1995/311     A.8

# TABLE OF CONVENTIONS

**References are to paragraph numbers.**

| | |
|---|---|
| European Convention for the Protection of Human Rights and Fundamental Freedoms | |
| 1950 | 4.15 |
| Art 6 | 5.26, 6.6 |
| Art 8 | 1.5, 4.8, 4.28 |
| Art 8(1) | 4.8 |
| Art 8(2) | 4.8 |
| | |
| United Nations Convention on the Rights of Persons with Disabilities 2007 | 1.6 |
| Art 23 | 4.15 |
| Art 23(2) | 1.6 |
| Art 23(4) | 1.6 |
| Optional Protocol | 1.6 |
| United Nations Convention on the Rights of the Child 1989 | |
| Art 18(2) | 4.15 |

# LIST OF ABBREVIATIONS

| | |
|---|---|
| CPR | Child Protection Register |
| CPR 1998 | Civil Procedure Rules 1998, SI 1998/3132 |
| CSDPA 1970 | Chronically Sick and Disabled Persons Act 1970 |
| FPR 2010 | Family Procedure Rules 2010, SI 2010/2995 |
| IASSID | International Association for the Scientific Study of Intellectual Disabilities |
| NHSCCA 1990 | National Health Service and Community Care Act 1990 |

# Chapter 1

# LEARNING DISABLED PARENTING: AN INTRODUCTION

**1.1** This book is a handbook for family lawyers involved in care proceedings in England and Wales where one or other of the parents has a learning disability (see **1.7–1.15** for the definition of 'learning disability' used throughout). As such it aims to equip the family lawyer, whether representing a parent, the local authority or the Children's Guardian, with knowledge of all the relevant legislation, statutory and policy guidance and an understanding of the range of issues that are likely to arise in such a case. In the author's experience there is all too often an inadequate appreciation of the types of support that a learning disabled parent might find beneficial, or which he or she is entitled to request, leading in some cases to a care order being sought as the easiest or most convenient outcome rather than the adoption of a more creative approach.

**1.2** Three developments underpin this handbook. First, the research showing that the children of learning disabled parents are over-represented in care proceedings (discussed at **1.22–1.31**). Whilst, on the one hand, this might suggest that there is something inherent in the fact of a learning disability which means that learning disabled parents are likely to fail to meet their children's needs adequately, the weight of the sociological, psychological and psychiatric research base suggests that negative stereotyping, inadequate training of professionals in learning disability issues and disparate support services provide a better explanation for such a trend (see discussion in Chapters 2 and 3). Secondly, there has been in recent governmental policy documents an increasing awareness of the issues affecting learning disabled parents, culminating in the publication in 2007 by the Department of Health and the Department of Education and Skills of the *Good Practice Guidance on Working with Parents with a Learning Disability*. Thirdly, and perhaps because of the increasing political interest in the issue, there has been since *Re L*[1] in 2006 an emergent body of case-law where the common thread is the learning disability of the child's parent or primary carer together with a submission that they have been treated less than fairly on that basis. The issue before the Court of Appeal in *Re L* was whether the judge below, having rejected the allegation of physical abuse which had led to the children's removal from home, had been wrong to find the threshold criteria proven simply on the basis of the opinion of the jointly instructed chartered clinical psychologist as to the risks likely to

---

[1] *Re L (Children) (Threshold Criteria)* [2006] EWCA Civ 1282.

be posed by the parents if the children were to be returned. In allowing the parents' appeal and remitting the case to the High Court, Lord Justice Wall commented that:

> '... the case ... seems to carry with it the danger that the court and the local authority can both be accused of engaging in the impermissible process of social engineering ... the family courts do not remove children from their parents into care because the parents in question are not intelligent enough to care for them or have low intelligence quotas.'

The point was addressed more obliquely by Hedley J in the High Court hearing[2] which followed, where he referred to the fact that the care system allows public law mandatory orders to be made only in exceptional circumstances and that society must as a result tolerate diverse standards of parenting, including the 'eccentric, the barely adequate and the inconsistent'. Taken as a whole, it is suggested that both the Court of Appeal and the High Court judgments in this case represent the real starting point of a jurisprudence in this area.

**1.3** In focusing on the parental learning disability as the common denominator in these cases, and in constructing parental learning disability as a sub-category of family law, there is perhaps a risk of overlooking the fact that the children of learning disabled parents rarely become the subject of child protection proceedings as a result of the learning disability itself, but often as a consequence of other problems such as neglect, chronic alcohol or drug abuse or domestic violence. In the *Care Proceedings Statistics 2008*,[3] for example, whereas 58.4% of the sample cases included concerns about maternal neglect, only 12.8% referred to concerns about maternal learning disability, and whereas 48.5% included concerns about paternal neglect, only 6.8% referred to concerns about paternal learning disability. Similarly, Cleaver and Nicholson found that the learning disability itself was the primary reason for the referral in 19.7% of child protection cases involving learning disabled parents.[4] It might be suggested that there is therefore nothing 'special' about 'learning disability' cases and that the task for the court in these cases is the same as the task for the court in all care proceedings, which is to consider the capacity of the parents to care for the child adequately, and their ability to change their parenting style if their care is found to be not good enough.

**1.4** However, for three reasons 'learning disability' merits consideration in its own right as a branch of public family law. First, the reality for many adults with learning disabilities is that 'the violation of their human rights is seen as a normal part of their everyday lives'.[5] As a consequence, public law proceedings where the case against the parents is that they lack the intellectual and other

---

[2] *Re L (A Child) (Care: Threshold Criteria)* [2007] 1 FLR 2050.
[3] Ministry of Justice, Research Series 4/08 (TSO, March 2008).
[4] Cleaver and Nicholson *Parental Learning Disability and Children's Needs: Family Experiences and Effective Practice* (Jessica Kingsley Publishers, 2007).
[5] Joint Committee on Human Rights *A Life Like Any Other? Human Rights of Adults with Learning Disabilities* HL 40-1; HC 73-1 (TSO, 2008).

resources with which to provide the child with adequate physical and emotional care become what Lord Justice Wilson in *Re L*[6] found to be 'one of the most difficult categories' of case. Secondly, there appears to be a perhaps inevitable gap between rhetoric and reality in the reasoning used in these cases. It is clear from *Re L*, for example, that the presence of a parental learning disability does not justify the removal of children from their parents, yet it is not unusual for care orders to be made where the parent, due to his or her limitations, is found by a parenting assessment to be unable to improve their parenting beyond a level below 'good enough'. Similarly, whereas it is a central tenet of family law that a child can only be removed if the standard of care has fallen below 'good enough', it is not unusual for *better than good enough* parenting to be demanded of the learning disabled parent on the basis that their child has been found to have global developmental delay and therefore requires a higher than average level of care. Further, the *Good Practice Guidance*[7] emphasises that the need for long-term support does not mean that a learning disabled parent should be ruled out as a carer for his or her child, yet the court may find that the extent and duration of the support package required is detrimental to the child's welfare because the child as a result is likely to be 'parented' by several people. In *Re G and A*,[8] for example, the likely impact on the children of multiple carers and a changing staff group supporting their parents throughout their childhood was held to be prejudicial to the children's need for security and stability and their capacity to form healthy attachments to their primary carers.

**1.5** Thirdly, the issues raised have already become the subject of international human rights law. The European Court of Human Rights in *Kutzner v Germany*[9] has stated that the decision to remove a child from learning disabled parents must take into account whether it would be more appropriate to provide additional support to the family, and that the failure in that case to give sufficient consideration to alternative methods of support which might have helped the parents keep the children at home meant that the interference with the parents' Article 8 rights was disproportionate. The judgment also emphasises at para 69 that the fact that it would be more beneficial for a child to be brought up in a different environment does not by itself justify a removal from the care of his or her parents, a point which applies to public law cases in general but is of particular relevance to cases where it is argued that the parents' learning disability makes it difficult for them to care for the child adequately.

**1.6** Further, the right of all disabled people to access parenting support is protected by the United Nations Convention on the Rights of Persons with Disabilities, which was ratified by the UK on 8 June 2009 (together with the Optional Protocol on 7 August 2009). Article 23(2) provides that:

---

[6] *Re L (Children) (Threshold Criteria)* [2006] EWCA Civ 1282; *Re L (A Child) (Care: Threshold Criteria)* [2007] 1 FLR 2050.
[7] Department of Health and Department for Education and Skills *Good Practice Guidance on Working with Parents with a Learning Disability* (TSO, 2007) p 20, at para 1.4.
[8] [2006] NI Fam 8.
[9] (2002) 35 EHRR 25.

'States Parties shall ensure the rights and responsibilities of persons with disabilities, with regard to guardianship, wardship, trusteeship, adoption of children or similar institutions, where these concepts exist in national legislation; in all cases the best interests of the child shall be paramount. States Parties shall render appropriate assistance to persons with disabilities in the performance of their child-rearing responsibilities.'

The same theme is picked up in Article 23(4), which protects the right of the child not to be removed from his or her parents on the basis of a disability of either the child or of one or both of the parents. It provides that:

'States Parties shall ensure that a child shall not be separated from his or her parents against their will, except when competent authorities subject to judicial review determine, in accordance with applicable law and procedures, that such separation is necessary for the best interests of the child. In no case shall a child be separated from parents on the basis of a disability of either the child or one or both of the parents.'

Similarly, the United Nations Standard Rules on the Equalization of Opportunities for Persons with Disabilities 1993, whilst not a legally binding instrument, sets out the right of persons with disabilities not to be denied the opportunity to experience sexuality, have sexual relations and experience parenthood,[10] and encourages states to promote measures to challenge the negative attitudes to their marriage, sexuality and parenthood. A 2005 supplement to the Rules refers – albeit indirectly – to measures promoting the rights of parents with learning disabilities rather than simply to the generic category of 'disabled parents': paras 91–93 of the proposal suggest the specific inclusion in disability public awareness programmes of those with 'invisible disabilities', where this means:

'... those who have disabilities that are not easily discovered by others ... the following may be mentioned: persons with psychiatric or developmental disabilities; those with disabilities from chronic diseases; and those who are hard of hearing or deaf.'

## LEARNING DISABILITIES OR LEARNING DIFFICULTIES?

**1.7** Throughout this book the term 'learning disabilities' rather than 'learning difficulties' has been used even though it is recognised that many learning disabled people would prefer to use the latter rather than the former nomenclature.[11] Whilst the terms are often used interchangeably,[12] there are

---

[10] Rule 9.
[11] See *Good Practice Guidance*, n 7 above, at p 36.
[12] See, for example, Tarleton et al *Finding the Right Support? A Review of Issues and Positive Practice in Supporting Parents with Learning Difficulties* (The Baring Foundation, 2006); and note the interchangeable use of 'learning difficulties' and 'learning disabilities' in the cases referred to in Chapter 6. On balance, however, the reported cases tend to favour the term 'learning difficulties'.

three reasons for the use of the term 'learning disabilities' rather than 'learning difficulties' here. First, because since 2000 the British Psychological Society has used this label to replace what it had previously – and perhaps pejoratively – referred to as 'mental impairments' or 'severe mental impairments'; secondly, because this is the language used by the government in the policy papers which are considered in Chapter 2; and, thirdly, so as to avoid confusion with specific learning difficulties associated with education such as dyslexia, or dyspraxia, which by themselves do not amount to an impairment of intellectual and social functioning and which do not entitle those adults suffering from such conditions to any assistance or support from adult social care.

**1.8** This book does, however, refer interchangeably to 'parents with learning disabilities' and 'learning disabled parents' in recognition of the fact that those who prefer the former wish to emphasise that the learning disability is secondary to their parenthood and not their major defining characteristic, whilst those who prefer the latter wish to avoid the implication that the learning disability is inherent to the individual and instead to locate the cause of the disability in the social arrangements which impede equality of opportunity and access to facilities. There is a link here with the 'social model' of disability, under which the limitations of cognitive or physical impairment are said to derive not from the fact of the impairment itself, but from the social arrangements and obstacles that restrict the activities of and access to facilities by disabled people. Under this definition, disability is something which is imposed upon people by oppressive and discriminatory social structures and not something which inevitably follows from the impairment.[13] The far-reaching implications of the social model of disability in providing a basis for anti-discrimination legislation are plain to see, although the theory is not without its critiques: commentators have pointed to its underplaying of the factual reality of some impairments and to the difficulties involved in securing rights to independent living and specialised services which follow from the model's rejection of any concept of 'normality'. An engagement with the debates in the field of moral and political philosophy is beyond the scope of this book, but it is argued that the social model of disability simply highlights the arbitrary injustice of the outcome for the client who falls – but only just – outside the definition of learning disability conventionally used by adult social care services and who as a result will struggle to obtain parenting support. Recent research[14] shows that adults who fail to meet the diagnostic criteria for learning disability but whose functioning is referred to as 'borderline' face very similar challenges to those who meet the diagnostic criteria for learning disability but who have higher-range IQs. For many commentators, it is this group of parents, which Edgerton referred to as 'the hidden majority',[15] who are most at risk of having their right to a fair assessment and support

---

[13] See Terzi 'Vagaries of the Natural Lottery? Human Diversity, Disability and Justice: A Capability Perspective' in Brownlee and Cureton (eds) *Disability and Disadvantage* (Oxford University Press, 2009).
[14] Snell et al 'Characteristics and Needs of People with Intellectual Disabilities who have Higher IQs' (2009) 47(3) *Journal of Intellectual and Developmental Disabilities* 220–223.
[15] Edgerton 'The Hidden Majority of Individuals with Mental Retardation and Developmental

overlooked – although they would have received specialised support and services during their school years, the adult lives of the 'hidden majority' tend to be characterised by unmet need.

## DEFINING LEARNING DISABILITIES

**1.9** Where the parent's legal representative is uncertain as to whether or not their client has a learning disability and suspects that the client's level of cognitive and social functioning has not been taken into consideration within the core assessment, the initial assessment or any local authority decision-making that has taken place, a psychological assessment should be sought. The attachment of the label of 'learning disability' to the client should not be seen as prejudicial, but as the starting point for a recognition by all the professionals involved of the obstacles that may have faced the parent in the task of unsupported parenting and for the instruction of an expert trained in working with parents with learning disabilities to carry out an individualised and realistically structured parenting assessment. Without such a specialised parenting assessment there is likely to be insufficient evidence for the court to make a final care order and the refusal of an application for such a parenting assessment may result in a successful appeal.[16]

**1.10** The Professional Affairs Board of the British Psychological Society has set out guidelines on the definition of learning disability for use in a health and personal social services setting. Whilst it is difficult to envisage the situation where a family lawyer will be required to make submissions as to whether or not a parent is learning disabled,[17] a working knowledge of the guidelines may be useful in considering whether to seek clarification as to a client's presentation in a specific case.

**1.11** In *Learning Disability: Definitions and Contexts*[18] the three core criteria which must be met for a person to be considered to have a learning disability are: (a) a significant impairment of intellectual functioning; (b) a significant impairment of adaptive or social functioning; and (c) the age of onset must have arisen before adulthood. Accordingly there will not be a diagnosis of learning disability if a person has a significant or even profound impairment in one of the two domains of intellectual and social/adaptive functioning but no significant impairment in the other. Moreover, the further sub-classification of a 'learning disability' into one of the categories of *mild, moderate, severe* or *profound* is only possible if there is a correspondence between the level of intellectual functioning and adaptive/social functioning. Importantly, however, this method of sub-classification of learning disability is not used universally across the different disciplines. Whilst psychological and educational

---

Disabilities' in Tymchuk et al *The Forgotten Generation: The Status and Challenges of Adults with Mild Cognitive Limitations* (Paul H Brookes Publishing Co, Inc, 2001).

[16] See *M v Neath Port Talbot CBC* [2010] EWCA Civ 821.
[17] As distinct from submissions as to a client's litigation capacity, for which see Chapter 5.
[18] The British Psychological Society, 2000.

researchers are likely to sub-classify into the *mild, moderate, severe, profound* groupings, some of those providing health or social care services for adults with learning disabilities are more likely to classify according to the differing levels of support needs.

**1.12** The principal method for determining whether there is an impairment of intellectual functioning is by means of a psychometric assessment based on an explicit model of normal distribution of general intelligence. Under these tests a 'significant impairment' of intellectual functioning has become defined as a performance of more than two standard deviations below the population mean, equating to an IQ of 69 or less.[19] A 'severe impairment' of intellectual functioning is said to correspond with an IQ performance of less than 55 (more than three standard deviations below the mean). The British Psychological Society sounds three notes of caution here: first, there is a need for a high degree of care and some flexibility when a person's impairment falls at the borderlines between significant and non-significant, or between significant and severe; secondly, there is a need to differentiate between an impaired performance as a result of a learning disability and an impaired performance arising out of emotional or psychological distress, medication, alcohol or drug use, all of which need to be ruled out if possible; and, thirdly, the interpretation of psychometric assessments of intellectual functioning should be carried out only in the light of the individual's personal and cultural circumstances, clinical status and other assessment information. For that reason, assistance should always be sought from a chartered psychologist.

**1.13** The assessment of an individual's adaptive or social functioning is to be measured according to how much assistance they need for their own survival on a day-to-day basis (ie in keeping themselves clean, warm and clothed) and/or for their social or community adaptation (ie social problem-solving and social reasoning). Such an assessment is usually carried out by direct observation in conjunction with observations made by at least one informant, whether a family member or carer, who knows the person well. There is a variety of tests available, whether norm-referenced, criterion-referenced or simply by way of checklist, and a lack of consensus in this area as to which is the most appropriate to use. The British Psychological Society recommends therefore that in order to obtain as complete and objective an assessment as possible more than one type of assessment should be carried out, with more than one informant and on more than one occasion.

**1.14** Sub-classification of the impairment of adaptive or social functioning can be facilitated by the use of psychometric testing such as the Vineland Adaptive Behaviour Scales, which classifies 'adaptive' levels into 'mild, moderate, severe and profound deficit'. However, the British Psychological Society recommends that as a guide to making a judgment as to the degree of impairment of social/adaptive functioning, consideration is given instead to

---

[19] Under the Wechsler Adult Intelligence Scale – Revised (WAIS-R) and the more recent WAIS-III (1999) the mean is 100 and the standard deviation is 15.

classification on the basis of the intensity and frequency of the assistance required. It is suggested that whereas a significant impairment is characterised by the need for 'intermittent' to 'limited' support (where 'intermittent' refers to short-term supports during a life-time transition and 'limited' refers to time-limited but not intermittent support), a 'severe' impairment arises where the needs are 'extensive' to 'pervasive' (where 'extensive' refers to regular support, not time-limited, and only required in some domains,[20] and 'pervasive' refers to potentially life-sustaining, high-intensity needs across all domains).

**1.15** For the impairment to be labelled as a learning disability it is also necessary for the cognitive limitation to have arisen during the developmental period, ie before adulthood. The British Psychological Society notes, however, that this definition would also include those who suffer cerebral injury later in childhood but before the age of 18, even though their needs would arguably be more appropriately supported through services designed for people with acquired brain damage rather than through generic adult learning disability support.

**1.16** The British Psychological Society definition of learning disability has been adopted by the key policy documents on adult learning disabilities.[21] In para 1.5 of *Valuing People*, learning disability is therefore said to include the presence of:

> 'A significantly reduced ability to understand new or complex information, to learn new skills (impaired intelligence); with a reduced ability to cope independently (impaired social functioning); which started before adulthood, with a lasting effect on development.'

Paragraph 1.5 of *Valuing People* has in turn been adopted by the Department of Health's *Good Practice Guidance on Working with Parents with a Learning Disability*; and by the Joint Committee on Human Rights in *A Life Like Any Other? Human Rights of Adults with Learning Disabilities*.[22]

**1.17** Similarly, the Equality Act 2010 deems a person to be 'disabled' for the purposes of the Act if they have either a physical or a mental 'impairment' and if that impairment has a 'substantial and long-term adverse effect on [a person's] ability to carry out normal day–to-day activities' (s 6(1)). The Equality Act 2010 applies to all organisations providing a service to the public and prohibits 'direct discrimination' if, because of a protected characteristic, A treats B less favourably than A treats or would treat others. It also prohibits discrimination against B on the basis of something arising in consequence of B's disability (s 15) as well as prohibiting indirect discrimination (s 19). Under s 20, there is a duty on the relevant authority to make reasonable adjustments where a provision, criterion or practice puts a disabled person at a substantial

---

[20] Such as, for example, at work or at home.
[21] Department of Health, *Valuing People, A New Strategy for Learning Disability for the 21st Century*, Cm 5086 (2001): the first White Paper on adults with learning disabilities since 1971.
[22] Seventh Report of Session 2007–08, HL 40-1; HC 73-1 (TSO, 2008).

disadvantage in relation to a relevant matter in comparison with people who are not disabled. 'Substantial' in this context means 'more than minor or trivial' (s 212). It is this provision which is likely to be of most relevance to learning disabled parents in that it expressly contemplates that inaccessible information can be a cause of such a disadvantage (s 20(6)). Guidance has been issued under s 6(5) and Sch 1, para 4 as to the matters to be taken into account by an adjudicating body in determining whether a person is a disabled person under the Act.[23] To that end it proposes an illustrative and non-exhaustive list of factors which it would be reasonable to regard as having a substantial adverse effect on normal day-to-day activities. Those factors perhaps most relevant to 'learning disability' include: 'difficulty asking specific questions to clarify instructions'; 'taking longer than someone who does not have an impairment to say things'; 'difficulty in adapting after a reasonable period to minor changes in work routine'; 'persistent and significant difficulty with reading'; 'persistent difficulty in remembering the spelling and meaning of words in common usage'; 'considerable difficulty in following a short sequence such as a simple recipe or a brief list of domestic tasks'; 'considerable difficulty in taking part in normal social interaction or forming social relationships'; 'disordered perception of reality'; 'persistent difficulty in crossing a road safely', 'persistent failure to nourish oneself, where nourishment is available'; and 'inability to recognise the physical dangers of touching an object which is very hot or cold'.

**1.18** Whereas the court in a care case involving a learning disabled parent is unlikely to be involved in determining the definition of 'learning disability', issues relating to the parent's capacity under the Mental Capacity Act 2005 are far more common. Having a learning disability is not the same thing as lacking capacity to conduct proceedings, and many learning disabled clients will be deemed to have capacity for the purposes of instructing their own legal teams. The issues arising in cases where the learning disabled parent does not have litigation capacity and requires representation by a litigation friend are dealt with in Chapter 5.

## DISCRIMINATION AGAINST LEARNING DISABLED PARENTS AND THEIR CHILDREN?

**1.19** No one knows exactly how many learning disabled adults there are in England and Wales, although there have been a number of estimates. In 2004 it was suggested that there were 985,000 people with learning disabilities in England,[24] consisting of 190,000 aged under 20 and 795,000 between the ages of 20 and 65. The most recently available information from the Health and Social Care Information Centre shows that as at 31 March 2009 there were a total of 1.047 million receiving community-based services, of whom around

---

[23] Office for Disability Issues, HM Government *Guidance on matters to be taken into account in determining questions relating to the definition of disability* (TSO, 2010).
[24] Institute for Health Research *Estimating Future Need/Demand for Supports for Adults with Learning Disabilities in England* (2004).

10% received services due to a learning disability.[25] In addition, there will be many more learning disabled people who are ineligible for adult social care and who will be relying instead solely on the support of family and friends. Figures for the number of *parents* with learning disability are equally unclear, with estimates varying from anywhere between 60,000 and 200,000.[26] A study in 2009 by Learning Disability Wales estimated that 12% of people with learning disabilities are parents and that there were 1,210 families in Wales where at least one parent had learning disabilities.[27] Despite the uncertainty as to how many learning disabled parents there are, which, it is argued, is itself is a symptom of the lack of co-ordination between children's and adults' services, there is a consensus that the number of parents with learning disabilities is likely to be on the increase. This is thought to be evidenced by the rising number of people reported to be seeking support from professional services[28] (community learning disability teams, clinical psychology departments and local advocacy schemes). The increase in the number of learning disabled people as a whole is attributed in part to the upward trend in the fertility of women above the age of 35 in the past three decades, and to the decreased mortality rates amongst children with severe and complex needs.[29]

**1.20** Figures suggest that the children of learning disabled parents are overrepresented in public law applications under the Children Act 1989. In the Social Services Inspectorate's *Jigsaw of Services*[30] it was noted, for example, that whilst there were child protection issues in less than 20% of all cases where the parents were receiving social care support, this figure rose to almost two-thirds of the families receiving services in cases where the parent had learning disabilities. Similarly, Booth and Booth found that at least one parent had mild to severe learning disabilities in 66 out of the 437 (15.1%) public law applications made to the Leeds and Sheffield Family Proceedings and County Courts in 2000, rising to 87 out of 437 (19.9%) if parents functioning at the borderline level were included. On the basis of a crude estimate that less than 1% of all parents in any given population have learning disabilities,[31] the

---

[25] Health and Social Care Information Centre *Community Care Statistics 2008–2009, Social Services Activity Report, England* (NHS, 2010).
[26] See Booth and Booth 'Temporal Discrimination and Parents with Learning Disability in the Child Protection System' (2006) 36 *British Journal of Social Work* 997–1015.
[27] *Being a Family: Parents with Learning Disabilities in Wales* (Learning Disability Wales, 2009).
[28] See Booth and Booth 'Temporal Discrimination and Parents with Learning Disability in the Child Protection System' (2006) 36 *British Journal of Social Work* 997–1015. See also Emerson *Estimating Future Need for Adult Social Care Services for People with Learning Disabilities in England*: CeDR Research Report 2008:6 (November 2008) and Department of Health, *Valuing People Now* (Department of Health, 2009) suggesting that the number of people using services is set to increase by more than 50% by 2018.
[29] Emerson *Estimating Future Need for Adult Social Care Services for People with Learning Disabilities in England*: CeDR Research Report 2008:6 (November 2008).
[30] Social Services Inspectorate *A Jigsaw of Services, Inspection of Services to Support Disabled Adults in their Parenting* (Department of Health, 2000).
[31] Emerson, Malam, Davies and Spencer *Adults with Learning Difficulties in England, 2003/4* (Department of Health, 2005); see also Aunos, Feldman and Goupil 'Mothers with Intellectual Disability who Do or Do Not have Custody of their Children' (2003) 10(2) *Journal of Developmental Disabilities* 65–80.

children of learning disabled parents are therefore vastly overrepresented in care proceedings. Furthermore, the children of learning disabled parents are statistically more likely to be placed away from their home and outside of their kinship network than are the children of parents without learning disabilities. Whereas almost three-quarters of the children with at least one learning disabled parent were placed outside their home or kinship network, the same outcome arose for only 52.4% of the children whose parents did not have learning disabilities. This disproportionately high rate of removal for the children of learning disabled parents is reported to be an international feature[32] rather than peculiar to England and Wales alone.

**1.21** Whilst the removal of a child from his or her parents' care is justifiable if the child is in need of care and protection which cannot be provided by any other outcome, the overrepresentation in care proceedings of children with at least one learning disabled parent raises two possibilities: either the impact of learning disability on parenting genuinely makes it largely impossible to carry out the parenting task, or there are negative assumptions being made as to parental capacity and inadequate supports and services being put in place on order to enable the children to remain at home. The research studies outlined below have been significant in drawing attention to the disproportionate outcomes for the children of learning disabled parents and in rooting the problem in the failure of services adequately to address their needs for more than short-lived support.

## THE RESEARCH STUDIES

**1.22** In *Parents with Learning Difficulties, Child Protection and the Courts*,[33] Booth and Booth published their 2-year investigation of parents with learning disabilities involved in care proceedings. The purpose of their study, which comprised a review of court records and social services files, observation of court proceedings and interviews with professionals, practitioners and parents, and focused on the 437 public law applications by local authorities coming before the Family Proceedings Court and the County Court in Leeds and Sheffield in 2000, was 'to explore the process and outcome of child protection work with parents who have learning difficulties and to evaluate the implications for policy and practice'. The records revealed that the children of parents with learning disabilities were significantly more likely to be placed outside the home and wider family than were the children of parents without learning disabilities: in 15.1% of the 437 cases at least one parent had learning disabilities, and of these children only 13 (10.2%) were returned home to their

---

[32] In Australia: McConnell 'Disability and Discrimination in Statutory Child Protection Proceedings' (2000) 15(6) *Disability and Society* 883; in the US: Glaun and Brown 'Motherhood, Intellectual Disability and Child Protection: Characteristics of a Court Sample' (1999) 24(1) *Journal of Intellectual and Developmental Disability* 95–105. Most of the research on the outcomes for children of learning disabled parents is, however, limited to high-income nations.
[33] 'Report to The Nuffield Foundation' (2005) 9(2) *Journal of Intellectual Disabilities* 109–129.

parents, with 74.8% being placed outside the home and outside the kinship network. Whilst the fact of the poor outcomes for these children does not lead inexorably to the conclusion that the learning disabled parents have been treated less favourably than the other parents, the authors conclude that there is a significant degree of indirect discrimination within the care system, and that 'it remains an open question' whether the right to a family life for these parents is compatible with the courts' interpretation of the paramountcy principle in such cases.[34] Their main findings were as follows.

**1.23** Most of the children with at least one learning disabled parent became known to the local authority due to concerns arising out of 'neglect', this being the central feature of the care order application for 61.4% of these children, with a further 38 children (29.9%) being identified as 'at risk' of neglect. The authors comment that the high number of cases alleging neglect perhaps reflects the professionals' negative assessments of the prospects of change.

**1.24** The court files made no reference in 80% of the cases to any support from statutory services being given to the parents, nor in 61.2% of the cases was there any reference to the support that was either being given or could be given by the grandparents or other family members. The authors concluded that:

> 'In this context, the absence of any comment on the services provided to families in such a high proportion of cases encourages the view that, in the eyes of many professionals, including judges, parents with learning difficulties are expected to cope standing alone.'

**1.25** There was indirect discrimination in the assessment process in that most parenting assessments were carried out by social workers who had very little training or experience in working with parents with learning difficulties.

**1.26** There was further entrenched and indirect discrimination in that the learning disabled parents appeared to have to demonstrate that the local authority's presumption of parental inadequacy was ill-founded, 'turning on its head the presumption that children's interests are best served by seeking wherever possible to preserve the bond between them and their parents'.

**1.27** The research by Booth and Booth was followed in November 2007 by Hedy Cleaver and Don Nicholson's work which explored the needs and outcomes of children living with a parent with learning disabilities who have been referred to children's social care services.[35] Like Booth and Booth, they found that these cases were more likely than others to result in the children not living at home, but by contrast they found that there was no evidence to suggest that the parental learning disability itself was the real reason the children were

---

[34] McConnell and Llewellyn argue similarly that the discretionary nature of the threshold test and the welfare principle allows for discrimination against learning disabled parents. See discussion in Chapter 4.
[35] Cleaver and Nicholson *Parental Learning Disability and Children's Needs: Family Experiences and Effective Practice* (Jessica Kingsley Publishing, 2007).

removed from their parents' care. Significantly, the authors found that the removal of the children was very much a 'last resort' and a decision taken after a substantial input of services had failed to bring about the required changes. Nonetheless, they made some criticisms and recommendations. These are set out below.

**1.28** Whilst there were considerable efforts made on the part of the child protection social workers to try to ensure that the parents were fully involved in the process of assessment and planning, there was little evidence of social work practitioners using specialist toolkits for working with learning disabled adults to assess the parents or of collaborative working with learning disability adult services teams.

**1.29** There was a failure routinely to record whether or not a planned service had been provided and, if so, whether the families had engaged with it. This was considered essential if the factors affecting the children's progress were to be fully reviewed and monitored. However, reviews did not take place regularly in all cases and as a consequence the children's progress and development were not overseen. This was of particular importance for the children of learning disabled parents, who had significantly higher levels of need than a comparison group of other children: 51.8% of the children living with a learning disabled parent had severe developmental needs as contrasted with only one-third of those in the comparison group.

**1.30** There was also little evidence of contingency planning or of the provision of long-term ongoing support and training to compensate for the parents' learning disabilities.[36] The involvement of children's social care was time-limited and in most cases had terminated within 3 years of the referral. This policy of short-term interventionism resulted in cyclical crisis episodes for families, with over half the cases closed to social services being re-referred at least once within 3 years. The authors recommended that a long-term package of services was necessary to meet the diverse needs of families where a parent or parents have learning disabilities and that resources must be committed for the duration of the children's childhood.

**1.31** More recently, the Baring Foundation funded research which reviewed the issues facing parents and professionals in this area,[37] and identified the best practice strategies to enable children to remain with their parents as a family. Amongst their many findings the authors identified the following key themes emerging as barriers to a constructive approach. First, in common with the earlier research by Booth and Booth, they found that the persistence of negative or stereotypical attitudes about learning disabled parents was a considerable obstacle to the provision of appropriate support, and that this was

---

[36] See *Re S (A Child)* [2008] EWCA Civ 1284 for a decision where the child's need for permanence was arguably prioritised over the uncertainty of the child's future at home with long-term support.

[37] Tarleton et al *Finding the Right Support? A Review of Issues and Positive Practice in Supporting Parents with Learning Difficulties* (The Baring Foundation, 2006).

underscored by a failure to provide child care social workers with training and specialist experience of working with people with learning disabilities. Moreover, this was compounded by the fact that adult social care professionals who supported parents with learning disabilities felt that the child protection professionals expected them to be 'perfect parents'.[38] This is a continuing criticism, with the Commission for Social Care Inspection finding in 2009[39] that the expectations placed on learning disabled adults in planning for the care of their children were higher than those placed on everyone else. Secondly, the authors noted a polarisation in outlook between child and family social workers, on the one hand, and the professionals in adult social care services, on the other, with the former believing that the children living with learning disabled parents would almost inevitably be at risk, and the latter concerned predominantly with the support needs of the parents. This historic tension might, however, be more apparent than real on the basis that the parents themselves also wanted to promote and protect the care of their children, and were more likely to do so if they were provided with appropriately targeted support.[40] Thirdly, they noted that the tightening of the eligibility criteria for adult social care meant that many learning disabled parents did not reach the thresholds for community care services or support, with the result that their children were being failed. What was needed was for procedures to be put in place so that 'children do not have to be perceived as clients of social services in order for their parents' support needs as parents to be met by local agencies'.

## OUTLINE

**1.32** This book develops the themes referred to above, aiming to provide the family lawyer with the contextual background to the legal issues likely to arise in this area. Chapter 2 therefore considers the origins and evolution of policy and legislation affecting care proceedings where at least one of the parents has a learning disability. The research base as to the risks and the mitigating factors associated with learning disabled parenting are set out in Chapter 3 in order to challenge the negative stereotyping which has been identified by Tarleton et al[41] and in the evidence subsequently received by the Joint Committee on Human Rights.[42] This chapter also considers the types of practical support which are considered to enhance long-term parenting for learning disabled parents. Chapter 4 turns to the legal framework and in particular to the application of the threshold test in the context of learning disabled parenting, focusing on the relevance to both the threshold criteria and the welfare principle of the parents' ability to parent with support. Chapter 5 provides an overview of practice and procedure in cases where a learning disabled parent is represented by the Official Solicitor or another 'litigation friend'. Finally, Chapter 6 returns to the

---

[38] Ibid, at p 24.
[39] *Supporting Disabled Parents: A Family or a Fragmented Approach* (CSCI, 2009) at para 4.4.
[40] See also similar comments made by McGaw and Newman in *What Works for Parents with Learning Disabilities?* (Barnardos, 2005).
[41] Above n 37.
[42] Above n 23.

body of case-law referred to above, analysing the judgments where possible in the light of the implications of the preceding chapters.

## Chapter 2

# SUPPORTING LEARNING DISABLED PARENTING: THE POLICY AND THE LAW

## INTRODUCTION

**2.1** The development of policy relating to learning disabled parenting in England and Wales has to date had a very short history. This is a reflection of the fact that it is only really in the last decade that there has been any acknowledgement that disabled people have parenting responsibilities and that parental disability in its widest sense has been included in policy and research agendas on the provision of parenting support and parenting education services.[1] The invisibility of disabled parenting in general may be due to a tendency within policy and practice to 'fragment' families in terms of 'cared for' and 'carer' relationships and to an assumption that disabled parents are the recipients rather than the providers of 'care' (with a focus, for example, on elderly disabled parents and the role of their children in looking after them, or on the care provided for disabled parents by 'young carers'). It is also perhaps a product of the fact that UK family policy and practice has for many years adopted the stance that the key to effective parenting rests on an individual's capacities and attributes, rather than on ensuring equal access for all to the supports and services which can assist parents in carrying out their parenting roles.[2] Whilst the introduction of the *Framework for the Assessment of Children in Need and their Families*[3] signified a move away from a narrow approach, by requiring assessments under the Children Act 1989 to have regard to the social and economic context in which the parents operate, the parents who are the subject of an assessment are still required to demonstrate their ability to adapt and learn quickly enough to meet the developing needs of their children. This focus on individual capacity and deficit tends to sideline disabled parenting in general (and learning disabled parenting in particular), where the tendency is to make negative assumptions about the skills an individual parent may have and their ability to provide 'good enough' care for their children. The *Good Practice*

---

[1] Richard Olsen and Harriet Clarke *Parenting and Disability, Disabled Parents' Experience of Raising Children* (The Policy Press, 2003), at p 2. See also Commission for Social Care Inspection *Supporting Disabled Parents: A Family or a Fragmented Approach?* (Commission for Social Care Inspection, 2009) at para 1.3.

[2] Although providing support for parents to help them bring up their children was said to be at the core of governmental family policy by 2000, there was considerable evidence of inadequate service provision for disabled parents in particular: see Social Services Inspectorate *A Jigsaw of Services, Inspection of Services to Support Disabled Adults in their Parenting* (Department of Health, 2000).

[3] Department of Health, 2000.

*Guidance on Working with Parents with a Learning Disability*[4] was therefore significant not only because it marked the emergence of the first ever policy guidance targeted specifically at learning disabled parenting, but also because of its role in challenging these stereotypical assumptions.

**2.2** What follows is a summary of those aspects of adult social care policy and child protection policy which have implications for learning disabled parenting. It is suggested that a working knowledge of current policy and the criticisms made of it is a useful tool for the family practitioner who may need to understand the background to and source of the supports and services to which a learning disabled parent may be entitled.

## *VALUING PEOPLE*, 2001

**2.3** The 2001 White Paper *Valuing People*[5] was the first White Paper since 1971 to address the needs of people with learning disabilities. Whereas the focus of *Better Services for the Mentally Handicapped*[6] had been on moving away from the care of the learning disabled in long-term hospitals and towards the increased provision of services for learning disabled people in the community, the aim of *Valuing People* was to improve the life chances of children and adults with learning disabilities so that they would be able to lead full and independent lives. Four key 'principles' were stated to lie at the root of the new proposals: 'rights', 'independence', 'choice' and 'inclusion'. These refer in turn to the concept that rights conferred on all people through disability discrimination and human rights legislation are equally applicable to people with learning disabilities; the idea that people with additional needs are not dependent upon public or social care services but have a right to services supporting them towards independent living; the right of disabled people to exercise choice over aspects of their care; and the right of learning disabled people to have access to and to be included within mainstream services.

**2.4** The White Paper accordingly set out 11 objectives for public services working with people with learning disabilities. These objectives were backed by the creation of a Learning Disability Development Fund of up to £50 million; and an implementation support fund of £2.3 million a year for the next 3 years. Further, the burden of implementation fell on local authorities, which under para 2.9 were required to set up new Learning Disability Partnership Boards in order to bring within the overall framework local public, voluntary and independent agencies. The needs of learning disabled parents are addressed on a limited basis within paras 7.40–7.43 as part of Objective 7 ('to enable people with learning disabilities to lead full and purposeful lives in their communities and to develop a range of friendships, activities and relationships').

---

[4] Department of Health, Department of Education and Skills, 2007.
[5] Department of Health, *Valuing People, A New Strategy for Learning Disability for the 21st Century*, Cm 5086 (2001).
[6] Department for Health and Social Security, 1971.

'7.40 The number of people with learning disabilities who are forming relationships and having children has steadily increased over the last 20 years. Parents with learning disabilities are amongst the most socially and economically disadvantaged groups. They are more likely than other parents to make heavy demands on child welfare services and have their children looked after by the local authority. People with learning disabilities can be good parents and provide their children with a good start in life, but may require considerable help to do so. This requires children and adult social services teams to work closely together to develop a common approach. Social services departments have a duty to safeguard the welfare of children, and in some circumstances a parent with learning disabilities will not be able to meet their child's needs. However, we believe this should not be the result of agencies not arranging for appropriate and timely support.

7.41 Support for disabled parents, including those with learning disabilities, is patchy and underdeveloped, as confirmed in the Social Services Inspectorate inspection. There are tensions and even conflicts within social services departments between those whose focus is the welfare of the child and those concerned with the parent.

7.42 The Government's Framework for the Assessment of Children In Need and their Families is intended for use with all children in need and their families. Further work is needed to help staff use the Assessment Framework when working with parents with learning disabilities and ensure that assessments result in appropriate services being provided to the child and their family. The Department of Health will commission the development of training materials to assist in this process. Parents with learning disabilities will be a priority for follow-up work on the Assessment Framework. We shall also ensure that their needs and those of their children are addressed in future Quality Protects initiatives. The Department of Health will work with Sure Start and the National Parenting Institute to ensure that the needs of parents with learning disabilities are recognised within the Government's wider initiatives to improve parenting and family support.

7.43 At local level, it will be the responsibility of the Director of Social Services, as part of his/her responsibilities for ensuring quality under the social care Quality Framework to ensure effective partnership working for parents with learning disabilities between children's and adult's teams. Partnership Boards should ensure that services are available to support parents with a learning disability.'

**2.5** Paragraph 7.41 above refers to the Social Services Inspectorate's *A Jigsaw of Services*,[7] which analysed the results of a review of services to support disabled parents provided by eight councils between November 1998 and July 1999 (and involving 621 disabled adults). Whilst the 113 disabled parents who responded to the questionnaire sent out as part of the survey were largely happy with the services they had received, they were nevertheless concerned that there was no recognition of the support they needed to help them in their parenting role. The report highlighted several shortcomings, many

---

[7] Social Services Inspectorate *Inspection of Services to Support Disabled Adults in their Parenting Role* (2000).

of which continue to dominate in the critique of adult social care policy a decade later.[8] First, there is a concern that for the majority of local authorities taking part in the survey the eligibility criteria for obtaining support services did not include being a parent.[9] This was found to be a particular issue in the context of parental learning disability, where some of the parents were recognised by the children's services teams as having limited parenting capacity yet were ineligible for support from the adult learning disability team because their IQ was higher than the cut-off point that had been set. Secondly, whilst in some local authorities there were examples of multi-agency coordination of services aimed at disabled adults, there was little evidence of inter-agency coordination between children's and adults' services in relation to disabled *parents*. This was exacerbated by the fact that the child care teams failed to record routinely that one or other of the parents had a learning disability whilst adult social services teams failed to record the presence of a child in the family. Moreover, social work staff appeared to concentrate either on the children in the family or on the impact of the parental disability on the adult's needs, seldom focusing on the needs of the family as a whole and how to support it. Thirdly, there was little evidence of parenting assessments being carried out by staff who had the skills and training to work with learning disabled adults, with the result that there was a risk that child protection decisions might be made on the basis of inadequate or inappropriate information.

**2.6** In view of the conclusion drawn in *A Jigsaw of Services* to the effect that a philosophical and practical shift in the approach to working with disabled parents was required, it is perhaps surprising that *Valuing People* did not address the support needs of learning disabled parents in any greater detail or with any greater urgency. In addition, it is arguable that the commitment to providing learning disabled parents with additional support in order to help them retain their children was more apparent than real, with the Social Care Institute for Excellence reporting as late as 2006[10] that even by that stage very little appeared to have been done about it, and that paras 7.40–7.43 of *Valuing People* seemed therefore to have been added as an afterthought.

# SUPPORTED PARENTING WITHIN ADULT SOCIAL CARE

**2.7** The starting point for ascertaining the type and extent of any available statutory support for the learning disabled parent is to request from the local authority an assessment of the parent's needs under s 47 of the National

---

[8] See, for example, Commission for Social Care Inspection *Supporting Disabled Parents: Family or Fragmented Approach* (2009).
[9] The Fair Access to Care Services framework (2003) and *Putting People First* (2010) – see **2.7** – each include parenting needs as one of the factors to be included within the eligibility criteria operated by the local authority.
[10] In Social Care Institute for Excellence *Supporting Disabled Parents and Parents with Additional Support Needs* (2006).

Health Service and Community Care Act 1990.[11] In drawing up its own eligibility criteria for determining whether a person's 'presenting needs' are also 'eligible needs' for which service provision may be made, the local authority is required to apply the Fair Access to Care Services guidance,[12] issued under s 7 of the Local Authority Social Services Act 1970 and therefore binding upon the local authority unless it considers that there is good reason for not doing so.[13] The current Guidance is now set out in *Putting People First: A Whole System Approach to Eligibility for Social Care*,[14] and its primary aim, like that of its 2003 predecessor, is that all local authorities should determine their criteria for access to social care support upon the basis of an assessment of needs and of the risks to independence over time, in a way that is fair and proportionate to the impact it will have on individuals and the wider community. 'Becoming a parent' is expressly recognised within the Guidance as amounting to a social care need. In para 26 of *Putting People First* it is acknowledged that 'adults who have parenting responsibilities for a child under 18 years may require help with these responsibilities'. Further, the ability to carry out family or other social roles if needs are not addressed remains a factor relevant to the categorisation of a person's eligible needs: the need is 'low' where '*one or two* family or other social roles or responsibilities cannot or will not be undertaken'; 'moderate' where '*several* family and other social roles cannot or will not be undertaken'; 'substantial' where '*the majority* of family or other social roles cannot or will not be undertaken'; and 'critical' where '*vital* family or other social roles cannot or will not be undertaken'. On the other hand, under the heading 'Children and Families' in paras 24–28, the Guidance tends to dwell on the need to avoid relying on the input of an inappropriate level of care from the children or young people in the family when considering the assessment of a disabled person's needs. The Guidance in this way seems to give more weight to the concept of 'parent as cared for' rather than the 'parent as carer'. Moreover, learning disability remains invisible within this statutory guidance.

**2.8** Similarly, the needs of learning disabled parents are recognised only to a limited extent in the new Direct Payments Guidance, also issued under s 7 of the Local Authority Social Services Act 1970.[15] The Guidance provides a framework to assist the local authority in its duty[16] to offer direct payments to

---

[11] See more detailed analysis in Chapter 4.

[12] *Putting People First: A Whole System Approach to Eligibility for Social Care* (Department of Health, 2010). In Wales, where adult social care is devolved, similar Guidance is set out in Welsh Assembly Government *Health and Social Care for Adults: Creating a Unified and Fair System for Assessing and Managing Care – Guidance for Local Authorities and Health Services* (2002).

[13] *R v Islington LBC ex parte Rixon* (1997) 1 CCLR 119, at 123.

[14] Department of Health, 2010.

[15] Department of Health *Guidance on Direct Payments: For Community Care, Services for Carers and Children's Services* (TSO, 2009).

[16] Under s 57(1) of the Health and Social Care Act 2001 and reg 7 of the Community Care, Services for Carers and Children's Services (Direct Payments) (England) Regulations 2009, SI 2009/1887; reg 5 of the Community Care, Services for Carers and Children's Services (Direct Payments) (Wales) Regulations 2004, SI 2004/1748 (W.185); Community Care, Services for Carers and Children's Services (Direct Payments) (Wales) Amendment Regulations 2006, SI 2006/2840 (W.256).

certain categories of people to enable them to obtain and control the provision of social care services for themselves. Under s 57 of the Health and Social Care Act 2001:

> '(1) Regulations may make provision for and in connection with requiring or authorising the responsible authority in the case of a person of a prescribed description who falls within subsection (2) to make, with that person's consent, such payments to him as they may determine in accordance with the regulations in respect of his securing the provision of the service mentioned in paragraph (a) or (b) of that subsection.
>
> (2) A person falls within this subsection if a local authority ("the responsible authority") have decided –
>
> (a) under section 47 of the 1990 Act (assessment by local authorities of needs for community care services) that his needs call for the provision by them of a particular community care service (within the meaning of section 46 of that Act), or
> (b) under section 2(1) of the Carers and Disabled Children Act 2000 (c. 16) (services for carers) to provide him with a particular service under that Act.'

**2.9** Section 58 of the Health and Social Care Act 2001 substitutes a new s 17A of the Children Act 1989, enabling direct payments to be made to a person with parental responsibility for a disabled child, a disabled person with parental responsibility for a child, or to a disabled child aged 16 or 17:

> '(1) The Secretary of State may by regulations make provision for and in connection with requiring or authorising the responsible authority in the case of a person of a prescribed description who falls within subsection (2) to make, with that person's consent, such payments to him as they may determine in accordance with the regulations in respect of his securing the provision of the service mentioned in that subsection.
>
> (2) A person falls within this subsection if he is –
>
> (a) a person with parental responsibility for a disabled child,
> (b) a disabled person with parental responsibility for a child, or
> (c) a disabled child aged 16 or 17,
>
> and a local authority ("the responsible authority") have decided for the purposes of section 17 that the child's needs (or, if he is such a disabled child, his needs) call for the provision by them of a service in exercise of functions conferred on them under that section.'

**2.10** The Direct Payments Guidance further expands the concept – recognised expressly in s 58(2)(b) of the Health and Social Care Act 2001 – that the parenting needs of disabled adults should be a factor for consideration in the drawing up of a local authority's eligibility criteria for direct payments. In this way, para 159 recognises that:

'Needs assessments for disabled adults should include parenting responsibilities, and councils should ensure a co-ordinated approach between adult and children's services and with other agencies.'

Further, in para 160:

'Disabled people who are parents could be assessed as needing services under community care legislation and/or the 1989 Act to assist them in their parenting role. This means that direct payments can be used to meet the social care needs of them, their children or their family that arise from their disability. It is important that the needs of the disabled person and their family are looked at holistically, bearing in mind that specific duties may arise under particular legislation.'

Finally, in para 161 it is stated that:

'Where there is a disabled parent, the council may be under a duty to assist the family if they are assessed as needing help in bringing up their child.'

On the other hand, the apparent commitment to the support of the disabled parent does not necessarily translate into reality: whilst s 17(1) of the Children Act 1989 imposes on the local authority a general duty to safeguard and promote the welfare of children in its area who are in need, and, so far as is consistent with that duty, to promote the upbringing of such children by their families by providing a range and level of appropriate services for them, it does not impose a mandatory duty on a local authority to take specific steps to satisfy the assessed needs of a particular individual child in need, regardless of the local authority's resources.[17] A child in need is eligible for the provision of services but has no absolute right to them, and the local authority has considerable latitude in determining what level of services are 'appropriate' to the needs of a child in need in any given case. In the same way, the disabled parent or person with parental responsibility for a child will not have an absolute right to financial assistance even if he or she has been assessed under the Children Act framework as needing it. Further, where the disabled parent has been assessed under community care legislation as being eligible for parenting support, his or her right to a remedy in the event that the services are not forthcoming remains limited (see Chapter 5 for further discussion).

## SUPPORTED PARENTING UNDER THE CHILDREN ACT 1989 AND THE CHILDREN ACT 2004

**2.11** The ideology underpinning the Children Act 1989 is that children's needs are best met by their families and that state intervention in the family ought to be kept to a minimum. Alongside this was a recognition that the previous law had not been effective in providing support to enable children to remain with their families in appropriate circumstances. Whilst s 1 of the Child Care Act 1980 imposed on local authorities the duty to make available such

---

[17] *R (on the application of G) v Barnet LBC* [2004] 2 AC 208, HL.

assistance as might promote the welfare of children by reducing the need to receive children into care or to bring them before a juvenile court, the provision of services for children was covered by disparate health and welfare legislation which dealt with responsibilities towards particular groups of people of all ages. Part III of the Children Act 1989 therefore aimed to bring together the two sets of legislation in order to ensure that all children received an appropriate standard of care and to increase the focus on the provision of family support rather than the reception of children into care. Section 17(1) of the Children Act 1989 seeks to combine the principle of minimum intervention with supportive measures designed to buttress the family in order to maximise the chances of the children remaining at home, and provides that:

> 'It shall be the general duty of every local authority (in addition to the other duties imposed on them by this Part) –
>
> (a) to safeguard and promote the welfare of children within their area who are in need; and
> (b) so far as is consistent with that duty, to promote the upbringing of such children by their families, by providing a range and level of services appropriate to those children's needs.'

Further, under Sch 2 to the Act every local authority is required to make such provision as it considers appropriate:

> '... for the following services to be available with respect to children in need within their area while they are living with their families –
>
> (a) advice, guidance and counselling;
> (b) occupational, social, cultural or recreational activities;
> (c) home help (which may include laundry facilities);
> (d) facilities for, or assistance with, travelling to and from home for the purpose of taking advantage of any other service provided under this Act or of any similar service;
> (e) assistance to enable the child concerned and his family to have a holiday.'

**2.12** It has been well documented elsewhere that during the 1990s the already overstretched local authorities struggled with the dual purpose of providing support to families whilst at the same time safeguarding the children from harm, with the consequence that priority was given to children considered to be at risk of significant harm and to the conducting of s 47 assessments rather than to assessments under s 17.[18] The overlooking of the interests of children 'in need' has been a recurrent theme and one which is particularly pertinent to disabled parents, for whom it has been said that it is often easier to access services by becoming the target of child protection measures than it is to access services available for the purpose of supporting effective parenting.[19] The implementation of a new s 17A of the Children Act 1989, which, as discussed,

---

[18] See Parton *Governing the Family: Child Care, Child Protection and the State* (Macmillan Education, 1991).
[19] Olsen and Clarke, n 1 above, at p 21.

enables direct payments to be made to a disabled parent in order to meet the parent's needs for supported parenting, goes some way – at least in theory – towards redressing this balance.

**2.13** Moreover, it is notable that there has been in recent years an increasing awareness of the impact upon parenting capacity not only of a diverse range of personal factors (domestic violence, alcohol and drug abuse, learning disability), but also of the part played by wider structural factors such as social isolation, poverty and unemployment. The increasing focus on the need to support children by supporting their parents is also reflected in the introduction of the Framework for the Assessment of Children in Need and their Families (2000), which set down national guidance for the carrying out of assessments of children in need by considering three aspects of 'the child's world': the child's developmental needs; the capacity of parents or carers to support their child's development and respond appropriately to his or her needs; and the wider family and environmental factors that may have an impact on both the child's development and the capacity of their parents and carers to support the child's development and respond to the child's needs. Despite these advances, however, it was not until *Every Child Matters* in 2003 that there was an express governmental objective to 'put supporting parents and carers at the heart of its approach to improving children's lives where support is needed or wanted'.[20]

**2.14** Yet there is only a very limited recognition within *Every Child Matters* that the support needs of *disabled* parents might be an area where additional services are required. Whilst para 3.6 refers indirectly to disabled parents in highlighting the importance of providing 'support to parents and carers who are facing particular difficulties because of their, or their children's, circumstances and experiences', the remainder of the chapter on Supporting Parents and Carers deals with the specific needs of parents and carers of (a) disabled children, (b) young carers and (c) children with parents in prison. Moreover, s 10 of the Children Act 2004, which places a duty on children's services authorities to promote co-operation between themselves and other agencies and therefore seems to address one of the long-standing obstacles facing the provision of support for learning disabled parents in particular, does not go far enough: s 10 provides that each children's services authority in England must make arrangements to promote co-operation between the authority and each of the authority's relevant partners. Yet, the exclusion of adult social care teams from the definition of 'partner services' set out in s 10(4) illustrates the continued sidelining of disabled parenting within the child welfare framework.

---

[20] Cm 5860, p 8.

## GOOD PRACTICE GUIDANCE ON WORKING WITH PARENTS WITH A LEARNING DISABILITY, DEPARTMENT OF HEALTH, 2007

**2.15** Set against the preceding background, the publication by the Department of Health and Department for Education and Skills of the *Good Practice Guidance on Working with Parents with a Learning Disability* is an important development. As Good Practice Guidance, it has no statutory force, although it purports to assist local authorities to fulfil their disability equality duty[21] to promote equality of opportunity for disabled people. Its recommendations will now assist local authorities in complying with their duties under the Equality Act 2010.

**2.16** The Good Practice Guidance represents a significant policy shift for three reasons. First, it represents a wholesale change from the course taken since *Valuing People*, in which the support of disabled people as parents has been largely sidestepped; secondly, in being expressly designed for the assistance of children's and adult's services it reunites both aspects of social care policy in a common purpose; thirdly, it deals solely and exclusively with learning disabled parents rather than learning disabled adults or disabled parents in general, and specifically recognises the need to improve the chances of the children of learning disabled parents remaining with their families by improving the quality of the support services available to them.

**2.17** The Guidance establishes five key features of good practice:

- Making information and communication accessible to enable parents with learning disabilities to engage with services and maximise the chances of their children's needs being met. This means, for example, that learning disability services should take steps to ensure that parents with learning disabilities know about the kinds of support available; and that any such information with which they are provided is in formats suitable for people with learning disabilities.
- Ensuring that there are jointly agreed protocols[22] between adult and children's services, and health and social care, so that the needs of learning disabled parents and their children can be responded to promptly and appropriately. The need for this level of coordination arises out of the fact that parents with learning disabilities may experience a range of needs and difficulties (from housing problems to issues concerning mental health, domestic violence and substance abuse). Moreover, a co-operative approach is of particular importance in order to ensure that low levels of

---

[21] Under the Disability Discrimination Act 2005 and now replaced by the Equality Act 2010.
[22] Page 11, para 1.2.1 outlines the issues which should be included in the jointly agreed protocols: referrals, information sharing, provision of information to parents and children, assessment responsibilities, provision of assistance and support to enable the parents and children to take part in the assessment, eligibility for different services, financial responsibilities and joint funding provision, charging, service provision, service reviews and training on the implementation of the protocol.

need are identified and addressed before they lead to difficulties for the parents and undermine the children's welfare.[23] The risk that a jointly agreed protocol is designed to avoid is that of parents and children falling between adults' and children's services,[24] such as where a parent is deemed not to be eligible by adult services for support with his or her parenting responsibilities, yet struggles without such support so that the children become children in need or are even considered likely to suffer significant harm. The Guidance suggests that agencies in drawing up their protocols may need to recognise 'that a combination of learning disability and parenting responsibilities creates a higher level of need than if needs only relating to learning disability are considered'.[25]

- Ensuring that support designed to meet the needs of parents and children is based on a realistic assessment of their needs and strengths. In particular, the Guidance stresses the importance of services taking a long-term view of the needs of learning disabled parents:[26]

   'It is against children's interests if support is provided to enable their parents to look after them while they are young but the necessary support is not then provided as children grow older and needs change.'

- Recognising the need to provide long-term support where necessary, and accepting that the need for long-term support does not mean that parents cannot look after their children.
- Ensuring that parents have access to independent advocacy and to self-advocacy support to enable them to build confidence and self-esteem, without which parenting difficulties might arise. It is recommended that independent advocacy should always be provided where the children are the subject of a child protection plan and/or care proceedings are instituted.

## Promoting children's best interests

**2.18** The Guidance specifically sets out the fundamentals of good practice in circumstances where safeguarding procedures are necessary and suggests the following measures to promote the best interests of the relevant children:

- complying with the duty to ascertain the wishes and feelings of children when carrying out assessments and making decision about service responses (s 17 of the Children Act 1989, as amended by s 53 of the Children Act 2004);
- ensuring that a child's needs are met under s 17 of the Children Act 1989 or under community care legislation in cases where s 47 inquiries have

---

[23] Page 10.
[24] Paragraph 1.2.3.
[25] Paragraph 1.2.4.
[26] Paragraph 1.3.4.

established that the child is not at risk of significant harm, ie ensuring that sufficient support is provided to the family so as to prevent the standard of care deteriorating;
- subject to the child's age and understanding, inviting the child to the child protection conference;
- ensuring, where a key worker is appointed for a child whose parent has a learning disability, that the worker has some understanding of learning disability or, if not, that the worker has access to such expertise;
- providing an independent advocate to a child who is accommodated under s 20 of the Children Act 1989; and
- promoting contact with family members for the child living away from the family, where it is in the best interests of the child for these links to be maintained.

## Ensuring equitable treatment for parents with learning disabilities

**2.19** The following measures are proposed to ensure equitable treatment for parents with learning disabilities:

- providing the parents with information about independent sources of local and national advice and advocacy;
- making every effort to ensure that independent advocates have skills and expertise in both learning disability and child protection;
- sharing information with the parents in a form which is accessible to them, unless sharing information would place the child at risk of significant harm;
- ensuring that core assessments involving families affected by learning disability include specialist input concerning the impact of learning disability;
- where the partner of a learning disabled parent is considered to pose a risk of harm, addressing the possible vulnerability of the learning disabled parent and their need to be protected from harm, and supporting the non-abusing parent to protect their child;
- drawing up a child in need plan where a child protection plan is not considered necessary, in order to prevent the standard of parental care from deteriorating due to a lack of support;
- inviting parents to attend child protection conferences and providing them with an independent advocate if they wish to attend;
- appointing a key worker for the parent where the children are subject to a child protection plan, and ensuring that the key worker has training in learning disability;
- ensuring that the parents are fully supported to understand what is required of them in a child protection plan, and the support that will be provided to help them achieve this;
- continuing to support the parents according to assessed need even where the child is no longer the subject of a child protection plan;

- where children are placed in foster care, providing the parents with practical support in order to maximise their chances of improving their parenting capacity;
- if the child is to be placed in foster care, placing the child wherever possible with carers who have experience and/or training in working in partnership with parents with learning disabilities;
- conducting the complaints procedure in ways which ensure that people with learning disabilities have equal access to it;
- making reasonable adjustments to care proceedings to avoid discrimination against parents with learning disabilities, ie giving them enough time to understand what is going on; involving them fully in any assessments and care planning; making reasonable adjustments to timetables for assessments, if necessary; and
- providing access to both emotional and practical supports where a care plan ends with children being removed.

**2.20** Despite the potential of the Good Practice Guidance to procure change, the Commission for Social Care Inspection reported in 2009 a failure by many local authorities to address the issues.[27] Sixty-six per cent of the local authorities consulted reported that their policies still tended to cover children's and adult's needs separately, with only 12% adopting a whole family focus and only 34% having begun to collect information on the numbers and profiles of disabled parents and families in their area, and only 30% having developed any kind of protocol to establish a shared understanding of roles and responsibilities within the local authority and with other partner agencies. This lack of joint co-operation was found to hamper the provision of preventative services, which was made worse by the fact that limited resources meant that there was no opportunity to support those with less than critical needs. In summary, it found that:[28]

> '... councils are failing to achieve the right balance of interventions to support disabled persons and the family. Extra efforts are required to overcome the new silos that have been created by the separation of children's and adults' services so that there is not a disjointed approach to supporting the family.'

The Joint Committee on Human Rights was similarly critical of the lack of progress,[29] finding that for adults with learning disabilities 'the violation of their human rights is seen as a normal part of their everyday lives'. Within the context of 'Parenting and Family life', Chapter Six of the Report observed that:

- The children of people with learning disabilities are still more likely to be removed from their parents' care than are the children of people who do not have learning disabilities (para 159).

---

[27] *Supporting Disabled Families, A Family or a Fragmented Approach* (February 2009).
[28] At p 6.
[29] Joint Committee on Human Rights *A Life Like Any Other – Human Rights of Adults with Learning Disabilities* Seventh Report 2007–2008, HL 40-41 (2008).

- The evidence received suggested that decisions about the future placement of children of parents with learning disabilities are taken without adequate information, arrangements or support being put in place to allow parents to demonstrate that they can look after their children satisfactorily (para 165).
- Adult social services and children's services often do not work together well to ensure that families have the support they needed (para 165).
- Assessments fail to test the parents' abilities and support needs effectively (para 165).
- Supports which parents with a learning disability may require to help them look after their children satisfactorily may not be available from local authorities, due to the application of increasingly narrow eligibility criteria as a result of resource constraints (para 165).
- If the Good Practice Guidance recommendations were implemented effectively, this could significantly reduce the risk that parents and children would be separated in breach of the European Convention on Human Rights (para 169).
- However, effective implementation of the Good Practice Guidance requires its widespread dissemination by central government and effective implementation by local authorities backed by sufficient resources (para 179).
- The proposals for monitoring progress in improving support to parents with learning disabilities are weak and lack precision (para 181).
- Learning disability partnership boards should be required to report annually on local commissioning of services to support parents with learning disabilities; and to collect data on the numbers of parents with learning disabilities supported by services and the number of children taken into care each year (para 181).

**2.21** The Labour Government's response to those concerns was set out in *Valuing People Now: A New Three-Year Strategy for People with Learning Disabilities*,[30] which set out key policy objectives for the next 3 years (ie 2009–2012). In the context of learning disabled parenting it was intended that by 2012 'all people with learning disabilities will have the choice to have relationships, become parents and continue to be parents, and will be supported to do so'. Reviewing the progress made in this area since *Valuing People*, it acknowledged that people with moderate and severe learning disabilities were still one of the most excluded groups in our society and that such parents still remained at a disproportionate risk of losing their children into care. The challenging of stereotypes and changing of attitudes was seen, however, as a major stumbling block to progress (para 3.54). To that end it recommended:

- That more should be done to ensure that adults' and children's services work more effectively together to improve the identification of families needing extra support and to carry out more effective assessments of their needs.

---

[30] Department of Health, 2009.

- That the Parenting Implementation Project continues to work with a number of local authorities to develop good practice in relation to the commissioning and implementation of parenting and family support services for learning disabled parents.
- That relevant professionals share good practice around joint working to best support vulnerable parents and are trained in the 2007 Good Practice Guidance.
- That parents with a learning disability receive support and benefit from all mainstream initiatives aimed at parents, including receiving the same level of information and advice.

## WALES

**2.22** In 2007 the Welsh Assembly Government published *a Statement of Policy and Practice for Adults with a Learning Disability*. The policy scarcely addresses the position of learning disabled adults as *parents* and the chapter on 'Families and Carers' is restricted to a recognition that the families and unpaid carers of learning disabled people are likely to need support. However, the Welsh Assembly Government has introduced a far more holistic response to the needs of learning disabled parents through the rolling out of a programme of integrated family support teams under the Children and Families (Wales) Measure 2010 (passed by the National Assembly on 10 November 2009). The aim, through co-operation between health services and social services in the establishment of local integrated family support teams, is to reduce the inequities existing for the most vulnerable children and families, in which the children of learning disabled parents are included by virtue of s 58(6)(d). Under s 58(6) of the Measure, a local authority may refer the family to an integrated family support team if it reasonably believes or suspects that a parent of a child in that family (or a prospective parent): '(a) is dependent on alcohol or drugs; (b) is a victim of domestic violence or abuse; (c) has a history of violent or abuse behaviour, or (d) has a mental disorder.' For the purpose of sub-s (6) '"mental disorder" means any disorder or disability of the mind'.

**2.23** As part of the consultation period for the Children and Families (Wales) Measure 2010 the Welsh Assembly Government commissioned Learning Disability Wales to provide more information about the experiences of learning disabled parents in Wales. The findings, set out in *Being a Family: Parents with Learning Disabilities in Wales, 2009,* echo the English experience:

- All of the respondents found that the practical support offered by their extended families had been invaluable in assisting them to retain the care of their children.
- Most of the parents felt that they had received poor support from Children's Services.
- None of the parents identified social workers from the child care teams as being good sources of support.

- Where practical support was provided by Children's Services it was likely to work more effectively if the workers were trained in best practice ways of working with people with learning disabilities.
- There was a lack of communication between the child and family team and the learning disabilities team.
- There was a general perception amongst learning disability social workers and parents that what was regarded as an acceptable standard of parenting depended on the professional's own personal standards rather than on an agreed set of standards within the department. Children's Services should therefore consider and outline the standards that are necessary for parents and children to continue to live together, and once these standards have been set for individual families, they should be shared with the family and with all those working with them.
- Independent advocacy services fulfilled a vital need, especially around the issues involved in care cases. As such, they should be funded by the Welsh Assembly Government rather than relying on charitable funding as at present.
- None of the respondents to the interview were aware of any learning disability policies or joint protocols in their locality for working with parents with learning disabilities.
- Local authorities should produce their own protocols on working with parents with learning disabilities.
- The Welsh Assembly Government should produce similar guidelines to the Department of Health's *Good Practice Guidance*.
- Where the first language of the family is Welsh, the case conferences should also be conducted in Welsh: it is well known that stress can increase an impairment and cause a deterioration in communication skills, and the stress of going through child care proceedings should not be underestimated.

## SUMMARY

**2.24** By far the most important policy document on learning disabled parents is the 2007 *Good Practice Guidance*, which focuses on the provision of services to support the parents in their parenting task and to try to enable the parents to keep their children at home. Commentators point repeatedly, however, to two ongoing areas of concern which unless remedied will tend to undermine the effective implementation of the Guidance: first, the ever-tightening of the eligibility criteria for access to social care services, which means that parents with mild to moderate learning disability might be especially vulnerable to failure to meet the standard of good enough care; and, secondly, the failure of children's services and adult learning disability teams to work together to ensure that an holistic view is taken. It is suggested as a consequence that as one of the first, practical steps in the representation of a learning disabled parent in care proceedings, the lawyer should request a copy of the authority's learning disability protocol. In a case where there is no agreed protocol between children's and adult's social care services the burden will be on the local authority to show that the learning disability of the parent has been appropriately taken into consideration and that he or she has received all the support to which they might be entitled.

# Chapter 3

# LEARNING DISABLED PARENTING: THE RESEARCH BASE

## INTRODUCTION

**3.1** Where a child is the subject of a child protection plan, a successful outcome depends upon the parents' ability to engage with, and to work in partnership with, the social work team. This will require the parents, first, to acknowledge and accept the concerns of the local authority; secondly, to be willing to co-operate with the local authority in the implementation of the child protection plan; and, thirdly, to be committed to bringing about a change in their parenting. The latter is of overriding importance since the fundamental aim of the social work assessment in care proceedings is to see how capable of change the parents are. Yet, demonstrating a commitment to change and a capacity for doing so is of particular significance for learning disabled parents in the light of the enduring preconceptions about them that they may face: first, that it is inevitable that a learning disabled parent will – albeit unintentionally – harm their child or expose him or her to a risk of harm from others; and, secondly, that there is as a result little point in offering them any preventative or support services.[1] At the same time, demonstrating commitment is a problematic area for the learning disabled parent for three reasons: due to his or her cognitive limitations the parent may be an unreliable timekeeper and repeated missed appointments might be viewed as non-engagement; the child protection workers may not have spent enough time developing a rapport with the parent in order to overcome his or her resentment of and resistance to the local authority, fear of engaging with social services being commonplace amongst the learning disabled;[2] and the parent might have acquiesced in what was being asked of him or her without properly understanding it, such that their failure to follow through is seen as non-co-operation.[3]

**3.2** In *Dundee City Council v McL*[4] the enduring power of the negative stereotype of the learning disabled mother and the inferences that may be drawn from her non-co-operation are well illustrated. The court had the benefit of neither a psychological assessment to determine the level at which the mother was functioning nor a careful social work assessment of the impact of

---

[1] McConnell and Llewellyn 'Stereotypes, Parents with Intellectual Disability and Child Protection' (2002) 24(3) *Journal of Social Welfare and Family Law* 297–317.
[2] Traustadottir and Sigurjonsdottir in Llewellyn et al *Parents with Intellectual Disabilities, Past, Present and Futures* (John Wiley & Sons, 2010), at p 111.
[3] Traustadottir and Sigurjonsdottir, n 2 above, at p 180.
[4] [2005] Scot SC 34.

the mother's learning difficulties on her parenting. Instead, the judge simply noted the conflict of opinion between the child's former social worker, who thought that the mother did not have the ability to learn basic skills, and that of the current social worker, who thought that the mother had such an ability but could not be bothered to engage with the local authority, and concluded that the views of the former social worker were 'nearer the mark': the mother was *'inherently incapable of learning sufficient basic parenting skills* to be able to care for a child without, by omission rather than act, putting that child's welfare at risk'. Although the judge criticised the local authority for failing to carry out a proper assessment of the mother, this criticism was not based on any sense of unfairness to the mother, but rather on the waste of resources and the risks to which the child had been exposed by an ill-judged attempt at rehabilitation:[5]

> 'If that had been effectively explored at the outset by the social work department, then they would have learned that there was no merit in pursuing a policy of attempting rehabilitation of the child ... and would not have exposed the child to the risks she was exposed to ... had J declined to co-operate with assessment of her intellectual capacity, then the department should have assumed she was inherently incapable and let her demonstrate the contrary rather than put the child at risk. They did not.'

**3.3** This chapter considers the multi-disciplinary research base, its identification of the possible risks to the child arising as a consequence of learning disabled parenting and the mitigating factors that might result in an outcome whereby the child remains at home. This is useful for two reasons: first, so that the lawyer representing any party has a better understanding of the sorts of psycho-social issues that are likely to arise in any given case; and, secondly, in order to provide a tool for challenging the kind of assumptions that can permeate some cases, such as in *Dundee City Council v McL*.[6] All of the research (summarised in tabular form at the end of this chapter) shares the same basic premise: that parental IQ is not by itself an indicator of inadequate parenting unless it falls towards the lower end of what is considered to be a mild learning disability, that is, below 55–60.[7] Most of the research also focuses on learning disabled *mothers*, whether by design or whether as a reflection of the reality that most of the primary carers were single mothers.

---

[5] Per Sheriff Davidson.
[6] [2005] Scot SC 34.
[7] However, it has been pointed out that the view that an IQ below 55 relates directly to inadequate parenting is based upon only three research studies: see discussion in Bernard 'Parents with Learning Disabilities – The Assessment of Parenting Ability' (2007)3 *Advances in Mental Health and Learning Disabilities* 14; and in Dowdney and Skuse 'Parenting Provided by Adults with Mental Retardation' (1993) 34(1) *Journal of Child Psychology and Psychiatry* 25–47.

# THE RISK FACTORS

## Choice of partner

**3.4** The vulnerability of the learning disabled mother in her choice of a partner, as evidenced by the fact that women with learning disabilities are reported as being four to ten times more likely to experience sexual violence, physical violence and homicide from their partners than are women without learning disability,[8] is a concept with which the family courts are very familiar. Also familiar is the tendency for learning disabled mothers to be targeted by Sch 1[9] offenders, who gain access to their children though offering practical and emotional support to the family.[10] There has, however, been very little research in relation to the characteristics of the partners of learning disabled parents and to any associated risks. Abuse by a learning disabled parent has been considered to be more likely where the partner is also learning disabled and therefore unlikely to provide effective parenting support.[11] Yet, McGaw et al found that there was an increased risk of abuse or neglect to the children of learning disabled mothers when their partners were known to have a criminal history, and that this risk became more significant in parallel with increasing levels of intelligence in the partners. The more intelligent the mother's partner, the greater the risk of harm to the child, with the risk being higher when the partner had a combination of an IQ of 85 or above and a criminal history than when the partner had a low IQ (between 60 and 84) and a criminal history.[12] Further, abuse or neglect was reported more frequently by the children taking part in their study when they lived in households where the mother's partner was known to have or to have had anti-social behavioural problems. An increased risk was also associated with partners who had suffered some form of childhood trauma in their past. Aunos et al,[13] although working with a much smaller study group than McGaw et al, also reported facts suggesting a direct relationship between the mother's choice of partner and the risk to the child: in eight out of 17 of their sample of learning disabled mothers whose children no longer lived with them there had been allegations of abuse or neglect, and in five of those eight cases the allegations had been directed against the mother's new partner. Their study did not, however, address the IQ level of any of the partners.

**3.5** On the other hand, it is important not to over-generalise these findings since there is evidence that the presence in the home of a partner without

---

[8] McGaw, Scully and Pritchard 'Predicting the Unpredictable? Identifying High-risk versus Low-risk Parents with Intellectual Disabilities' (2010) 34 *Child Abuse and Neglect* 699–710, at p 707.
[9] Children and Young Persons Act 1933.
[10] Cleaver and Nicholson *Parental Learning Disability and Children's Needs: Family Experiences and Effective Practice* (Jessica Kingsley Publishers, 2007).
[11] Dowdney and Skuse, n 7 above.
[12] McGaw et al, n 8 above.
[13] Aunos, Goupil and Feldman 'Mothers with Intellectual Disabilities who Do or Do Not have Custody of their Children' (2003) 10 *Journal on Developmental Disabilities* 65–80.

learning disabilities can in some cases be protective.[14] Cleaver and Nicholson, for example, concluded that the children were likely to achieve better outcomes where the learning disabled parent had the continuing and day-to-day support of a capable and non-abusive adult.[15] In other words, in these cases the presence in the home of a partner without learning disabilities mitigated the other risk factors likely to impact upon the children of learning disabled parents, which McGaw et al found were associated with the mother having had a history of childhood trauma, the mother having additional disabilities on top of the learning disability and the child having special needs.[16]

## Parental childhood history

**3.6** The ability of all parents to respond to their children is often linked to their having had positive emotional experiences in their own childhoods. As yet, the effects on learning disabled parents of their own experiences of being parented have been largely unexplored, since most research on the lifespan of learning disabled parents involves parents who have been brought up in institutional care. McGaw et al have recently considered the childhood experiences of learning disabled parents in their study of 49 parents who received support from a special parenting service in Devon over a 5-year period (2000–2005). They found that 79.6% of their sample of parents reported abuse or neglect of some form during their childhood, with 55.1% citing multiple abuse/neglect categories,[17] that severe to extreme abuse or neglect was the most common level of trauma experienced by the parents and that emotional abuse was the most prevalent.[18] As to the effect of this on the *children* of learning disabled parents, the analysis of their results showed that 79% of those parents who had suffered childhood abuse had children who were or who had been registered on the Child Protection Register (CPR),[19] and that there was a significant relationship between the number of parents who had suffered childhood emotional abuse and the number of children who were or had been registered under the same category. In addition, there was evidence that the children of learning disabled parents who had reported childhood trauma were themselves at increased risk of mental health difficulties.[20] McGaw et al accepted, however, that the reliability and validity of the parents' reports of childhood abuse might be questioned on the basis of their intellectual functioning (and their poor memory capacity, comprehension and processing speed in particular), since in some cases the parents were recalling events that had happened some 20–50 years earlier. On the other hand, they surmised that

---

[14] McGaw et al, n 8 above.
[15] Above n 10.
[16] See further below.
[17] McGaw, Shaw and Beckley 'Prevalence of Psychopathology across a Service Population of Parents with Intellectual Disabilities and their Children' (2007) 4(1) *Journal of Policy and Practice in Intellectual Disabilities* 11–22.
[18] Ibid.
[19] Ibid, at p 17.
[20] Ibid, at p 19.

adults with learning disabilities tended to under-report the abuse they had experienced, perhaps out of fear that their own children might be removed from their care.

## Maternal stress

**3.7** 'Stress' is experienced when the subjective demands of a situation are incompatible with a person's response capabilities. Most research on stress caused by parenting has been carried out in relation to mothers and has shown an association with negative mother-child interactions; low development scores for very young children; and emotional maladjustment, behavioural problems and school problems in older children. Whilst it is the case that parenting stress can be experienced by anyone regardless of their cognitive abilities, there is a clinically significant correlation between mothers with learning disabilities and extremely high stress levels. In 1997, Feldman et al[21] tested the hypothesis that learning disabled mothers would report significantly higher stress levels than a normative sample of parents without disabilities, using a field of 82 'intellectually disabled' mothers (with an IQ of less than 80). Whilst they acknowledged what might be seen as the inherent bias within their study (in that all the participants were already known to social services and were perhaps predisposed to stress on that basis), they found that all 82 mothers reported considerable stress and scored significantly higher than the normative sample of non-learning-disabled mothers. Moreover, they found that maternal stress increased when the children reached school age, probably reflecting their increasing inability to manage the children's behaviour as the children grew older. On the other hand, the authors also noted that there were other factors that could account for this, referring to their findings that the mothers of the school-age children were older, had lower IQs, lived in more crowded conditions and were subject to less child welfare scrutiny than the mothers of the pre-school children. A further study, by Feldman, Verghese, Ramsay and Rajska,[22] found similarly that mothers with learning disabilities were highly stressed and socially isolated, that the mothers of older children experienced more stress than did those of younger children, and that there was no difference between the (high) stress levels experienced by those mothers living in small population centres and those living in the city.

## Mental health

**3.8** Adults with learning disability have a higher rate of psychiatric disorder than do adults in the general population, with the research suggesting that the prevalence rates for learning disabled people is two to three times higher than for the general adult population.[23] There is some evidence, however, that there

---

[21] Feldman, Leger and Walton-Allen, 'Stress in Mothers with Intellectual Disabilities' (1997) 6(4) *Journal of Child and Family Studies* 471–485.
[22] Feldman, Varghese, Ramsay and Rajska 'Relationships between Social Support, Stress and Mother-child Interactions in Mothers with Intellectual Disabilities' (2002) 15 *Journal of Applied Research in Intellectual Disabilities* 314–323.
[23] McGaw et al 2007, n 17 above.

is a higher prevalence rate of psychiatric disorder amongst those adults with profound and severe learning disabilities than amongst those with mild to moderate learning disabilities. Cooper and Bailey in 2001[24] found that whereas 62.5% of adults with profound and severe learning disabilities had a psychiatric disorder, 42.2% of those with moderate and mild learning disabilities did so. They conceded, however, that since their research population was drawn from the community learning disability register, and that those with milder learning disabilities were not all registered on it (those with mild learning disabilities being notoriously difficult to reach), their study was perhaps not representative of the entire learning disability population.

**3.9** It follows that many learning disabled *parents* will also suffer from mental illness: McGaw et al found, for example, that 45% of their subject group of 49 learning disabled parents demonstrated some form of psychopathology, whether depression (33%), anxiety (20%), psychosis (10%), obsessive compulsive disorders (12%) or hypomania/mania (4%) and that mothers were significantly more likely to report psychopathology than were fathers. Feldman, Vargehese et al[25] found, similarly, that a higher proportion (70%) of mothers with learning disability have depression or anxiety, and have greater and more severe depression symptomatology than do mothers who do not have learning disabilities. Likewise, Tymchuk[26] found that learning disabled mothers scored significantly higher on the Beck Depression Inventory than did the control group of those who were not learning disabled, that the symptoms they identified with on the Beck Inventory were those giving rise to greater clinical concern (with 31% of the learning disabled mothers and only 8% of the control group mothers having had suicidal thoughts) and that almost 40% of the learning disabled mothers scored above the cut-off point for depression. As to whether or not the poor mental health of the learning disabled parent has an effect upon the outcome for the child, Aunos et al,[27] in considering the variables between learning disabled mothers who had lost the care of their children and those whose children remained at home, found that the mental health of the mother was not a significant factor. The mothers of the children who were not removed from the home generally reported greater community involvement and greater satisfaction with the services and support they could access, yet there was no statistically significant relationship between the different outcomes for the children and any differences between their mothers' mental and physical health. McGaw et al found that the risk to the children of learning disabled parents was greater if the parents were also physically disabled or otherwise additionally impaired than it was if they suffered from poor mental health but had no other disability.[28]

---

[24] Cooper and Bailey 'Psychiatric Disorders amongst Adults with Learning Disabilities – Prevalence and Relationship to Ability Level' (2001) 18(2) Ir J Psych Med 45–53.
[25] Above n 22.
[26] Tymchuk 'Depression Symptomatology in Mothers with Mild Intellectual Disability: An Exploratory Study' (1994) 19(2) *Australia and New Zealand Journal of Developmental Disabilities* 111–119.
[27] Above n 13.
[28] McGaw et al 2010, n 8 above.

**3.10** On the other hand, whilst the mental health of the learning disabled mother may not be statistically relevant to the question of whether her parenting is 'good enough', a significant relationship has been found between the presence of psychopathology in learning disabled parents and mental disorders in their children, with 69% of the children in McGaw's research sample having one or more problems showing the presence of some kind of mental disorder.[29] More specifically, 40% of the children had multiple problems; 41% had poor attention spans; 40% had conduct disorders; and 24% had either anxiety or acute problems. The authors controlled for the fact that learning disabled children are reported as being two to three times more likely to experience severe emotional and behavioural disorders or psychiatric illnesses than are children without learning disability and that there is a relationship between poverty and psychiatric problems in children with learning disabilities in that it increases their exposure to and vulnerability to stressors: first, the parents in their study were all claiming benefits and income support and so fell into the same socio-economic category which, albeit low, meant that 'poverty' was unlikely to be a variable affecting outcome; secondly, the results showed that the children taking part in the study who were themselves learning disabled were no more likely to suffer from mental disorders than were those who were not learning disabled.

## Developmental delay

**3.11** There is some evidence, primarily from researchers in Canada and Australia, that the children of learning disabled parents are in reality at risk of poor developmental outcomes.[30] For example, in 1999 Keltner et al[31] analysed the developmental status of 38 children born to low-income mothers with learning disability and 32 children born to low-income mothers without learning disability, and found that 42% of the former and only 12% of the latter were assessed as developmentally delayed. A similar relationship was found by Feldman, Leger and Walton-Allen[32] when they analysed the outcomes for children aged between 6 and 12 years and concluded that, on average, the educational performance of the children of learning disabled mothers was poorer than that of the children whose mothers were not learning disabled but who were recruited from the same low-income neighbourhood. More recently, in 2003 Aunos, Goupil and Feldman[33] found that 41% of the children of learning disabled mothers who still lived at home, and 45% of those who had been placed outside the family, attended special classes, in contrast to the 10%

---

[29] McGaw et al 2007, n 17 above, at p 19.
[30] 'Parents Labelled with Intellectual Disability: *Position of the International Association for the Scientific Study of Intellectual Disabilities (IASSID)* Special Interest Research Group (SIRG) on Parents and Parenting with Intellectual Disabilities' (2008) *Journal of Applied Research in Intellectual Disabilities* 296–307.
[31] Keltner, Wise and Taylor 'Mothers with Intellectual Limitations and their 2 Year Old Children's Developmental Outcomes' (1999) 24 *Journal of Intellectual and Developmental Disability* 45–57.
[32] Above n 21.
[33] Aunos, Goupil and Feldman 'Mothers with Intellectual Disabilities Who Do or Do Not have Custody of their Children' (2003) 10(2) *Journal on Developmental Disabilities* 65–80.

of children attending elementary school nationwide. Moreover, 14% of the children of learning disabled mothers still living with their mother and 23% of the children placed outside the family had a developmental diagnosis, as compared with 3.3% of children aged 0 to 14 nationwide. Again, Cleaver and Nicholson[34] found that over half of the children in their study group (cases involving a parent with learning disability) were classified as having severe developmental needs, whereas only 32.9% of the comparison group (cases where parents did not have a learning disability) met those criteria. Language delay is a particular area of concern, with a range of research studies identifying a high incidence of expressive language delay amongst the children of learning disabled parents. This is thought to derive from a reduced tendency by the learning disabled parent towards using verbal interaction with their children, a reduced tendency towards making descriptive statements to them and a limited tendency to use praise.[35]

**3.12** It is unclear from the research how far it can be argued that the developmental delay in any given case is attributable to the care (or lack of it) being given by the parent or whether it is genetically linked to the fact of the parent's own learning disability.[36] A study in 1965 found that when neither parent had a learning disability only 1% of their children had a learning disability, but that this figure rose to 15% where one parent had a learning disability and to 40% when both parents were learning disabled.[37] On the other hand, a follow-up study found that the risk was greater when the mother rather than the father was the only parent with a learning disability, suggesting that the likelihood of the child having a learning disability was directly linked to whether or not the primary care-giver (usually the mother) was so affected.[38] More recently, however, McConnell et al[39] have widened the question of causation by suggesting that the variations observed in the developmental outcomes of the children of learning disabled parents are possibly associated with poor antenatal and maternity care rather than with differences in the quality of the home environment. In their study of 37 pre-school-aged children born to learning disabled mothers they found that between 35% and 57% of the children showed developmental delay of at least 3 months. Whilst there was a wide variation in the developmental status of the children, there was no significant relationship between the developmental level of the child and the quality of the home environment, the latter being assessed on the basis of the level of maternal responsiveness and involvement and the stimulation available.

**3.13** The raising of a child with special needs appears to be a significant factor affecting the differences in outcomes between those learning disabled

---

[34] Above n 10.
[35] James 'Promoting Effective Working with Parents with Learning Disabilities' (2004) 13 *Child Abuse Review* 31–41.
[36] Ibid.
[37] Reed and Reed *Mental Retardation: A Family Study* (Philadelphia, Saunders, 1965).
[38] James, n 35 above, at p 33.
[39] McConnell, Llewellyn, Mayes et al 'Developmental Profiles of Children Born to Mothers with Intellectual Disability' (2003) 28(2) *Journal of Intellectual and Developmental Disability* 122–134.

mothers who retained the care of their children and those who had their children removed. A comparison of the outcomes suggested that the former were more satisfied with the level of services they had received; were more involved in the community; had younger children; had a higher income; and were more likely to have a child who was receiving additional services for special needs.[40] Conversely, raising a child with special needs or developmental delay[41] has been identified as a factor less conducive to a successful outcome along with the parents having additional physical or sensory impairment on top of their learning disability, or themselves reporting a history of childhood abuse or neglect. Cleaver and Nicholson[42] also found that since the presence of a child with learning disability or special needs was an extra challenge for any parent, the tendency of parents with learning disabilities to acquiesce in and fail to challenge the provision of services for them meant that it was much less likely that these children would have their needs adequately met. The identification of the child's special needs or developmental delay as both a mitigating factor and a factor indicating a less successful outcome is perhaps explained by the relatively small populations contained in the different research studies. Alternatively, its presence as both a positive and a negative risk factor perhaps depends on whether or not the child's special needs have been identified at a sufficiently early stage for appropriate resources to be provided, in that where sufficient support has not been provided, the parent is likely to struggle. What is clear, however, is that it is not uncommon for the local authority to seek to use the child's developmental delay as a factor justifying the child's removal from home on the basis that the developmental delay has arisen as a consequence of learning disabled parenting. Whilst a local authority might seek to rely on any educational progress or developmental progress made by the child who has been placed in foster care, Hedley J has warned against such an approach, commenting in *Re L*[43] that it would be 'very surprising indeed' if a child who had been removed from the care of learning disabled parents into the care of more able foster parents did not make some progress in the new environment. As Cleaver and Nicholson found, all the children in their research study made educational and behavioural progress once they had been removed from home and placed with foster carers. The point made in *Re L*, however, is that this in itself does not prove that the standard of care provided by the parents was intolerable or even inadequate.

## IMPLICATIONS

**3.14** There are two consequences for policy and practice arising out of the summary of the research base set out above. The first point is that since many of the learning disabled parents in these studies presented with additional problems, such as poor mental and physical health, substance misuse, domestic violence, inadequate housing and social isolation, the need for multi-agency

---

[40] Aunos et al, n 13 above.
[41] McGaw et al 2010, n 8 above, at p 707.
[42] Above n 10.
[43] *Re L (A Child) (Care: Threshold Criteria)* [2007] 1 FLR 2050.

coordination and support in assisting them to achieve better outcomes is crucial. Yet, as discussed in Chapter 2, the failure of adults and children's social services departments to communicate effectively with one another has been repeatedly identified as an obstacle standing in the way of effective support for learning disabled parents. Moreover, the research base in fact highlights the need for multi-agency communication and coordination amongst a range of agencies extending beyond children's and adult's social care to include housing and mental health or psychiatric services. In fact, it is arguable that in view of the prevalence of mental health needs amongst parents with learning disabilities, the psychiatric needs of parents with learning disabilities have perhaps been overlooked: the *Good Practice Guidance on Working with Parents with a Learning Disability 2007* is, for example, surprisingly silent on the role to be played by psychiatric services in the assessment of learning disabled parents and their support.[44] Furthermore, the co-morbidity of mental health problems in learning disabled parents suggests that it might be more appropriate in the context of care proceedings to instruct a psychiatric expert rather than a psychological expert to provide a report assessing the parent's intellectual functioning; the extent of any mental health problems; the impact of any such illness on the child; and the attachment between parent and child. Whilst a psychiatric or a psychological report is more or less routine in such cases, psychological reports appear to be more commonly sought.

**3.15** Secondly, in considering whether or not different background variables are of statistical significance to the outcomes for children of learning disabled parents, there is a tendency to lose sight of the fact that it is now well established that learning disabled parents can successfully raise their children if they are provided with appropriate supports.[45] The summary set out in the position paper of the International Association for the Scientific Study of Intellectual Disabilities (IASSID) points to a consistent research finding that many learning disabled parents can learn, apply new knowledge and maintain new skills if provided with appropriate parenting education and training. Successful parenting education programmes[46] for parents with learning disabilities contain the following attributes: first, they should be home based, if possible, or take place in home-based settings, so that the skills are taught in the environment in which they are to be applied;[47] secondly, they should be skills based, with the parent first undergoing an assessment in order to ascertain the skills the parent already demonstrates and the skills which need further training; thirdly, training should be on a one-to-one basis, with group

---

[44] O'Keefe and O'Hara 'Mental Health Needs of Parents with Intellectual Disabilities' (2008) 21 Curr Opin Psychiatry 463–468; Bernard 'Parents with Learning Disabilities – The Assessment of Parenting Ability' (2007) 1(3) *Advances in Mental health and learning disabilities* 14–18.
[45] Above, n 30.
[46] See Feldman 'Parenting Education Programmes' in Llewellyn et al *Parents with Intellectual Disabilities, Past, Present and Futures* (John Wiley & Sons, 2010).
[47] See Tarleton et al, *Finding the Right Support* (The Baring Foundation, 2006): whilst the residential assessment of learning disabled parents is sometimes an appropriate step within care proceedings, it is thought that being away from home can distract the parent from focusing on learning how to parent, and can cause them to lose contact with valuable community support networks.

teaching formats being avoided; fourthly, the work should be based on a competence-enhancing behavioural approach, where the task is presented, prompts are used to promote correct responding, correct responding is reinforced and a maintenance programme implemented. The characteristics of successful teaching strategies for use in assessments and parenting education programmes are contrasted with the characteristics of ineffective teaching methodology in Table 3.1:[48]

**Table 3.1 Best practice in parenting education programmes**

| **Negative teaching strategies** | **Effective teaching strategies** |
| --- | --- |
| Didactic instruction: use of reading materials and discussion of abstract concepts. | Use of pictorial posters and manuals; audio and videotapes. Use of role play and game formats. |
| Teaching too much at one time or too quickly. | Modelling – especially when focusing on the specific sub-step of the skill the parent is missing. |
| Focusing only on mistakes. | Positive feedback and reinforcement; increasing introduction of corrective feedback over time. |
| Assuming correspondence between knowledge and skills. | Repeating topics regularly and offering opportunities for frequent practice. |
| Doing things for the participants. | Corrective feedback; working with the parents themselves to find and develop helpful resources. |

**3.16** Furthermore, as Cleaver and Nicholson identified, the most successful outcomes are those where there is an acknowledgement by the local authority that the family will require low-level but long-term support. Two cases illustrate the point. First, where the mother had learning disabilities, the father suffered from poor mental health and where the provision of services included: a parenting programme; family support three times a week concentrating on issues such as hygiene and safety; family support work to assist the mother with shopping and budgeting; social work support; health visitor support; and psychological support. Of note was the fact that the family was heavily supported by the paternal grandmother, who looked after the child for one day per week. In a second case, the mother had moderate learning disabilities, two children with autism and challenging behaviour and one with speech

---

[48] Adapted from Feldman, n 46 above, and Tarleton et al, n 47 above.

difficulties. Again, there was support from both sets of grandparents and the provision of a support package from the local authority, which included children's social care; health; housing; and educational input. The authors concluded that the common thread to both these cases was that there was a considerable amount of family support and a recognition from the local authority that there was a need for low-level agency support on a long-term basis. Notably, they found that where an extensive support network was lacking, the cases tended to ricochet between children's social care and various statutory and non-statutory agencies as the concerns about the children's safety fluctuated as a result of the impact of short-term targeted interventions.

## APPENDIX: SUMMARY OF RESEARCH STUDIES

**3.17** The key points of the research studies are set out in the following tables.

| Authors | Purpose of research | Sample characteristics | Findings |
|---|---|---|---|
| Aunos, Feldman, Goupil 'Mothers with Intellectual Disabilities Who Do or Do Not have Custody of their Children' (2003) 10(2) *Journal of Developmental Disabilities* 65–80 | To consider how learning disabled mothers who keep their children differ from those who lose their children. | 47 learning disabled mothers living in Quebec and receiving services from specialist agencies, of whom 30 had their children living with them. All lived under the poverty line. | • Children remaining at home were significantly younger than the children removed from their parents' care.<br>• In over half of the families where the children were no longer living at home, the removal of the children followed an allegation of abuse or neglect.<br>• Mothers who had their children living with them had younger children; were more involved with their community; had a higher income; and received more special needs services than mothers living apart from their children.<br>• Not significant to outcome: the mother's mental health; her physical health; the number of people in her social network; her adaptive behaviours; the number of children she had. |
| Aunos, Feldman, Goupil 'Mothering with Intellectual Disabilities: Relationship between Social Support, Health and Well-being, Parenting and Child Behaviour Outcomes' (2008) 21(4) *Journal of Applied Research in Intellectual Disabilities* 320–330 | To examine potential determining factors of different outcomes for learning disabled parents: maternal social support; psychological well-being; parenting style; quality of the home environment; child problem behaviours. | 32 mothers recruited through learning disability support services. | • 87% of the mothers were satisfied with the services they received.<br>• Participating mothers reported poorer mental and physical health than reflected in the normative sample of American women.<br>• 53% reported borderline to significantly high stress levels.<br>• A significant relationship existed between maternal parenting stress and parenting style and child problem behaviour. |

| Authors | Purpose of research | Sample characteristics | Findings |
|---|---|---|---|
| Cleaver and Nicholson *Parental Learning Disability and Children's Needs: Family Experiences and Effective Practice* (Jessica Kingsley Publishers, 2007) | To explore the needs and outcomes of children who were living with a parent with learning disabilities and who had been referred to children's social care. | 76 cases where one or both parents had a learning disability and a comparison group of 152 cases where neither parent had a learning disability. | • A greater proportion of children living with parents with learning disabilities had needs in every developmental dimension of the 'Framework for the Assessment of Children in Need and their Families', difficulties in each of the parenting capacity dimensions and problems in relation to every family and environmental factor.<br>• One third of the study group experienced severe problems in all three domains: developmental needs; parenting capacity; family and environmental needs.<br>• A high proportion of parents with learning disabilities (95.7%) also experienced issues such as mental illness or substance misuse.<br>• The broad age range of the children removed from the care of their parents belies the widely held assumption that children's social care is likely to remove babies from the care of parents with learning disabilities.<br>• Where children remained at home the learning disabled parent had the day-to-day support of a capable, non-abusive adult, such as a partner, relative or committed foster carer (under a shared care arrangement) and were taking full advantage of universal and specialist services when necessary. |

| Authors | Purpose of research | Sample characteristics | Findings |
|---|---|---|---|
| Feldman, Leger, Walton-Allen 'Stress in Mothers with Intellectual Disabilities' (1997) 6(4) *Journal of Child and Family Studies* 471–485 | To consider the extent to which learning disabled parents experience considerable stress and its effect on their parenting problems. | 82 learning disabled mothers (those with IQ less than 80) all of whom were welfare recipients. | • Learning disabled mothers raising infants/toddlers, pre-school or school-age children endured clinically significant levels of stress which increased when the child reached school age.<br>• This could be explained by the other significant variables: mothers of school-age children being older, having lower IQs, living in more crowded conditions and being subject to less child protection scrutiny than mothers of younger children. |
| Feldman and Walton-Allen 'Effects of Maternal Mental Retardation and Poverty, on Intellectual, Academic and Behavioural Status of School-age Children' (1997) 101 *American Journal on Mental Retardation* 352–364 | To examine the effect on a child's intellectual, academic and behavioural development of being brought up by a learning disabled mother. | Comparison of 27 children of mothers with mild learning disability with 25 children of mothers without learning disability. All mothers were of the same, low socio-economic status. Referrals came from community agencies supporting learning disabled adults. | • Social isolation score of learning disabled mothers was significantly higher than that of non-learning disabled group.<br>• Children's IQs significantly lower for children of learning disabled mothers, with significantly lower scores for reading ability, spelling and mathematics.<br>• Higher percentage of children of learning disabled mothers scoring above the clinical level for conduct disorders and emotional disorders.<br>• Children of learning disabled mothers were five times more likely to receive special educational services than the children of non-learning disabled mothers.<br>• Recognition that since the prevalence of depression is relatively high in adults with mild learning disability, depression may have had a significant association with the outcomes. |

| Authors | Purpose of research | Sample characteristics | Findings |
|---|---|---|---|
| Feldman, Vargese, Ramsay, Rajska 'Relationships between Social Support, Stress and Mother-Child Interactions in Mothers with Intellectual Disabilities' (2002) 15 *Journal of Applied Research in Intellectual Disabilities* 314–323 | To examine the relationships between parenting stress, social-support and mother-child interactions in 30 learning disabled mothers. | 30 mothers from small cities in Ontario, recruited from social services learning disability agencies; all living independently in the community and many below the official poverty line. 62 children were involved. | • Mothers with intellectual disabilities are highly stressed and socially isolated, social support being negatively correlated with parenting stress.<br><br>• High need for but low satisfaction with social participation and involvement of others. The parents' perception of supports may be more important than actual resource size in counteracting the effects of stress, since having a large support network does not necessarily mean that the parent considers all those involved to be helpful.<br><br>• Satisfaction with social support was related to positive maternal behaviours, thereby highlighting the crucial role of perceived competency enhancing supports in promoting positive parenting practices for parents with learning disabilities. |

| Authors | Purpose of research | Sample characteristics | Findings |
|---|---|---|---|
| McGaw, Scully, Pritchard 'Parenting the Unpredictable? Identifying High-risk versus Low-risk Parents with Intellectual Disabilities' (2010) 34 *Child Abuse & Neglect* 699–710 | To identify any factors distinguishing between high risk and low-risk parenting for learning disabled parents; to identify whether parent relationships and partner relationships associate with risk of harm to the child. | Retrospective study of 101 learning disabled parents who had used an NHS special parenting service between 1999 and 2004 and who were the main carers of the children. Parents were categorised as either high risk or low risk according to whether or not their children had at any point been either 'looked after' or placed on the CPR. | • IQ, age, relationship status and access to support/resources were not relevant to categorisation as high risk or low risk.<br>• High-risk parents were significantly more likely to have experienced childhood trauma (emotional abuse and physical neglect in particular); to have a child with special needs; and to have other impairments as well as learning disability.<br>• Partner IQ was significantly associated with an increase in risk to the child, with the odds of risk associating with partners with IQ>85 being nine times greater than for partners with IQ<70; the risk increased in parallel with increasing levels of intelligence in partners. |

| Authors | Purpose of research | Sample characteristics | Findings |
|---|---|---|---|
| McGaw, Shaw, Beckley 'Prevalence of Psychopathology Across a Service Population of Parents with Intellectual Disabilities and their Children' (2007) 4(1) *Journal of Policy and Practice in Intellectual Disabilities* 11–22 | To establish the prevalence of abuse and psychopathology in learning disabled parents; the prevalence of mental disorders and abuse/neglect in their children; the vulnerability of such children to abuse/neglect when their parents have histories of childhood trauma and or psychopathological disorders. | Retrospective study of 49 parents who had been referred to the special parenting service from 2000 to 2005. Average IQ 72.8. All were receiving statutory income support. | • 79.6% had experienced childhood abuse or neglect, with 55.1% citing multiple abuse/neglect categories.<br>• 'Severe or extreme' abuse/neglect was the most common level of trauma experienced (57%), with emotional abuse being the most prevalent (22%).<br>• Psychopathology findings: 33% of the learning disabled parents suffered from depression; anxiety (20%); obsessive compulsive disorders (12%); hypomania/mania (4%).<br>• Weak association between psychopathology and reports of past childhood abuse.<br>• Significant relationship between parents who reported childhood trauma and registration of their children on the CPR for maltreatment, with 82% of the parents reporting emotional abuse in their childhood having children who were registered or had been registered on the CPR.<br>• Children of learning disabled parents showed higher levels of mental disorders than those reported in other studies involving the general child population: 40% had multiple problems; 41% had a poor attention span; 40% had conduct disorders; 24% had anxiety or acute problems. |

| Authors | Purpose of research | Sample characteristics | Findings |
|---|---|---|---|
| Tymchuck 'Depression Symptomatology in Mothers with Mild Intellectual Disability: An Exploratory Study' [1994] *Australia and New Zealand Journal of Developmental Disabilities* 111–119 | To determine whether mothers with intellectual disability have greater depression symptomatology than do mothers without intellectual disability from similar backgrounds. | 33 learning disabled mothers and 97 non-learning-disabled mothers; all were receiving some form of public assistance. | • 39% of the learning disabled mothers and only 13% of the contrast group scored above the cut-off score considered under the Beck Depression Inventory to be indicative of clinical depression.<br>• The learning disabled mothers scored significantly higher on the Beck Inventory than did the contrast group of mothers.<br>• Learning disabled mothers exhibited more severe symptoms of depression than the non-learning disabled mothers.<br>• Few relationships were found between background variables and depression symptomatology of learning disabled mothers, although the best single indicator of high Beck scores in this group was whether there had been a family history of abuse or neglect. |

# Chapter 4

# THE THRESHOLD TEST: ESTABLISHING 'SIGNIFICANT HARM' AND THE NEED FOR PARENTING SUPPORT

## INTRODUCTION

**4.1** McConnell and Llewellyn identified[1] two commonly held presumptions about learning disabled parents in Australia: first, that it was inevitable that learning disabled parents would either harm their children or fail to protect them from harm from others; and, secondly, that there was therefore little point in offering such parents any support. They argued, further, that these attitudes endured elsewhere, referring, for example, to the research of North American scholars between 1985 and 1995 reporting the denial of parents' rights to be heard and the refusal of parenting support before their children were permanently removed. Several years after McConnell and Llewellyn's research, evidence received by the Joint Committee on Human Rights in the UK[2] was to the same effect: that 'professionals often had negative or stereotyped attitudes about people with a learning disability and their ability to be parents'. McConnell and Llewellyn went on to argue that since compulsory intervention in the family is based on non-specific statutory standards ('is suffering, or is likely to suffer significant harm' in the UK and failing to provide 'adequate provision ... for the child's care' in Australia), the inherent flexibility of these concepts allows those negative stereotypes about parents with learning disabilities to permeate the system.[3] In the same way, Booth et al[4] suggested that the child protection system also discriminates indirectly against learning disabled parents in that the time-limits on initial assessments, core assessments and parenting assessments, together with the need to move quickly and 'within the child's time-scales', do not take into consideration their slower rate of learning new skills.

**4.2** The focus of this chapter is on the legal issues that might arise upon the application of the threshold test where one or both of the parents is learning disabled. It is self-evident that the 'welfare' stage of care proceedings requires the court to consider whether or not the best interests of the child can be met

---

[1] McConnell and Llewellyn 'Stereotypes, Parents with Intellectual Disability and Child Protection' (2002) 24(3) *Journal of Social Welfare and Family Law* 297–317.
[2] *A Life Like Any Other? Human Rights of Adults with Learning Disabilities*, HL 40-1; HC 73-1 (2008).
[3] McConnell and Llewellyn, n 1 above, at p 308.
[4] T Booth, D McConnell and W Booth 'Temporal Discrimination and Parents with Learning Difficulties in the Child Protection System' (2006) 36 *British Journal of Social Work* 997–1015.

by supporting the parent to parent the child at home, and that this in turn will require a parenting assessment to be carried out by an assessor who is experienced in working effectively with learning disabled adults. What is suggested here, however, is that the parent's capacity to parent with the provision of appropriate support is a necessary consideration in determining whether or not the threshold criteria have been met. The chapter then sets out the framework of community care legislation which, together with the services offered by adult learning disability teams and children's services departments, represents – at least in theory – the sources of formal support available.

## THE THRESHOLD CRITERIA

**4.3** Under s 31(2) of the Children Act 1989 a court may only make a care order or supervision order if it is satisfied:

> '(a) that the child concerned is suffering, or is likely to suffer, significant harm; and
> (b) that the harm, or likelihood of harm, is attributable to –
> (i) the care given to the child, or likely to be given to him if the order were not made, not being what it would be reasonable to expect a parent to give to him; or
> (ii) the child's being beyond parental control.'

**4.4** The threshold test establishes the jurisdictional basis for the making of a care or a supervision order and when met enables the court to make an order under Pt IV of the Children Act 1989, provided it is satisfied that it is in the best interests of the child to do so. Since it is the tradition of the UK that children are best brought up within their birth families, the threshold test thereby represents – in principle – the point at which a variety of rights or interests converge: the right of the child to know and to be brought up by his or her parents; the right of the child to be protected by his or her parents from unacceptable risk; and the right of the parents to bring up their own child whatever their economic, social, religious or cultural circumstances.

**4.5** Yet, by itself, the Children Act 1989 is of limited assistance in determining the point at which intervention is required. 'Harm' is defined in s 31(9) as meaning the 'ill-treatment or the impairment of health or development including, for example, impairment suffered from seeing or hearing the ill-treatment of another'. Further, under s 31(10):

> 'Where the question of whether harm suffered by a child is significant turns on the child's health or development, his health or development shall be compared with that which could reasonably be expected of a similar child.'

Nor is there further detail provided by the *Review of Child Care Law*[5] which ultimately led to the public law provisions of the Children Act 1989, and in

---

[5] Department of Health and Social Security, 1985.

para 2 of which the purpose of the threshold test is put as follows: 'Only where their children are put at an unacceptable risk should it be possible compulsorily to intervene.'

**4.6** The failure of the Children Act 1989 to define 'significant harm' further or to provide a more detailed description of the point at which the mandatory powers can be exercised, reflects the reality that 'significant harm' needs to be fact-specific to prevent a set of circumstances from being considered to fall inside or outside of the concept of 'significant harm' simply because they have or have not been anticipated before.[6] Similarly, the courts too have refused to restrict the scope of 'significant harm': in *Humberside CC v B*[7] the Court of Appeal adopted the view that 'significant harm' was 'harm that the court should consider was either considerable or noteworthy or important ... harm which the court should take into account in considering a child's future'. Further, in *Re H (Minors) (Sexual Abuse: Standard of Proof)*[8] the House of Lords referred to the open-ended range of facts and parental behaviours that can be taken into consideration in determining whether a child is suffering or is likely to suffer significant harm:[9]

> 'I must now put this into perspective by noting, and emphasising, the width of the range of facts which may be relevant when the court is considering the threshold conditions. The range of facts which may properly be taken into account is infinite. Facts include the history of members of the family, the state of relationships within a family, proposed changes within the membership of a family, parental attitudes, and omissions which might not reasonably have been expected, just as much as actual physical assaults. They include threats, and abnormal behaviour by a child, and unsatisfactory parental responses to complaints or allegations. And facts, which are minor or even trivial if considered in isolation, when taken together may suffice to satisfy the court of the likelihood of future harm. The court will attach to all the relevant facts the appropriate weight when coming to an overall conclusion on the crucial issue.'

**4.7** In *Re MA (Children) (Care Threshold)*[10] the Court of Appeal was asked to consider for the first time the dividing line between harm and significant harm, where the judge at first instance had found that the subject children had not suffered and were not likely to suffer significant harm. On the facts before it, however, the Court of Appeal was divided, with Wilson LJ dissenting from the views of Ward LJ and Hallett LJ and departing from the view of the trial judge. In Wilson LJ's judgment: (a) the parents had on at least five occasions either slapped, kicked, pushed or hit the oldest child; (b) the two oldest children had been exposed to the 'shocking ill treatment' of another child living with the family, which had included failing to register that child with the medical or dental authorities because they wished to keep her presence a secret from the

---

[6] See per Hedley J in *Re L (A Child) (Care: Threshold Criteria)* [2007] 1 FLR 2050, at [51] and below.
[7] [1993] 1 FLR 257.
[8] [1996] 1 FLR 80.
[9] Ibid, at 101, per Lord Nicholls.
[10] [2009] EWCA Civ 853.

authorities, beating her and threatening to set a dog on her; and (c) the combination of the grossly abnormal conduct towards that child and the ill-treatment of the parents' oldest child was that all three of their biological children were likely to suffer significant physical and emotional harm. On the other hand, whereas Ward LJ did not condone the parents' behaviour, he considered that whilst the oldest child had suffered 'harm', she had not suffered 'significant harm' since despite outside intervention in the family's life she appeared to be 'well-nourished, well cared for and with close attachments to her parents'. Moreover, in his view, the judge below was best placed to determine the extent to which it was likely that the parents would treat their own children in the way they had treated the other child. Hallett LJ shared the view that this was a classic case for trusting the judgment of the trial judge before whom there had been good evidence that the parents had treated their biological children differently.

**4.8** Earlier, in *Re L (Care: Threshold Criteria)*[11] Hedley J in the Family Division of the High Court had also been required to consider the dividing line between 'harm' and 'significant harm'. In doing so, he cautioned against an all embracing definition of 'significant harm' and stressed the fact that the use of the phrase 'significant harm' is intended to entitle the state to intervene in 'exceptional' situations only, rather than in all situations of defective parenting where as a consequence the children experience disadvantage and harm:[12]

> 'What about the Court's approach, in the light of all that, to the issue of significant harm? In order to understand this concept and the range of harm that it's intended to encompass, it is right to begin with issues of policy. Basically it is the tradition of the United Kingdom, recognised in law, that children are best brought up within natural families. Lord Templeman, in *Re: KD (a minor ward) (termination of access)* [1988] 1AC806, at page 812 said this:
>
>> "The best person to bring up a child is the natural parent. It matters not whether the parent is wise or foolish, rich or poor, educated or illiterate, provided the child's moral and physical health are not in danger. Public authorities cannot improve on nature."
>
> There are those who may regard that last sentence as controversial but undoubtedly it represents the present state of the law in determining the starting point. It follows inexorably from that, that society must be willing to tolerate very diverse standards of parenting, including the eccentric, the barely adequate and the inconsistent. It follows too that children will inevitably have both very different experiences of parenting and very unequal consequences flowing from it. It means that some children will experience disadvantage and harm, whilst others flourish in atmospheres of loving security and emotional stability. These are the consequences of our fallible humanity and it is not the provenance of the State to spare children all the consequences of defective parenting. In any event, it simply could not be done.

---

[11] [2007] 1 FLR 2050.
[12] Ibid, at 2063.

That is not, however, to say that the State has no role, as the Children Act 1989 fully demonstrates. Nevertheless, that Act, wide ranging though the court's and social services' powers may be, is to be operated in the context of the policy I have sought to describe. Its essence, in Part III of the Act, is the concept of working in partnership with families who have children in need. Only exceptionally should the State intervene with compulsive powers and then only when a Court is satisfied that the significant harm criteria in Section 31(2) is made out. Such an approach is clearly consistent with Article 8 of the European Convention on Human Rights. Article 8(1) declares a right of privacy of family life but it is not an unqualified right. Article 8(2) specifies circumstances in which the State may lawfully infringe that right. In my judgment Article 8(2) and Section 31(2) contemplate the exceptional rather than the commonplace. It would be unwise to a degree to attempt an all embracing definition of significant harm. One never ceases to be surprised at the extent of complication and difficulty that human beings manage to introduce into family life. Significant harm is fact specific and must retain the breadth of meaning that human fallibility may require of it. Moreover, the Court recognises, as Lord Nichols pointed out in H & R that the threshold may be comparatively low. However, it is clear that it must be something unusual; at least something more than the commonplace human failure or inadequacy.'

**4.9** Hedley J went on to find that whilst the children in *Re L* had both suffered 'harm' and were likely to continue to do so in the future, and whilst they were both almost certainly children in need of services within the meaning of Pt III in s 17(1) of the Children Act 1989, they had not, in his judgment, suffered *significant harm*. He found that: (a) violence had been inflicted by the father against the mother on at least two occasions, resulting in visible bruising and injuries to the face, ear, shoulder, hands and wrists; (b) violence between the parents may have occurred on other occasions; (c) such violence might recur in the future; and (d) the children were likely to know of it and to be affected by that knowledge and experience. He further found that there was a 'fairly clear lack of boundaries and a worrying attitude from time to time displayed by the children towards their mother and which the father has been unable to check and has even appeared to encourage'. However, as Hedley J stated,[13] although it was therefore likely that the children would continue to suffer harm in the future and although that harm was attributable to the parenting they would receive, the circumstances were not such as to open the gateway to steps which could result in the permanent separation of the parents and the children. Whilst the case was 'close to the border', he was clear that in this case it had not been crossed.

**4.10** On one level, since the need to establish significant harm remains 'the hallmark of a free and democratic society in which diversity and individuality are valued'[14] these two cases illustrate the simple point that not all harm inflicted by parents on children, or inflicted by parents on others in front of their children, amounts to behaviour triggering the state's compulsory powers of child protection. On another level, the cases reveal that the non-specific definition of the concept of significant harm does allow a range of personal or

---

[13] Ibid, at 2064, [51].
[14] Per Lady Hale in *Re B (A Child) (Residence: Second Appeal)* [2009] UKSC 5.

subjective views to intrude. For example, in *Re MA (Children) (Care Threshold)*[15] Wilson LJ declared himself 'staggered' that the judge below had refused to hold that the three children would be likely to suffer significant physical and emotional harm, whilst Ward LJ and Hallett LJ, although finding the parents' behaviour 'deplorable', considered that they might well have come to the same conclusion as the trial judge himself. As suggested above, this flexibility is of particular significance in the context of learning disabled parenting where it has been observed that negative assumptions may be made about a parent's abilities and their capacity to learn.

## OBJECTIVITY OR SUBJECTIVITY?

**4.11** The need to refer back to the standards of the hypothetical reasonable parent[16] in determining whether or not the threshold criteria have been met suggests that test is an objective, rather than a subjective, one. In other words, if a child suffers significant harm, albeit as a result of objectively reasonable parenting, the threshold criteria will not have been crossed. However, to what extent, if at all, is the hypothetical reasonable parent endowed with any of the limitations of the particular parent whose parenting is in question? For example, in *Re K*[17] Munby J referred to the need, in evaluating parental conduct by reference to the objective standard of the hypothetical reasonable parent, not to ignore the underlying cultural, social or religious circumstances and to be slow to find:[18]

> '... that parents only recently or comparatively recently arrived from a foreign country, particularly a country where standards and expectations may be more or less different , sometimes very different indeed, from those with which they are familiar, have fallen short of an acceptable standard of parenting if in truth they have done nothing wrong by the standards of their own community.'

In his opinion, the sexual abuse of the 15-year-old girl from a Kurdish Iraqi family was not attributable to the care being given to her by her parents in arranging a marriage for her, since although she had been unlawfully married to a man some 12 years her senior, the marriage had not taken place against her wishes and had been facilitated in accordance with the family's religious beliefs and cultural mores. It is noted, however, that Munby J's comments were made *obiter*, since the threshold criteria had largely been conceded by both parents on other grounds and the issue before the court was as to whether a supervision order was going to be effective in the circumstances.

**4.12** It may follow by analogy with those comments in *Re K* that just as the parents' religious and cultural beliefs may be a relevant factor in considering whether or not the parental standard of care has fallen below that of the

---

[15] [2009] EWCA Civ 853.
[16] See s 31(2)(b)(i) of the Children Act 1989.
[17] [2007] 1 FLR 399.
[18] Ibid, at 406.

hypothetical reasonable parent, then so too are the functional and cognitive abilities of the learning disabled parent, since parenting inadequacies arising out of any such impairment do not arise through any 'fault' of that parent him- or herself. To judge the learning disabled parent by the standards of the non-disabled parent is therefore, it is said, discriminatory. However, this argument has been emphatically rejected by the Court of Appeal in *Re D (A Child) (Care Order: Evidence)*[19] on the basis that the risks of adopting such an approach would severely reduce the child protection functions of the court in that it would serve to protect only the limited group of children whose parents were able to care for them, and who either chose not to do so or neglected to do so. Hughes LJ was robust in clarifying that 'when the judge is addressing the threshold conditions it is absolutely clear that concepts of discrimination in relation to the parents are simply not helpful and should not be permitted to intrude', and in professing the reference of the judge below to discrimination to be 'generally puzzling':[20]

> '... the Disability Discrimination Act has nothing whatever to say about care proceedings ... it may be ... the judge was making no more than a general reference to the proposition that those such as the local authority or social workers dealing with any kind of handicap must tailor their approach to the person they are dealing with, but that is a mile away from bringing either the disability or the concept of discrimination into the exercise of deciding whether the threshold conditions for the making of a care order are satisfied.'

**4.13** It is suggested, however, that in cases involving parents with learning disabilities, the local authority will need to go further than simply tailoring its approach to the specific needs of the person it is working with if it is to succeed in establishing the threshold criteria. For example, in cases where the concerns arise out of the parental learning disability coupled with neglect, if the parent has not been provided with an appropriate package of parenting support the local authority will struggle to establish that significant harm caused or likely to be caused to the child is attributable to an unreasonable level of care from the parent. After all, a parent whose needs have not yet been assessed or who has not been provided with the support to which they are entitled can hardly be considered to be providing an 'unreasonable' level of care if he or she has attempted, to the best of his or her abilities, to parent alone. There is some support for this argument in *H (Local Authority) v KJ*[21] where Hedley J was concerned with an application for a care order in relation to a child whose multiple care needs meant that she would be permanently dependent on others. The court found that the Somalian mother had not co-operated with professional advice and support and that her decision to reject this advice had on occasion been contrary to the interests of the child; and, further, that the mother had failed to acknowledge the child's complex needs, leading to a lack of stimulation and a failure to provide the level of hygiene that her medical needs required. Nonetheless, in finding that the significant harm was

---

[19] [2010] EWCA Civ 1000.
[20] Ibid, at [37].
[21] [2007] EWHC 2798 (Fam).

'attributable to the care not being what it would be reasonable to expect a parent to give to him' the judge made the following observations: first, that:[22]

> '... it cannot be said that a single parent exposes herself to compulsory state intervention in family life simply on the grounds that a particular child's needs are beyond the capacity of one parent ... however assiduously they devote themselves to the care of the child ...'

and, secondly, that it cannot be the case that:[23]

> '... a local authority can fail to put in the support properly required to enable a child to be cared for at home (absent expert evidence that a child could never be cared for at home because of disability whatever reasonable support was provided) and then use that failure as grounds for compulsory intervention under Part IV of the Act.'

**4.14** Whilst *H (Local Authority) v KJ* was concerned with establishing the threshold criteria in relation to a disabled *child* rather than a disabled *parent*, it is arguable that a disabled parent must be entitled to reasonable support before the level of care provided to the child can be considered to be attributable to inadequate parenting and hence to meet the threshold criteria. Such an approach was adopted in *Re G and A (Care Order: Freeing Order: Parents with a Learning Disability)*,[24] where the court recognised that 'consideration must be given to the assessment phase by a Trust and in the application of the threshold test' and was careful to check whether the level of support required by the mother was available or practicable before concluding that the threshold criteria had been met. In this case there was a likelihood of significant harm to both of the children due to the parents' lack of insight and understanding of risk, and due to expert evidence that if the parents were to be supported in their parenting on a long-term basis, they would need to be provided with care on the impractical basis of 24 hours per day.

## SUPPORT UNDER COMMUNITY CARE LEGISLATION

**4.15** The right of the disabled parent to parenting support and services is promoted by the European Convention on Human Rights (see *Kutzner v Germany*[25]); by the United Nations Convention on the Rights of the Child, Article 18(2);[26] by the United Nations Convention on the Rights of Persons with Disabilities, Article 23;[27] by s 17 of the Children Act 1989; and by the

---

[22] Ibid, at [20].
[23] Ibid, at [21].
[24] [2006] NI Fam 8.
[25] [2002] ECHR 160.
[26] Article 18(2): 'For the purpose of guaranteeing and promoting the rights set forth in the present Convention, States Parties shall render appropriate assistance to parents and legal guardians in the performance of their child-rearing responsibilities and shall ensure the development of institutions, facilities and services for the care of children.'
[27] See Chapter 1, at **1.6**.

policy underlying the Children Act 2004 (see *Every Child Matters*,[28] at p 29: 'The Government intends to put supporting parents and carers at the heart of its approach to improving children's lives'). In reality, however, the experience of many parents with borderline learning disability is that they are considered ineligible for support from the adult learning disability team in their area because of the common adoption of an IQ of 70 as the cut-off point for access to services. Further, the experience of those learning disabled parents with higher levels of functioning is that their ability to access community care services is limited: the demands upon resources and budgetary constraints now mean that many local authorities' eligibility criteria provide services only for those whose needs are assessed as 'critical'. What follows is a summary of entitlement to support under current adult social care legislation.

**4.16** The starting point for ascertaining the level of support from community care services to which a learning disabled parent might be entitled, is to ask the local authority for an assessment under s 47 of the National Health Service and Community Care Act 1990 (NHSCCA 1990). This section acts as the gateway to the provision of community care services and provides that:

> '... where it appears to a local authority that any person for whom they may provide or arrange for the provision of community care services may be in need of any such services, the authority –
>
> (a) shall carry out an assessment of his needs for those services; and
> (b) having regard to the results of that assessment, shall then decide whether his needs call for the provision by them of any such services.'

'Community care services' are defined in s 46(3) of the Act as:

> '... services which a local authority may provide or arrange to be provided under any of the following provisions –
>
> (a) Part III of the National Assistance Act 1948;
> (b) section 45 of the Health Services and Public Health Act 1968;
> (c) section 21 of and Schedule 8 to the National Health Service Act 1977; and
> (d) section 117 of the Mental Health Act 1983.'

**4.17** Part III of the National Assistance Act 1948 makes provision under ss 21 and 29 for the provision of residential accommodation and 'welfare services' respectively. Section 21 requires local authority social services to make arrangements for the provision of residential accommodation when three conditions are met: (a) the person is in need of care and attention; (b) that need arises by reason of age, illness, disability or any other circumstances; and (c) care and attention is not available to him or her otherwise than by the provision of residential accommodation under this particular power.

**4.18** Under s 29(1) the local authority:

---

[28] *Every Child Matters*, Cm 5860 (2003).

'... may, with the approval of the Secretary of State, and to such extent as he may direct in relation to persons ordinarily resident in the area of the local authority shall, make arrangements for promoting the welfare of persons to whom this section applies, that is to say persons aged eighteen or over who are blind, deaf or dumb, or who suffer from mental disorder of any description and other persons aged eighteen or over who are substantially and permanently handicapped by illness, injury, or congenital deformity or such other disabilities as may be prescribed by the Minister.

...

(4) Without prejudice to the generality of the provisions of subsection (1) of this section, arrangements may be made thereunder –

(a) for informing persons to whom arrangements under that subsection relate of the services available for them thereunder;
(b) for giving such persons instruction in their own homes or elsewhere in methods of overcoming the effects of their disabilities;
(c) for providing workshops where such persons may be engaged (whether under a contract of service or otherwise) in suitable work, and hostels where persons engaged in the workshops, and other persons to whom arrangements under subsection (1) of this section relate and for whom work or training is being provided in pursuance of the Disabled Persons (Employment) Act, 1944, or the Employment and Training Act 1973 may live;
(d) for providing persons to whom arrangements under subsection (1) of this section relate with suitable work (whether under a contract of service or otherwise) in their own homes or elsewhere;
(e) for helping such persons in disposing of the produce of their work;
(f) for providing such persons with recreational facilities in their own homes or elsewhere;
(g) for compiling and maintaining classified registers of the persons to whom arrangements under subsection (1) of this section relate.'

**4.19** Section 45 of the Health Services and Public Health Act 1968 concerns the promotion of the welfare of 'old people' and is therefore likely to be irrelevant to an analysis of the community care arrangements for learning disabled parents. Section 21 of and Sch 8 to the National Health Service Act 1977 refer to services for the care of expectant and nursing mothers; for those who are ill or have been ill; and to the provision of a home-help for those requiring it owing to the presence of 'a person who is suffering from illness, lying-in, an expectant mother, aged, handicapped as a result of having suffered from illness or by congenital deformity'. Section 117 of the Mental Health Act 1983 refers to 'after-care' services for those who have been detained under that Act.

**4.20** The services available under s 29(1) of the National Assistance Act 1948 can also be provided by a local authority exercising its duty under s 2(1) of the Chronically Sick and Disabled Persons Act 1970 (CSDPA 1970). Section 2(1) requires the local authority to provide specific domiciliary and community-based services to people ordinarily resident in its area and to whom s 29(1) of the National Assistance Act 1948 applies, if satisfied that such services are necessary in order to meet that person's needs:

> 'Where a local authority having functions under section 29 of the National Assistance Act 1948 are satisfied in the case of any person to whom that section applies who is ordinarily resident in their area that it is necessary in order to meet the needs of that person for that authority to make arrangements for all or any of the following matters, namely –
>
> (a) the provision of practical assistance for that person in his home;
> (b) the provision for that person of, or assistance to that person in obtaining, wireless, television, library or similar recreational facilities;
> (c) the provision for that person of lectures, games, outings or other recreational facilities outside his home or assistance to that person in taking advantage of educational facilities available to him;
> (d) the provision for that person of facilities for, or assistance in, travelling to and from his home for the purpose of participating in any services provided under arrangements made by the authority under the said section 29 or, with the approval of the authority, in any services provided otherwise than as aforesaid which are similar to services which could be provided under such arrangements;
> (e) the provision of assistance for that person in arranging for the carrying out of any works of adaptation in his home or the provision of any additional facilities designed to secure his greater safety, comfort or convenience;
> (f) facilitating the taking of holidays by that person, whether at holiday homes or otherwise and whether provided under arrangements made by the authority or otherwise;
> (g) the provision of meals for that person whether in his home or elsewhere;
> (h) the provision for that person of, or assistance to that person in obtaining, a telephone and any special equipment necessary to enable him to use a telephone,
>
> then, ... subject to the provisions of section 35(2) of that Act (which requires local authorities to exercise their functions under Part III of that Act ... in accordance with the provisions of any regulations made for the purpose) and to the provisions of section 7(1) of the Local Authority Social Services Act 1970 (which requires local authorities in the exercise of certain functions, including functions under the said section 29, to act under the general guidance of the Secretary of State) and to the provisions of section 7A of that Act (which requires local authorities to exercise their social services functions in accordance with directions given by the Secretary of State) it shall be the duty of that authority to make those arrangements in exercise of their functions under the said section 29.'

**4.21** Under this complex legislative framework, which has been described by the Law Commission[29] in its report on *Adult Social Care* as 'inadequate, often incomprehensible and outdated', the provision of community care for those who are disabled runs alongside the provision of community care for others, albeit with some differences. First, the trigger for an assessment for the provision of community care services under s 47 of NHSCCA 1990 is that a

---

[29] Law Com No 192 (TSO, 2010).

person has the 'appearance' to the local authority of being in need of services. A person seeking such an assessment does not therefore have a 'right' to an assessment unless the local authority considers that this standard has been met. However, the statutory *Guidance on Eligibility Criteria for Adult Social Care (England) 2010*[30] sets the threshold at a very low level in that para 51 states that: 'Councils must not exempt any person who approaches or is referred to them for help from the process to determine eligibility for social care, regardless of their age, circumstances, apparent financial means or the nature of their needs' whilst para 76 warns similarly of the 'risks of screening people out of the assessment process before sufficient information is known about them'.

**4.22** By contrast, the trigger for the duty under s 2(1) of CSDPA 1970 to provide services for those who are disabled (those to whom s 29 of the National Assistance Act 1948 applies) is that the local authority is 'satisfied' that the services listed under s 2(1) are 'necessary' to meet the needs of the individual. There is no reference to the local authority being obliged to carry out an 'assessment' before being satisfied that it is necessary to provide the s 29 services, although s 4 of the Disabled Persons (Services, Consultation and Representation) Act 1986 requires the local authority to make a decision about service provision upon the receipt of a request to do so from a disabled person or from someone representing him or caring for him:

> 'When requested to do so by –
>
> (a)   a disabled person,
> (b)   his authorised representative, or
> (c)   any person who provides care for him in the circumstances mentioned in section 8,
>
> a local authority shall decide whether the needs of the disabled person call for the provision by the authority of any services in accordance with section 2(1) of the Chronically Sick and Disabled Persons Act 1970 (provision of welfare services).'

In addition, under s 47(2) of NHSCCA 1990, where it appears to a local authority carrying out an assessment that the person being assessed is disabled, it is required to consider whether that person is eligible for services under s 4 of the Disabled Persons (Services, Consultation and Representation) Act 1986 (which itself refers back to services under s 2(1) of the 1970 Act). This does not depend upon any prior request from the disabled person. The local authority must inform the disabled person that it will be deciding whether he or she needs any such services and of his or her rights under the Disabled Persons (Services, Consultation and Representation) Act 1986.[31] In summary, whereas a disabled person falling within the class of people covered by s 29 of CSDPA 1970 (the 'blind, deaf or dumb, or who suffer from mental disorder of any description and other persons aged eighteen or over who are substantially and permanently

---

[30]   *Prioritising Need in the Context of Putting People First: A whole system approach to eligibility for social care* (Department of Health, 2010).
[31]   NHSCCA 1990, s 47(2)(b).

handicapped by illness, injury, or congenital deformity or such other disabilities as may be prescribed by the Minister') must request an assessment of his or her welfare needs; the same person can receive an assessment of needs via NHSCCA 1990 without that person or his or her carer having to request it first.

**4.23** Secondly, there is at first sight a difference in the *nature* of the duty set out under s 47(1)(a) and (b) and that set out under s 2(1) of CSDPA 1970. Under s 47 the local authority is required only to (a) carry out an assessment; and (b) having carried out an assessment, decide whether or not the assessed needs call for the provision of any community care services. In other words, under s 47 the local authority, having carried out an assessment, has a duty to decide whether or not services will be provided, but a discretion as to whether or not services will in fact be provided. This is in stark contrast to the position under s 2(1) of CSDPA 1970, where if the local authority is satisfied that the provision of welfare services is necessary to meet a disabled person's needs, it is then under an absolute duty to meet those needs. There is, however, no private law remedy sounding in damages for the failure to comply with this duty: *Wyatt v Hillingdon LBC*.[32]

**4.24** The local authority's discretion under s 47 must be exercised in accordance with the governmental Guidance set out in the *Prioritising Need in the Context of Putting People First: A whole system approach to eligibility for social care*[33] (in England) and *Creating a Unified and Fair System for Assessing and Managing Care*[34] (in Wales). Both are issued under s 7 of the Local Authority and Social Services Act 1970 and are therefore binding upon the local authority unless there is good reason not to do so: *R v Islington LBC ex parte Rixon*.[35] The aim of the Guidance is to provide local authorities with a toolkit for determining their own eligibility criteria under which certain 'presenting' needs (defined as those needs which are identified when individuals approach the local authority seeking social care support) are considered to be 'eligible' needs (defined as presenting needs for which a local authority will provide help because they fall within the local authority's eligibility criteria) and which are therefore to be met by public service provision. The Guidance recognises that the demand on resources is such that services should be allocated according to individual need in a way that is as fair and transparent as possible, and allows local authorities setting eligibility criteria to 'take account of their own resources, local expectations, and local costs'.[36] Further, under para 46 of *Putting People First*:

---

[32] (1978) 76 LGR 727.
[33] Department of Health, 2010.
[34] Welsh Assembly Government *Health and Social Care for Adults: Creating a Unified and Fair System for Assessing and Managing Care – Guidance for Local Authorities and Health Services* (2002).
[35] (1996) 1 CCLR 119.
[36] *Putting People First*, para 44.

'Councils should review their eligibility criteria in line with their usual budget cycles. Such reviews may be brought forward if there are major or unexpected changes, including those with significant resource consequences.'

**4.25** Whereas the statutory Guidance approves and in fact enjoins the taking of resources into consideration in setting eligibility criteria for community care services, a shortage of resources will not excuse a failure to provide services under s 2 of CSDPA 1970 which a local authority is satisfied it is necessary to provide:[37] 'when [the duty] does arise then it is clear that a shortage of resources will not excuse a failure in the performance of the duty.' However, since the decision by the House of Lords in *R v Gloucestershire CC ex parte Barry*[38] to the effect that the local authority is entitled to consider resources in determining which 'needs' under s 2 of CSDPA 1970 it is satisfied should be met, the difference between the duty under s 2 and the s 47 discretion appears more illusory than real. The case concerned the issue of whether or not the local authority, having assessed Mr Barry as being entitled to the provision of home care twice a week and meals on wheels four times a week, had been entitled 2 years later for financial reasons to decline to meet his assessed needs, and the broader question of whether the local authority was entitled to take resources into consideration in (re)assessing an individual's needs under s 2 of the 1970 Act. Whilst the Divisional Court held that the local authority had acted unlawfully in withdrawing its services without carrying out a reassessment of Mr Barry's needs, it also found that 'a local authority would face an impossible task unless it could have regard to the size of the cake before deciding how to cut it' and that resources were therefore a lawful consideration in the determination of 'need'. The Court of Appeal allowed Mr Barry's appeal in relation to the broader question, holding that resources were not a relevant consideration. The House of Lords reversed the Court of Appeal's decision. By a majority it confirmed that notwithstanding the specific nature of the s 2 duty, the cost of providing a service was a relevant consideration for the local authority in determining whether there was an individual need for it. In the words of Lord Clyde:[39]

'... neither the fact that the section imposes the duty towards the individual, with the corresponding right in the individual to the enforcement of the duty, nor the fact that consideration of resources is not relevant to the question whether the duty is performed or not, means that a consideration of resources may not be relevant to the earlier stages of the implementation of the section which lead up to the stage when the satisfaction is achieved.'

The boundaries of the s 2 'duty' have been pushed even further by *R (on the application of McDonald) v Kensington and Chelsea RLBC*:[40] where it is possible to meet the assessed need in more than one way, the local authority is entitled to take its resources into consideration and to choose the most

---

[37] *R v Gloucestershire CC ex parte Barry* [1997] 2 All ER 1, per Lord Clyde. See also *R (on the application of JL (A Child)) v Islington LBC* [2009] EWHC 458.
[38] [1997] 2 All ER 1.
[39] Ibid, at 16.
[40] [2010] EWCA Civ 1109.

economic form of provision. Furthermore, the House of Lords has held that the local authority can take into consideration the resources of a third party when deciding whether or not to provide resources under s 2(1) of CSDPA 1970: *R (on the application of Spink) v Wandsworth LBC*.[41]

**4.26** It was suggested in argument on behalf of Mr Barry that the co-existence of the s 2(1) duty alongside the s 47 discretion created a distinct substantive regime for the provision of services for the disabled. Lord Lloyd (in his dissenting opinion) agreed, stating that the mandatory duty to provide 'necessary' services to disabled people under s 2(1) of CSDPA 1970 had been preserved and reinforced by its retention upon the implementation of s 47 of NHSCCA 1990 and that Parliament had thereby underlined its intention to treat the needs of the disabled as a special case in the consideration of which resources play no part. The majority of the House of Lords considered, however, that the intention in retaining s 2(1) was simply to create a separate procedure for access to services for disabled people and/or their carers. Lord Clyde commented that:[42]

> 'It seems to me that there is sufficient reason for the making of a distinct provision in subsection 2 [of s 47 of the 1990 Act] in the desire to recognise the distinct procedural situation relative to the disabled. But it does not follow that any distinction exists in the considerations which may or may not be taken into account in making an assessment in the case of the disabled as compared with any other case. What is significant is that s.2(1) is clearly embodied in the whole of the community care regime, distinct only in its particular procedure and the importing of an express duty of performance once the local authority has been satisfied regarding the necessity to make the arrangements.'

## UNMET NEEDS

**4.27** For the person whose needs have been assessed as falling outside the relevant eligibility criteria and whose community care needs therefore remain unmet, there are limited opportunities for redress. In *R (on the application of Chavda) v Harrow LBC*[43] the claimants sought judicial review of the local authority's decision to restrict adult care needs to people with critical needs only, since the decision meant that their own substantial needs would not be met. The application was brought partly on the basis of the alleged flaws in the consultation process, yet also on the basis that the local authority had 'by excluding large numbers of persons with substantial needs, fettered its discretion to consider whether to provide community care services individually'. The decision to restrict services to this level of need was also challenged on the grounds of *Wednesbury* unreasonableness. Whilst the court found that the local authority had not complied with its duty under s 49A of the Disability Discrimination Act 1995 (there was no mention of the disability equality duty in any of the documents prepared by the local authority in the

---

[41] [2005] EWCA Civ 302.
[42] *R v Gloucestershire CC ex parte Barry* [1997] 2 All ER 1, at 18.
[43] [2007] EWHC 3064.

consultation period), the other grounds of challenge failed: the local authority was held to be perfectly entitled under the Fair Access to Care Services 2003 (the statutory Guidance applicable at that time) to restrict the range of people for whom it provided social care and to take resources into account in doing so. Moreover, the judgment states that the statutory complaints system rather than judicial review should be used to address any individual grievances arising out of the decisions made.

**4.28** The court in *R (on the application of Ireneschild) v Lambeth LBC*[44] has urged a similar level of caution in seeking judicial review of the mechanics of the community care assessment process by arguing, for example, that a local authority has failed to take into consideration important factors or given improper consideration to those which are irrelevant:[45]

> 'It is not a final determination of a legal dispute by a lawyer which may be subjected to over zealous textual analysis. Courts must be wary, in my view, of expecting so much of hard pressed social workers that we risk taking them away, unnecessarily, from their front-line duties.'

Hallett LJ made the same point, drawing attention, at [72], to the fact that although the process of a community care assessment was 'operational and inevitably judgmental', representations could be made about the assessment after it had been completed and the statutory complaints procedure could be invoked if necessary. Further, in *R (on the application of F) v Wirral BC*[46] the court observed that if any of the claimants had had a proper claim that their eligible needs were not being met by the council on the basis that either the assessment or the care plan had been inadequate, the appropriate remedy was through the statutory complaints procedure rather than through judicial review. Neither is a human rights challenge to the local authority's failure to meet needs likely to be any more successful: even if a local authority's decision not to provide services amounts to a breach of an individual's Art 8 rights, it is likely to be justified by reference to the fact that 'the court is slow to interfere with decisions which involve a balance of competing claims on the public purse in the allocation of economic resources'.[47]

## SUMMARY

**4.29** The cases concerning the boundary between 'harm' and 'significant harm' should be seen in the context of the research discussed in Chapters 1 and 3, which has shown that parents with learning disability are far more likely than other parents to be the subject of local authority intervention, that 'neglect' is the most common reason for their coming to local authority attention[48] and

---

[44] [2007] EWCA Civ 234.
[45] Ibid, at [57].
[46] [2009] EWHC 1626.
[47] *R (on the application of Dudley) v East Sussex CC* [2003] EWHC 1093.
[48] Hedy Cleaver and Don Nicholson *Parental Learning Disability and Children's Needs: Family Experiences and Effective Practice* (Jessica Kingsley Publishing, 2007).

that negative value judgments may be unfairly made about the level of parenting the learning disabled parent has reached. In other words, particular attention is required in these cases in order to determine whether the family is in fact maintaining a just about acceptable standard of parenting, or whether the circumstances really are exceptional enough for the compulsory powers to be exercised. It is suggested that whether or not the learning disabled parent has received an adequate support package is a relevant consideration to both the threshold test and the welfare test. Unfortunately, however, whilst the *Good Practice Guidance 2007* is very clear about the types of support that can benefit learning disabled parents, their right to access appropriate community services support is likely to be limited.

## Chapter 5

# PROTECTED PARTIES AND THE LITIGATION FRIEND

**5.1** In some cases a learning disabled parent may lack the ability to understand the issues involved in the care proceedings and therefore to contest the local authority's application for a care order and a placement order by instructing a solicitor directly. In this situation, the parent is said to lack 'litigation capacity' and requires a 'litigation friend' to deal with the proceedings on his or her behalf.[1] Importantly, however, the two concepts – of being learning disabled and of having no capacity to litigate – are different: a parent with impaired intelligence and impaired social or adaptive functioning might also have limited cognitive functioning and be unable to make decisions, but this should not be presumed and depends perhaps upon the degree of learning disability they have. Conversely, a parent with an IQ of 70 or over and hence not diagnosed as learning disabled may nonetheless be considered to lack litigation capacity if, for example, his or her working memory is so poor that it cannot be relied upon within the context of a fact-finding hearing; or where the parent's borderline intellectual functioning combined with an ability to communicate only in British Sign Language is such that he or she would experience considerable difficulty in understanding and processing events taking place within a legal framework;[2] or where the parent's ability to understand and to take part in proceedings fluctuates according to his or her changing levels of emotional well-being and anxiety levels.[3] Mental incapacity may also arise for reasons other than learning disability (for example, dementia; mental illness; brain damage acquired in adulthood).[4]

**5.2** Yet, deeming a person to have no capacity to issue or defend proceedings in their own name and requiring someone else to make decisions on their behalf is a significant step which must be strongly justified, since it deprives that person of 'important rights, long-cherished by English law'.[5] The rationale for doing so is said to derive from the need to protect a defendant from having proceedings brought against him or her at the whim of someone of 'unsound

---

[1] Family Procedure Rules 2010, SI 2010/2955, r 15.2, referring to the need for a 'protected party' to have a 'litigation friend'. The Family Procedure Rules 2010 set out a unified set of rules for all levels of court: the new rules relating to litigation friends replace the previous rules in Pt 7 of the Family Procedure (Adoption) Rules 2005, SI 2005/2795; and Pt IX of the Family Proceedings Rules 1991, SI 1991/1247.
[2] *Re SA (Vulnerable Adult with Capacity: Marriage)* [2006] EWHC 2492.
[3] *Re W (Children) (Care Proceedings: Litigation Capacity)* [2008] EWHC 1188.
[4] *Learning Disability: Definitions and Contexts* (The British Psychological Society, 2000).
[5] *RP v Nottingham City Council* [2008] EWCA Civ 462, at [114].

mind' acting alone, and the need to protect someone who has impaired cognitive functioning from having to deal alone with proceedings brought against them.[6] In *Masterman-Lister v Brutton* Kennedy LJ put it this way:[7]

> 'In the context of litigation Rules as to capacity are designed to ensure that claimants and defendants who would otherwise be at a disadvantage are properly protected, and in some cases that parties to litigation are not pestered by other parties who should be to some extent restrained.'

The same point was made in *Folks v Faizey*,[8] where the court was unimpressed by the respondent's objections to the appointment of a litigation friend on behalf of the appellant, noting that in any case the appointment of the litigation friend for the appellant would provide the respondent with a 'degree of protection'. In this way the need for a person without capacity to have someone else deal with the proceedings on his or her behalf is said both to uphold the fairness of the legal system and to protect the right of both parties to a fair trial. It is therefore perhaps anomalous that the question of whether or not someone has litigation capacity can be decided solely on the basis of a medical opinion and even without reference to the court[9] (see *Folks v Faizey* at **5.20**) and that the appointment of a litigation friend on behalf of a party can take place without any scrutiny by the court as long as the protected party – who is considered to lack capacity – does not object.[10]

**5.3** The need for a protected party to have a litigation friend to conduct the proceedings on his or her behalf is now set out in r 15.2 of the Family Procedure Rules 2010 (FPR 2010): 'A protected party must have a litigation friend to conduct proceedings on that party's behalf.'[11] A 'protected party' under the FPR 2010 is defined in r 2.3 as 'a party, or an intended party, who lacks capacity (within the meaning of the 2005 Act) to conduct proceedings'. This single rule replaces the previous rules to similar effect set out in the Family Proceedings Rules 1991[12] and the Family Procedure (Adoption) Rules 2005.[13]

**5.4** Rule 15.3 goes further by preventing any substantive step from being taken by any party in any proceedings without the permission of the court until the protected party has a litigation friend:

---

[6] *RP v Nottingham City Council* [2008] EWCA Civ 462.
[7] [2002] EWCA Civ 1889, at [31].
[8] [2006] EWCA Civ 381.
[9] There is no requirement in the rules for a judicial determination of the question of whether or not capacity exists.
[10] See Family Procedure Rules 2010, SI 2010/2955, Pt 15, supplemented by Practice Direction 15A, which enables a person to become a litigation friend without a court order, provided that a certificate of suitability complying with certain specified requirements has been filed. See further below at **5.18–5.22**.
[11] The new rules are effective from 6 April 2011.
[12] SI 1991/1247, as amended by the Family Proceedings (Amendment) (No 2) Rules 2007, SI 2007/2187.
[13] SI 2005/2795, as amended by the Family Procedure (Adoption) (Amendment) Rules 2007, SI 2007/2189.

'(1) A person may not without the permission of the court take any step in proceedings except –

(a) filing an application form; or
(b) applying for the appointment of a litigation friend under rule 15.6,

until the protected party has a litigation friend.'

Rule 15.3(2) addresses the situation where the fact that there is a protected party was not known at the outset and becomes known only once proceedings have started, or where, capacity being a fluctuating concept, the need for a party to be protected changes during the course of proceedings:

'If during proceedings a party lacks capacity (within the meaning of the 2005 Act) to continue to conduct proceedings, no party may take any step in proceedings without the permission of the court until the protected party has a litigation friend.'

In addition, under r 15.3(4) any step taken before a protected party has a litigation friend 'has no effect unless the court orders otherwise'.

**5.5** Before the implementation of the Mental Capacity Act 2005 on 1 October 2007, the common-law test for whether or not a person had capacity to conduct proceedings on their own behalf was set out in the case of *Masterman-Lister v Brutton*.[14] The Code of Practice accompanying the 2005 Act states at paras 4.31–4.33 that:

'The Act's new definition of capacity is in line with the existing common law tests, and the Act does not replace them. When cases come before the court on the above issues, judges can adopt the new definition if they think it appropriate.'

Whilst this suggests that the court can *choose* whether or not to adopt the statutory definition of litigation capacity and in this respect appears to be in conflict with r 2.3 of FPR 2010 and its predecessor – which defines capacity in accordance with the definition in the 2005 Act – it is generally accepted[15] that the tests for litigation capacity propounded in *Masterman-Lister* and the statutory definition are essentially the same.[16]

## THE COMMON-LAW TEST OF CAPACITY

**5.6** In *Masterman-Lister v Brutton*[17] the Court of Appeal dealt with the issue of litigation capacity for the first time. The context in which it arose concerned a claimant who had settled proceedings arising out of a motorcycle accident in

---

[14] [2002] EWCA Civ 1889.
[15] Wall LJ in *RP v Nottingham City Council* [2008] EWCA Civ 462.
[16] Munby J in *Local Authority X v M* [2007] EWHC 2003 (Fam); *Saulle v Nouvet* [2007] EWHC 2902.
[17] [2002] EWCA Civ 1889.

which he had suffered a severe brain injury. Finding his negligence claim against his solicitors time-barred, he sought to re-open the compromised claim on the basis that at the time he had settled the matter he been a patient under the Mental Health Act 1983 and that the compromise had not received the approval of the court that it had therefore required under RSC Ord 80, r 10. At issue specifically was the question of whether the claimant was at any time a 'patient', defined under the 1983 Act as 'a person who by reason of mental disorder ... is incapable of managing and administering his own affairs' and who should under RSC Ord 80, r 10 have brought proceedings only by his next friend. On appeal from the judge at first instance, who had ruled that the claimant had not been a 'patient' at any time since 1983, the issue of litigation capacity arose.

**5.7** Chadwick LJ said this:[18]

> '... the test to be applied ... is whether the party to legal proceedings is capable of understanding, with the assistance of such proper explanation from legal advisers and experts in other disciplines as the case may require, the issues on which his consent or decision is likely to be necessary in the course of those proceedings. If he has capacity to understand that which he needs to understand in order to pursue or defend a claim, I can see no reason why the law whether substantive or procedural should require the interposition of a next friend or guardian ad litem (or, as such a person is now described in the Civil Procedure Rules, a litigation friend).'

Further, when considering whether a person has the capacity to pursue or defend a claim in relation to a particular matter Chadwick LJ stated:[19]

> '... a person should not be held unable to understand the information relevant to a decision if he can understand an explanation of that information in broad terms and simple language; and ... should not be regarded as unable to make a rational decision merely because the decision which he does, in fact, make is a decision which would not be made by a person of ordinary prudence.'

Kennedy LJ and Potter LJ agreed with this formulation of the test to be applied.

**5.8** In determining whether or not a person has litigation capacity, it is important to remember that litigation capacity is issue-specific. This means that the question of capacity needs to be considered in the context of the particular piece of litigation in which the question arises rather than being something to be considered in the abstract.[20] It follows, for example, that a person might have capacity to litigate in a case where the issues are simple but

---

[18] Ibid, at [75].
[19] Ibid, at [79].
[20] Ibid, per Kennedy LJ at [27]; Chadwick LJ at [75] (referring to the need to understand 'the issues on which his consent or decision is likely to be necessary in the course of *those* proceedings').

lacks the capacity to litigate in a case where the issues are more complex;[21] or that someone may lack litigation capacity in relation to whether they should have a particular form of surgical intervention yet at the same time retain the capacity to agree to a very simple surgical procedure. The latter point highlights not only the fact that litigation capacity is issue-specific, but also the fact that although a person may lack litigation capacity they may nonetheless have subject-matter capacity in relation to matters which are the subject of that litigation. For example, a parent without capacity to conduct placement proceedings may still have capacity to consent to adoption under ss 19 and 20 of the Adoption and Children Act 2002.[22] In *Re W (Children) (Care Proceedings: Litigation Capacity)*[23] McFarlane J highlighted the difference between litigation capacity and subject-matter capacity this way:[24]

> 'What is it that I am assessing? It is not issue specific in the sense that I have to look at whether he can give instructions and has capacity to be a litigant on particular parts of the case, for example, in due course, whether contact is to be on a Saturday afternoon or a Sunday morning or whatever the practical issues might be, it is to take part in the proceedings as a whole. The analogy that I offered yesterday was of someone being put in the driving seat of a car and the question for the court is whether he has sufficient capacity to be the driver for the whole leg of the procedural journey at least, through the fact-finding process, and not simply for different stretches of that journey. It has to be established on the balance of probability that he lacks capacity to undertake that task and to make the necessary decisions.'

**5.9** Whilst there is a consensus that a person lacking litigation capacity may have capacity with regard to the matters which are the subject of that litigation, it has been acknowledged that it is hard to imagine a situation where the converse is true and where a person has litigation capacity but no subject-matter capacity. No such case has been reported, and there is judicial recognition that this is only likely to arise in unusual circumstances.[25]

# CAPACITY UNDER THE MENTAL CAPACITY ACT 2005

**5.10** Section 1 of the Mental Capacity Act 2005 sets out some 'enabling' principles which apply for the purposes of determining capacity under the Act. These include the following: a person must be assumed to have capacity unless it is established that he lacks capacity (s 1(2)); a person is not to be treated as unable to make a decision unless all practicable steps to help him to do so have been taken without success (s 1(3)); a person is not to be treated as unable to make a decision merely because he makes an unwise decision (s 1(4)); an act done, or decision made, under this Act for or on behalf of a person who lacks capacity must be done, or made, in his best interests (s 1(5)); before the act is

---

[21] *Sheffield County Council v E* [2004] EWHC 2808, at [39].
[22] Ibid, at [40].
[23] [2008] EWHC 1188.
[24] Ibid, at [80].
[25] Munby J in *Sheffield County Council v E* [2004] EWHC 2808.

done, or the decision is made, regard must be had to whether the purpose for which it is needed can be as effectively achieved in a way that is less restrictive of the person's rights and freedom of action (s 1(6)).

**5.11** Section 2 of the Mental Capacity Act 2005 provides as follows:

'(1) For the purposes of this Act, a person lacks capacity in relation to a matter if at the material time he is unable to make a decision for himself in relation to the matter because of an impairment of, or a disturbance in the functioning of, the mind or brain.

(2) It does not matter whether the impairment or disturbance is permanent or temporary.

(3) A lack of capacity cannot be established merely by reference to (a) a person's age or appearance, or (b) a condition of his, or an aspect of his behaviour, which might lead others to make unjustified assumptions about his capacity.

(4) In proceedings under this Act or any other enactment, any question whether a person lacks capacity within the meaning of this Act must be decided on the balance of probabilities.'

**5.12** Section 3 of the Mental Capacity Act 2005 provides that:

'(1) For the purposes of section 2, a person is unable to make a decision for himself if he is unable –

(a) to understand the information relevant to the decision,
(b) to retain that information,
(c) to use or weigh that information as part of the process of making the decision, or
(d) to communicate his decision (whether by talking, using sign language or any other means).

(2) A person is not to be regarded as unable to understand the information relevant to a decision if he is able to understand an explanation of it given to him in a way that is appropriate to his circumstances (using simple language, visual aids or any other means).

(3) The fact that a person is able to retain the information relevant to a decision for a short period only does not prevent him from being regarded as able to make the decision.

(4) The information relevant to a decision includes information about the reasonably foreseeable consequences of –

(a) deciding one way or another, or
(b) failing to make the decision.'

**5.13** Further clarification of the above provisions is set out in the Code of Practice accompanying the Act. At para 4.11 the Code refers to a 'two-stage test' of capacity, where Stage 1 ('the diagnostic test') requires proof that a person has an impairment of the mind or brain, or some sort of disturbance that affects the way their mind or brain works. Stage 2 ('the functional test') requires that the impairment or disturbance must affect their ability to make the specific decision when they need to. As far as Stage 1 is concerned, the Code sets out examples of what might amount to an impairment: conditions associated with some forms of mental illness; dementia; significant learning disabilities; the long-term effects of brain damage; physical or mental conditions that cause confusion, drowsiness or loss of consciousness; delirium; concussion following a head injury; and the symptoms of drug or alcohol abuse. In relation to Stage 2, the Code clarifies at para 4.13 that all practical and appropriate support to help the person make the decision must have failed. Moreover, para 4.16 emphasises the need not to assess someone's understanding before every effort has been made to provide them with information in order to aid that understanding. It is suggested at para 4.18, for example, that:

'... a person with learning disability might need somebody to read to them. They might also need illustrations to help them to understand what is happening ... It might also be helpful for them to discuss things with an advocate.'

In addition, para 3.10 of the Code sets out a helpful summary of all the possible means of communication of which use should be made in order to help a person make a decision for themselves.

## PROCEDURE

**5.14** Since under r 15.3(4) of FPR 2010 any step taken before a protected party has a litigation friend 'has no effect unless the court orders otherwise', it is clear that the question of whether or not a parent has capacity to litigate needs to be determined at the earliest possible opportunity. This prioritisation reflects the provisions of the *Public Law Outline*,[26] para 11.4 of which requires the court *upon the issue of proceedings* to consider giving directions as to the representation of any protected party or non-subject child. Paragraph 7.2 confirms the need to deal with the question of capacity expeditiously, in that it states that 'any issue as to the capacity of an adult to conduct the proceedings must be determined before the court gives any directions relevant to that adult's role within the proceedings'. Further, para 12.3(6)(f) states that by the date of the first court appointment (ie Day Six) the 'court should be in a position to consider whether or not a protected party is competent to make his or her statement'. In addition, since at this stage the court will also be considering whether or not to join any other adult party to the proceedings, it must also consider whether the Official Solicitor should be invited to act on their behalf.

---

[26] *The Public Law Outline: Guide to Case Management in Public Law Proceedings* (Ministry of Justice, 2008).

**5.15** Since there were no provisions for protected parties under the Family Proceedings Courts (Children Act 1989) Rules 1991,[27] the Official Solicitor could only act in the High Court or in a county court pursuant to Part IX of the Family Proceedings Rules 1991. It followed that where there was a real possibility that a person lacked capacity to conduct proceedings within the meaning of the Mental Capacity Act 2005, the Family Proceedings Court was required to transfer the case to the care centre forthwith. The introduction by FPR 2010 of a unified set of rules for family proceedings in the magistrates' court, the county court and the High Court means that there is now no procedural obstacle to the appointment by the magistrates' court of a litigation friend for a protected party. Whether or not this results in fewer such cases being transferred to the county court remains to be seen. It is noted, however, that where the magistrates' court considers that 'there is a real possibility that a party to proceedings is a person lacking capacity within the meaning of the Mental Capacity Act 2005 to conduct the proceedings', this remains a valid reason for transfer to the county court under the Allocation and Transfer of Proceedings Order 2008.[28]

**5.16** A legal representative forming the view that their client might not be able to give them proper instructions is under a duty to have the issue resolved as quickly as possible. Indeed, to continue to take instructions from a person whom a legal adviser does not believe has the capacity to instruct them is a serious breach of their professional and ethical code.[29] The Bar Council suggests the following approach:[30]

- '• In the first place, Counsel should discuss the question of the client's capacity with Instructing Solicitor (who is likely to have had more contact with the client than Counsel has).
- • If, having discussed the question of the client's capacity with Instructing Solicitor, Counsel still reasonably suspects that the client lacks capacity and, if Counsel has not already met the clients, Counsel should, if practicable, meet the client. Whether or not Counsel meets the client, if Counsel's concerns about the client's capacity persist, Counsel should ensure that the client is informed of those concerns as tactfully as possible, and that any comments which the client has to make on the issue of capacity are obtained and taken into account.
- • If, at this stage, Counsel still reasonably suspects that the client lacks capacity, Counsel should advise that evidence about the client's capacity is obtained. Clearly, obtaining the necessary time, funding (particularly if there is doubt about the propriety of relying on private funding from the client), and co-operation from the client, may all be problematic. If an adjournment of a hearing is necessary, Counsel will obviously need to be discreet in informing the Court and any other party about the reason, but must not be misleading. Circumstances may justify simply saying that Counsel and Instructing Solicitor are in a situation of professional embarrassment which

---

[27] SI 1991/1395.
[28] SI 2008/2836, Sch 2, art 5.
[29] *RP v Nottingham City Council* [2008] EWCA Civ 462.
[30] Bar Council *Guidance on Client Incapacity*, http://www.barcouncil.org.uk/guidance/clientincapacity/.

- makes it impossible for them to proceed immediately, the nature of which they are not currently at liberty to reveal, and which they need time to resolve.
- Counsel should bear in mind in advising that it may be appropriate for Instructing Solicitor to seek advice and/or assistance from the Official Solicitor (or additionally, in family proceedings, CAFCASS Litigation). Evidence about capacity from lay people who know the client well may be useful, although, by its very nature, it may not be independent or disinterested. Evidence from the client's GP may be very helpful, if the client will permit it and the GP knows the client. A report from a suitably qualified Medical Expert (normally, a Consultant Psychiatrist approved for the purpose of section 12 of the Mental Health Act 1983), based on an examination of the client, the client's medical records and any of the other evidence obtained, is usually essential. Counsel is entitled to advise the client to co-operate in the obtaining of medical evidence, but is not entitled to insist on the client doing so.
- If, in the light of such evidence, if any, as can be obtained, Counsel still reasonably suspects that the client lacks capacity, Counsel should, if practicable, meet the client again, and should, in any event, ensure that any further comments which the client has to make are obtained and taken into account, and should discuss the issue of the client's capacity further with Instructing Solicitor.
- If, having done so, Counsel still reasonably suspects that the client lacks capacity, Counsel should at this stage advise that the appropriate Court be informed of the client's suspected lack of capacity.
- If this advice is accepted and followed, well and good.
- If the client rejects this advice but Instructing Solicitor nonetheless accepts it ... the Court should be informed of the client's suspected lack of capacity (which, in the absence of any special application, will normally mean informing any other party to the proceedings), even if the client purports to forbid this ... this is a situation where Counsel's duty to the Court overrides the client's purported instructions, even if the client subsequently turns out to have capacity. Disclosure of the client's suspected lack of capacity is necessary for the protection of the client, in case the client lacks capacity, and may be necessary for the protection of Counsel and Instructing Solicitor, since, as pointed out above, if the client lacks capacity to give instructions and/or to authorise private funding, Counsel and Instructing Solicitor cannot properly be acting on the basis of the client's instructions and/or any such funding.
- Once the client's suspected lack of capacity has been disclosed to the Court: ... if the client's capacity to conduct civil or family proceedings is in question, that question can be determined by the civil or family Court, and, if the client is a "patient" for that purpose, in civil proceedings a "litigation friend" or in family proceedings a "next friend" or "guardian ad litem" can be appointed to conduct the litigation on the client's behalf.[31]
- If, however, both the lay client and Instructing Solicitor reject Counsel's advice that the client's suspected lack of capacity be disclosed to the Court, Counsel will probably be in such a situation of professional embarrassment that the only proper course will be to withdraw from the case.'

---

[31] FPR 2010 now uses the term 'litigation friend'.

**5.17** In referring the client to an appropriate expert for assistance in assessing his or her level of cognitive functioning and capacity to conduct proceedings, it is important that the relevant expert has their attention drawn to the applicable legal criteria in the Mental Capacity Act 2005, ss 1–3, to the context and the background of the case, and to the need to consider the alternative ways of communicating with the client which might enable capacity to be retained[32] (see Appendix 6 for the Official Solicitor's draft letter of instruction to an expert). When asking the expert to assess the party's capacity, it is also good practice to ask the instructed expert to consider (if his or her assessment is that the party is a protected party) whether or not the party can give evidence or whether or not he or she requires special measures in this regard (see para 8.4 of the *Practice Direction: Guide to Case Management in Public Law Proceedings 2010*). There is no requirement for the protected party to give evidence, which remains a matter for the solicitor and the litigation friend (unless someone wishes to call him or her as a witness).

**5.18** The expectation in para 11.4 of the *Public Law Outline* that the court may be in a position to deal with the question of capacity by the time the proceedings are issued might suggest that the child protection team bringing the application should take a more proactive stance in commissioning an expert to consider the issue of litigation capacity at the pre-proceedings stage. In *RP v Nottingham City Council*,[33] however, Thorpe LJ considered that although the child protection team has a duty to try wherever possible and in accordance with the child's welfare to ensure that the child remains with his or her parents, the local authority had fulfilled its obligations by consenting to the joint instruction of a psychologist to determine whether or not the child's mother had capacity to litigate rather than obstructing it. There is no obligation on the local authority child protection team at the pre-proceedings stage to take on a more direct role in facilitating the representation of a parent who might be a protected party, although it is good practice for the child's social worker to refer the parent to the adult learning disability team.[34] Once proceedings have been issued, the question of representation then becomes a matter for the parent's legal team, who should, bearing in mind the fluctuating nature of capacity, seek to review it from time to time. That said, at the pre-proceedings stage, where the parent appears to the child protection social worker to be a protected party, the local authority should be extremely careful to ensure that the parent understands the concerns being raised as to their care of the child. In practice this means that the local authority should either ensure that the letter before action is written in plain language or in symbols that the parent will be able to understand, or should convey the local authority's concerns by means of a discussion with the parent rather than by a letter before proceedings. Moreover, in circumstances where a parent appears to be a protected party (or would be in the event that proceedings were issue) it would

---

[32] See Mental Capacity Act 2005 Code of Practice, paras 4.16–4.19.
[33] [2008] EWCA Civ 462.
[34] *RP v Nottingham City Council* [2008] EWCA Civ 462, at [181].

be inappropriate to accept the parent's consent to s 20 accommodation of the child and any such consent obtained would appear to be invalid.[35]

## THE APPOINTMENT OF THE LITIGATION FRIEND

**5.19** The appointment of a litigation friend can be made either by a court order under r 15.6 of FPR 2010, or without a court order under r.15.4. Protected parties in care proceedings are often represented by the Official Solicitor, but this need not always be the case since the Official Solicitor is an office of last resort whose consent is required before his appointment in any given case. Where the Official Solicitor is to act as the litigation friend, his appointment can only be made by court order (see FPR 2010, r 15.5(6)). Whether the appointment of the litigation friend is made with or without a court order, the person appointed must comply with the conditions set out in r 15.4(3):[36] that person must be able to conduct proceedings fairly and competently on the protected party's behalf; they must have no interest adverse to that of the protected party; and they must undertake to pay any costs ordered against the protected party, subject to any right to be repaid from the assets of the protected party. The latter condition, however, does not apply where the Official Solicitor is the litigation friend and in any event is largely irrelevant in care proceedings, where costs are rarely ordered against parents and where parents are entitled to public funding without reference to means, prospects of success or reasonableness.

**5.20** Where the appointment is made by court order, it can be made upon application by a person who wishes to become a litigation friend, upon application by a party to the proceedings or upon the court's own initiative (r 15.6(2)).[37] Any such application must be supported by evidence (r 15.6(4)), which will usually be the evidence as to cognitive capacity from the instructed psychological or psychiatric expert. Further, the person to be appointed must satisfy the court that they can comply with the r 15.4(3) conditions. Within the context of civil proceedings under the Civil Procedure Rules[38] (CPR) there is a subsidiary issue as to whether the notice of application for the appointment of a litigation friend needs to be served on the respondents to the proceedings, since r 23.4(1) requires service of an application notice on each 'Respondent' and CPR, r 23.11 defines 'Respondent' as a person against whom an order is sought. Since a litigation friend can act on behalf of a party without any need for a court order and without any facility for another party to object,[39] it can hardly be said that an order is being sought *against* the respondent and the court will need to consider whether a direction for service is required in each

---

[35] 'Parents who lack Capacity to Conduct Public Law Proceedings' [2010] Fam Law 745.
[36] Except where that person already has authority as a deputy to conduct the proceedings on the protected party's behalf: r 15.4(2). For 'deputy', see s 16(2)(b) of the Mental Capacity Act 2005.
[37] See further Practice Direction 15A (Protected Parties), supplementing Pt 15 of FPR 2010.
[38] SI 1998/3132.
[39] *Folks v Faizey* [2006] EWCA Civ 381.

case. Under FPR 2010, it seems that an application notice for a court order appointing a litigation friend need only be served on (a) a person who is the attorney of a registered enduring power of attorney, a donee of a lasting power of attorney or a deputy, or, if there is no such person, on the person with whom the protected party resides or in whose care the protected party is; and (b) the protected party unless the court directs otherwise.[40] Even where the appointment of the litigation friend is made by a court order, the court generally adopts a hands-off approach to the appointment of a litigation friend on behalf of a protected party. In *Folks v Faizey*,[41] for example, the Court of Appeal considered whether the judge below had been wrong to order a hearing as to the appointment on behalf of the appellant of a litigation friend under CPR, r 21.6 when there was appropriate medical evidence to support the application but where the consultant neuropsychiatrist instructed on behalf of the respondent had taken a different view. The relevant rule was r.21.6 of the CPR (the appointment of a litigation friend). The court referred to Chadwick LJ in *Masterman-Lister v Brutton*[42] in relation to the Supreme Court Rules 1980:

> '... the rule making body ... intended that the question of whether a party was required to act through a next friend or guardian ad litem (as the case may be) should be determined by the party ... and those caring for him.'

Accordingly, it was held that whilst there has to be evidence in support of an application for a court order appointing a litigation friend so that the court is acting as more than a mere rubber stamp, the other party is not entitled to submit evidence disputing the basis of the application. In other words, an order appointing the litigation friend should be made where the protected party and the litigation friend both consent to the appointment of the latter, where there is adequate evidence to support the application and no evidence that the application is anything other than genuinely motivated. Whilst *Folks v Faizey* is an application concerned with the appointment of a litigation friend under the CPR and does not concern family proceedings, it is suggested that, since the harmonisation of Family Law procedure with the CPR 1998 is one of the key objectives of FPR 2010, the same principles will apply. The appointment of a litigation friend for a parent in care proceedings is in this way not a matter which should trouble the other parties or become the subject of judicial decision-making unless a ruling on the issue is required because the protected party objects to not being permitted to represent him- or herself.

**5.21** Paragraph 4.5 of Practice Direction 15A (Protected Parties) does, however, place restrictions on those who may seek to become a litigation friend by way of court order. It states that, where an application is made for a court order appointing a litigation friend, 'the proposed litigation friend may be one of the persons referred to in paragraph 3.3 where appropriate, or otherwise may be the Official Solicitor'. Paragraph 3.3 refers to 'the person who is the attorney

---

[40] Practice Direction 15A, para 4.2.
[41] [2006] EWCA Civ 381.
[42] [2002] EWCA Civ 1889, at [66].

of a registered enduring power of attorney, donee of a lasting power of attorney or deputy, or, if there is no such person, to the person with whom the protected party resides or in whose care the protected party is'. There appears, however, to be no such restriction on those who can become a litigation friend without a court order.

**5.22** Where the appointment of a litigation friend is made without a court order, r 15.5 of FPR 2010 requires the person wishing to act as a litigation friend to file a 'certificate of suitability' confirming their compliance with the r 15.4(3) conditions at the time of taking the first step in the proceedings on behalf of the protected party.[43] The certificate of suitability must comply with the requirements set out in Practice Direction 15A, para 3.1(b). Where the person wishing to act as the litigation friend already has authority as deputy, he or she must simply file an official copy of the order, declaration or other document which confers that person's authority to act. The court does, however, retain the power to direct that a person cannot act as a litigation friend, to terminate the appointment of a litigation friend already appointed or to appoint a new litigation friend in substitution for an existing one (r 15.7).

**5.23** In practice the appointment of a person other than the Official Solicitor as a litigation friend is rare. In *RP v Nottingham City Council*,[44] for example, whilst it was stated, at [130], that there was no reason why a lay person should not be the litigation friend of the claimant, the Court of Appeal found a clear conflict of interest between the claimant and the family members the mother had suggested could act on her behalf, primarily because all three of them had put themselves forward as alternative carers for the child in opposition to her wishes. The judge was also influenced by the fact that none of the family members appeared able to conduct the proceedings 'fairly and competently', nor to be able to provide her with the clear and objective advice that in view of her learning disabilities she needed. Moreover, there was abundant evidence of the family's hostility to social services.[45] Again, in *A Local Authority v A*[46] the court considered it inappropriate for a family member to become the litigation friend in view of the fact that her strong feelings on the subject matter in dispute tended to cloud her judgment and ability to be objective.

**5.24** Where a legal adviser considers that the Official Solicitor should be invited to act on behalf of his or her client, they should contact the Official Solicitor without delay. If the case has already come before the court and it then becomes apparent that the parent is a protected party, the order inviting the Official Solicitor to act should be expressed as subject to his consent. The parent's representative should then forward a copy of the order to the Official Solicitor inviting him to act (with a note of the reasons approved by the judge if appropriate), together with the court file, a bundle with summary, statement of issues and chronology. The Official Solicitor will require medical or

---

[43] See further Practice Direction 15A (Protected Parties), para 3.1 (reproduced in Appendix 7).
[44] [2008] EWCA Civ 462.
[45] Ibid, at [133].
[46] [2010] EWHC 1549.

psychological evidence in order to consent to the request and will do so only if no other person is either willing or suitable. The 2001 Practice Note[47] states that upon receipt of an application the Official Solicitor will endeavour to respond within 10 working days and a directions hearing should therefore be listed within 28 days to deal with any issues arising out of the Official Solicitor's response.

**5.25** Guidance from the Official Solicitor and the President of the Family Division issued in December 2010 refers to the 'severe budgetary constraints' being experienced by the Official Solicitor's office and to the associated difficulties it has in accepting requests to act as a litigation friend in proceedings relating to children. To that end, the Guidance restates that the Official Solicitor will require (a) satisfactory evidence or a finding by the court that the party lacks capacity to conduct the proceedings and is therefore a protected party; (b) confirmation that there is security for the costs of the legal representation; and (c) confirmation that there is no other person suitable and willing to act as the guardian or the next friend. It is, however, not ultra vires for the Official Solicitor to continue to act if a family member has also put themselves forward.[48]

# THE ROLE OF THE LITIGATION FRIEND

**5.26** Where a litigation friend conducts a case on behalf of a protected party, several practical issues arise for the solicitor or legal adviser. First, the protected party is still the client, but the solicitor must take their instructions not from the client but from the litigation friend. This is the corollary of the fact that the function of the litigation friend is to supplement the protected party's want of judgment. Secondly, the client not being able to give *instructions*, it follows that the client cannot terminate the services of the legal adviser. Thirdly, the role of the litigation friend is to conduct proceedings on behalf of the protected party fairly and competently and all steps and decisions must be taken for the benefit of that protected party.[49] In determining the sort of action that may be for the benefit of the protected party, s 4(6) of the Mental Capacity Act 2005 requires consideration of (a) the person's past and present wishes and feelings (and, in particular, any relevant written statement made by him or her when he or she had capacity), (b) the beliefs and values that would be likely to influence his or her decision if he or she had capacity, and (c) the other factors that he or she would be likely to consider if he or she were able to do so. Further, under s 4(7) decision-making must take into account, if it is practicable and appropriate to do so, the views of (a) anyone named by the person as someone to be consulted on the matter in question or on matters of that kind, (b) anyone engaged in caring for the person or interested in his or her welfare, (c) any donee of a lasting power of attorney granted by the person, and (d) any deputy appointed for the person by the court, as to what would be

---

[47] *The Official Solicitor: Appointment in Family Proceedings* [2001] 2 FLR 155.
[48] *A Local Authority v A* [2010] EWHC 1549.
[49] Practice Direction 15A (Protected Parties), para 2.1.

in the person's best interests and, in particular, as to the matters mentioned in s 4(6). Whilst the provisions of the Mental Capacity Act 2005 do not purport to set out the *role* of the litigation friend, it is suggested that s 4(6) and (7) provide a useful checklist for avoiding a potential breach of the protected party's rights under Article 6 of the European Convention on Human Rights. To this end, the Official Solicitor has commented that:[50] 'the litigation friend must act properly and with due regard to the person's rights and wishes [and] ... when departing from the person's wishes, to oppose, frustrate or negate them to the least necessary extent.' The same point has been made in *Local Authority X v M*:[51]

> 'The nearer to the borderline the particular adult, even if she falls on the wrong side of the line, the more weight must in principle be attached to her wishes and feelings, because the greater the distress, the humiliation and indeed it may even be the anger she is likely to feel the better she is able to appreciate that others are taking on her behalf decisions about matters which vitally affect her matters, it may be, as here, of an intensely private and personal nature.'

**5.27** In practice the Official Solicitor will depart from the client's own wishes only where it is considered that those views will inevitably be rejected by the court; or where on medical evidence, it is thought to be detrimental to the party's own welfare to oppose the case. Moreover, the Official Solicitor considers that the appropriate course to take is to:[52]

> '... present any realistic arguments and relevant evidence that may be available on behalf of (ie in support of) the parent in relation to the issues before the court ... the criterion should be whether the point is reasonably arguable, not whether it is likely to succeed.'

In order to have a full understanding of the reasonableness of the issues involved, the Official Solicitor or litigation friend should seek further evidence in most cases as to how the disability is likely to affect the party's ability to care for the children, or to have contact with them. To this end the litigation friend, in addition to seeking expert evidence,[53] should seek a statement from the local authority as to the parenting support that has been offered by the protected party and as to the outcome of any assessment under the National Health Service and Community Care Act 1990. Where, however, there are no realistic arguments to be made, it is thought to be more appropriate not to oppose than to make explicit concessions.[54]

---

[50] *RP v Nottingham City Council* [2008] 2 FLR 1516.
[51] [2007] EWHC 2003.
[52] *RP v Nottingham CC* [2008] 2 FLR 1516, at 1584.
[53] See cases discussed in Chapter 6: *Re M* [2009] EWCA Civ 315; *Re B* [2010] EWCA Civ 363.
[54] *RP v Nottingham CC* [2008] 2 FLR 1516, at 1585.

## ADOPTION PROCEEDINGS

**5.28** Where a respondent to placement proceedings has no litigation capacity, he or she may nonetheless have capacity to consent to adoption under either s 19 or 20 of the Adoption and Children Act 2002. Under FPR 2010, r 14.10, consent under s 19 or 20 must be given in the form referred to in the Practice Direction 5A or form to like effect. If the parent does not consent to adoption, the court cannot under s 52 of the Adoption and Children Act 2002 dispense with the parent's consent to the child being placed for adoption or to the making of an adoption order in respect of the child unless the court is satisfied that (a) the parent or guardian cannot be found or is incapable of giving consent, or (b) the welfare of the child requires the consent to be dispensed with. A reference to an appropriate expert for an assessment of the parent's capacity to consent to adoption should therefore be sought. It is suggested that the parent will not have capacity to consent to adoption unless he or she understands that (a) the adoption of their child removes the child from his or her family on a permanent basis; and (b) that the child will then in law become the child of the adoptive family.

## SUMMARY

**5.29** Establishing whether or not the learning disabled parent has litigation capacity in care proceedings is an important step which raises issues of procedural fairness as well as of substantive human rights. The main practical points arising out of the discussion above are as follows:

- The issue of whether or not a parent is a 'protected party' must be dealt with expeditiously; the instructed expert should be referred to the relevant provisions of the Mental Capacity Act 2005 and the accompanying Code of Practice.
- Legal representatives of the protected party in placement proceedings should ensure, notwithstanding that the parent has no litigation capacity, that there is also an assessment of the parent's capacity to consent to the child's placement for adoption.
- It appears that there is now no obstacle to the appointment of a litigation friend in the magistrates' courts.
- A person other than the Official Solicitor can be appointed as a litigation friend (although securing funding for any other professional to act in this capacity may be problematic).
- Where a parent is represented by a litigation friend, the first steps to be taken on their behalf should include (a) ascertaining whether there has been an assessment under s 47 of the National Health Service and Community Care Act 1990 and, if so, its outcome; (b) requesting a copy of the local authority's protocol on working with parents with learning disabilities; and (c) ensuring that the client has received a specialist parenting assessment.

# Chapter 6

# LEARNING DISABILITY: CASE SUMMARIES

## DISCRIMINATION AND SOCIAL ENGINEERING

6.1

*Re L (A Child) (Care: Threshold Criteria)* **[2006] EWCA Civ 1282, [2007] 1 FLR 2050**

*Whether the threshold criteria had been crossed in relation to the learning disabled parents of two children – judge finding the threshold proven on the basis of expert psychological evidence – meaning of 'significant' in 'significant harm' – risk of social engineering if the threshold is set too low*

Both parents were described as having learning difficulties, with the mother being represented by the Official Solicitor. The parents appealed against the threshold findings in relation to their 10-year-old daughter and 7-year-old son, both of whom had been removed into foster care several months previously following an allegation that the father had seriously assaulted them ('the belting incident'). The judge at first instance had found the threshold criteria proven solely on the basis of the opinions and evidence of the jointly instructed chartered psychologist. The Court of Appeal held that he was wrong to do so and remitted the case to be re-heard by a different judge. By the time of the re-hearing, the local authority had accepted that the belting incident was unlikely to be substantiated against the father and sought to prove the threshold on the basis of historical allegations of domestic violence and the general inadequacy of the father and mother as parents.

(1) The chartered psychologist had been jointly instructed by the parties not in relation to whether the threshold had been crossed but in relation to the final determination of the care order applications in the event that it had been crossed. However, the Court of Appeal concluded that the judge should not have based his conclusion that the threshold criteria were satisfied solely on the psychologist's recommendation that the children were likely to suffer significant harm if they were to be returned to their parent's care: the expert had departed from the obligation not to deal independently with any one party without reference to the others, and not to have informal, unrecorded discussions with any of the professionals, as she had had access to the children's special educational needs files and the

local authority's files, neither of which had been seen by the parents, and had had unrecorded interviews with the children's teachers. The discussions with the latter had been influential in the formation of her opinion in that they referred to a marked improvement in the behaviour and educational progress of both children since they were accommodated. In addition, the expert relied heavily on the results of the psychometric tests of the father, notwithstanding that he had a borderline learning disability and could scarcely read and write. Her opinion had been further devalued by her concession that she would have needed to carry out further work if she had been instructed on the threshold issue, and her concession that she was unable to conclude that the parents did not now provide 'good enough parenting'.

(2) In the Court of Appeal, in order to assuage the parents' concerns that they had already been written off by the local authority as parents, Wall LJ confirmed that:

> '... family courts do not remove children from their parents into care because the parents in question are not intelligent enough to care for them or have low intelligence quotas. Children are only removed into care (a) if they are suffering or likely to suffer significant harm in the care of their parents; and (b) if it is in their interests that a care order is made. Anything else is social engineering and is wholly impermissible.'

That said, whilst there are no reported cases where a child has been removed from his or her parents as a result of the learning disability alone, there are cases where the effect of the learning disability appears to be a dominant reason for the making of a public law order. Moreover, the number of children removed into care who have at least one parent who is learning disabled is disproportionately high (see **1.19–1.21**).

(3) At the re-hearing, Hedley J found that the father had been violent to the mother on at least two occasions and that there was a fairly clear lack of boundaries and a worrying attitude by the children towards their mother which the father had been unable to stop and had appeared to encourage. However, although the children had suffered 'harm' and although the local authority had good reason to be concerned about the children and their circumstances, this did not amount to 'significant harm', which must be 'something more than the commonplace human failure or inadequacy'. This was the first time that the difference between 'harm' and 'significant harm' had been considered in any reported case – see Chapter 4, at **4.7–4.10** for further discussion. At p 50 of the judgment, Hedley J referred to the policy of minimal intervention in the family, arising out of the principle that children are best brought up within their natural families wherever possible, and concluded as a consequence that 'society must be willing to tolerate very diverse standards of parenting including the eccentric, the barely adequate and the inconsistent'. The case serves as a valuable reminder that the parents in learning disability cases, as in all others, need to be judged by whether or not their parenting is 'good enough', a point which needs reinforcing in the light of the fact that the Commission for Social Care Inspection found in 2009 that the

expectations placed on learning disabled parents were routinely higher than the expectations placed on others.[1]

## 6.2

## *Re S (A Child)* [2008] EWCA Civ 1284

*Father with a mild learning disability putting himself forward as a carer for his 6-year-old son – whether or not the judge was plainly wrong to approve the care plan for long-term fostering rather than rehabilitation especially when the father had a very good relationship with the child and was wholly committed to him and his welfare*

The father of a 6-year-old boy was assessed by a clinical psychologist as having litigation capacity, although he had 'learning difficulties' (functioning at the borderline between the upper end of a mild learning disability and the lower end of the normal range) and was considered to be anxious, vulnerable and highly suggestible. The view of the clinical psychologist and the local authority was that in spite of the positives of his relationship with and commitment to his son (with whom he had had very regular contact since the child was accommodated following the parents' separation), he was likely to experience difficulties in boundary-setting and behaviour management and in understanding the child's social and emotional needs as the child grew up and became more challenging. The father's application for permission to appeal against the making of the care order (in which ongoing contact was part of the care plan) was dismissed.

(1) The Court of Appeal approved the decision of the judge at first instance, who it considered had not been wrong to approach the case on the basis that it was all about risk, nor to balance the competing risks to the child in staying at the foster placement where he had settled, on the one hand, and returning to his father, on the other. The risks to his welfare if he were to remain with his father were considered to be that his father would be less able to manage him as he grew older and more challenging. This need for permanence outweighed any detriment he might suffer in not being placed in his father's care.

(2) Of note is the fact that short shrift was given to the (perhaps bold) argument on behalf of the father that he was being discriminated against due to his intellectual shortcomings, and that as a learning disabled parent he had not been given the same chance to care for his child as would be given, for example, to a recovering alcoholic. In rejecting that argument, Lord Justice Wall added, at [20], that:

> 'This case, like so many others, turns on its facts and there is nothing in this case ... which even begins to come near discrimination or indeed does anything other than obey principles laid down in the [Children] Act.'

---

[1] *Supporting Disabled Parents: A Family or a Fragmented Approach* (CSCI, 2009), at p 37.

(3) It is suggested, however, that this case highlights the difficulties faced by those parents with even mild learning disability in rebutting the argument that they will not be able to deal with the particular challenges posed by the increasingly independent child as he grows up. Rather than accepting that such a parent will require long-term targeted support in order to manage their child to a good enough standard, the tendency is to prioritise the child's permanency needs. Put another way, the case perhaps reflects the resource-driven tendency of local authorities implementing the Children Act 1989 framework to focus on a solution avoiding the provision of long-term services and support under s 17 of the Act.[2] Moreover, whilst it was considered to be of particular importance to the outcome in this case that the child's early years had been very damaging and that he was considered to be a 'very vulnerable child' badly in need of certainty, permanency and security, it is suggested that such a description can be made of children in the majority of care cases.

## 6.3

### Re D (A Child) (Care Order: Evidence) [2010] EWCA Civ 1000

*Care proceedings – children removed from home for the third time after a long history of local authority involvement – learning disabled mother but no history of drug or alcohol abuse, no history of significant violence, no sign of children being disturbed or out of control, no issues with sexual boundaries, no issue with ability to protect from third parties – local authority seeking permanent removal on the basis of the expert psychological evidence*

The mother had a full-scale IQ of 73, a significant discrepancy between her verbal IQ and her performance IQ, and 'quite substantial learning difficulties'. The father was 'submissive or dependent and rather naïve'. Together they had six children who at the time of the appeal were aged from 16 months to 9 years and had been the subject of care proceedings since 2005. Care orders were made in relation to the four oldest children in January 2007, although they were returned home later that year, and the parents made sufficient changes so that the local authority in 2008 proposed that the care orders were discharged. The children were, however, removed again on a temporary basis in 2009 following one of the children having told a teacher that the father had hit him with a belt, which was subsequently found not to have taken place. Following a red mark being found on the neck of one of the children, which he reported to have been caused by his mother, the children were removed for the last time in January 2010 and the local authority changed its plan to one of permanent removal from the home. Whilst the local authority's case rested mainly upon a

---

[2] See Olsen and Clarke *Parenting and Disability: Disabled Parents' Experiences of Raising Children* (The Policy Press, 2003), at p 20: 'a common concern shared by many disabled parents that, while it is extremely difficult to access services that support effective parenting (on grounds of budgetary constraints, the division of adult and child social work, and so on), it is very easy to become a target of social work with regard to the adequacy of parenting and the perceived risk of child neglect and significant harm.'

psychological assessment of the parents to the effect that they were unlikely to be able to parent the children adequately during their minority, the judge preferred the positive evidence of the independent social worker, the family support worker and the health visitor. The local authority's appeal was dismissed.

(1) The Court of Appeal held that the judge below was entitled to have preferred the empirical evidence provided by the independent social worker, the family support worker and the health visitor to the recommendations of the child and adult psychologist and of the Guardian, and had provided reasons for doing so. The empirical evidence was of significance because it showed, contrary to the experience of the local authority, that the parents appeared to have abilities to cope and were willing to co-operate and accept advice. Where there is evidence of different kinds it is the job of the judge to weigh the overall effect of it taken together.

(2) The judge had been entitled to conclude that if these children were to be removed from the home, then so too would large numbers of families with parents with learning disabilities and psychological profiles similar to the mother's. However, whilst there were some features of the local authority's actions which demanded robust criticism, namely the peremptory removal of the children on two occasions, the judge's criticisms of the psychologist and the guardian for a lack of professionalism were unjustified.

(3) The Court of Appeal clarified, for the avoidance of doubt, that the test under s 31(2) of the Children Act 1989 is an objective one. If it were otherwise, and 'the care which it is reasonable to expect a parent to give' were to be judged by the standards of the parent with the characteristics of the parent in question, 'the protection afforded to children would be very limited indeed, if not entirely illusory' (per Hughes LJ at [35]). As discussed in Chapter 4, however, whilst the threshold test applies an objective standard by which the reasonableness of the parental behaviour should be judged, it is suggested that an individualised parenting assessment will be required in order to determine whether the significant harm is attributable to the care being given by the parent, or whether it is attributable to that parent being provided with an inadequate level of support.

(4) Whilst Hughes LJ was very clear that the Disability Discrimination Act 1995 was not relevant to care proceedings and that the concept of discrimination should not be brought into the exercise of deciding whether the threshold conditions have been satisfied, there is – as discussed in earlier chapters – a body of evidence to the effect that children with at least one learning disabled parent are more likely to be removed from their home than others, that the numbers of children removed are disproportionate to their representation in the general population, and that discriminatory attitudes – even after the 2007 Good Practice Guidance – can still prevail.

**6.4**

## Re G and A (Care Order: Freeing Order: Parents with a Learning Disability) [2006] NI Fam 8

The parents of two children, who by the time of the final hearing were aged 2 and one, each had 'a severe mental handicap'. The oldest child was placed as an unborn baby on the Child Protection Register and was removed some 2–3 weeks after birth due to the parents' failure to co-operate with the local authority and to allow access to the child. In March 2004 there was a parenting assessment in a residential unit in Peterborough, this having been chosen by the local authority on the basis that it was thought better able to facilitate a couple with learning disabilities than anywhere in Northern Ireland, although it was terminated prematurely and the child was returned to foster carers. A second child born in September 2004 was also placed in foster care, and the plan for both children became adoption. The judge, Gillen J, set out a number of principles which were applicable to learning disability cases and which he had taken from the Nuffield Foundation Report by Booth and Booth;[3] the Review of Mental Health and Learning Disability (Northern Ireland) *Equal Lives: Review of Policy and Services for People with a Learning Disability in Northern Ireland* (September 2005); and general documentation from Mencap:

- It is important that a court approaches these cases with a recognition of the possible barriers to the provision of appropriate support to parents including negative or stereotypical attitudes about parents with learning difficulties on the part of staff in some trusts or services.
- Parents with learning difficulties can often be 'good enough' parents when provided with the ongoing emotional and practical support they need. The courts should: scrutinise the possibilities of support from the extended family; examine the approach of the local authority to ensure that there has been effective multi-agency coordination; ensure that parents with learning disabilities are not judged against harsher or stricter criteria than other parents; and give careful consideration to the assessment phase and to the application of the threshold test to ensure that there has been no discrimination against the parents, whether direct or indirect.
- It is important not to focus exclusively on the child's welfare without addressing the parents' needs arising from their disability which might impact adversely on their parenting capacity: the parents should therefore be advised of the benefits to them of using an advocate; and local authorities should give careful consideration to providing child protection training to staff working in services for adults with learning disabilities and training about adults with learning disabilities for those working in child protection.
- The court should also take steps to ensure that there are no barriers to justice within the process itself: allowing the parents extra time with their

---

[3] See Chapter 1, at **1.22–1.26**.

legal representatives; adjourning the proceedings at intervals to give the parents the opportunity to have matters explained; ensuring the language and vocabulary used is appropriate; ensuring that the supposed inability of the parents to change is not an artefact of professionals' ineffectiveness in engaging with the parents in appropriate terms.

- In summary, a shift must be made from the old assumption that adults with learning disabilities could not parent their children to a process of questioning why appropriate levels of support are not provided to them so that they can parent successfully and why their children should often be taken into care: the concept of 'parenting with support' must move from the margins to the mainstream.

(1) Applying these principles to the case before him, the judge found that the social workers had not applied stricter criteria to these parents than they would have done to parents without a learning disability; that there was a significant risk of neglect to the children because of the parents' lack of insight into the dangers that existed for them; that it would therefore be necessary to provide services on a 24-hour basis for these parents; and that support of such a level was not available in Northern Ireland or elsewhere. Moreover, even if such intensive support were available, the evidence was that in view of the fact that neither of the parents accepted that they had a learning disability, they would be likely to reject the need for support and intervention. Only adoption was able to safeguard and promote the welfare of the children throughout their childhood: it would not be possible to train the parents to meet every eventuality of risk; and the expert psychological evidence to the court was that adults with a learning disability tended to find the parenting task harder as the children mature. The possibility of extended family care was not available in this case.

(2) This remains the only reported case where a court has clearly considered the research findings as to best practice for working with parents with learning disabilities (or perhaps the only reported case where these findings have been drawn to its attention). Not only did the judge in this case set out the principles, but he also considered whether they had been applied by those working with the parents in the case before him. Notably, Gillen J suggests that the issue of discrimination is of direct relevance to the question of whether or not the threshold criteria have been met:

> 'Courts must be acutely aware of the distinction between direct and indirect discrimination and how this might be relevant to the treatment of parents with learning difficulties in care proceedings. In particular careful consideration must be given to the assessment phase by a Trust and in the application of the threshold test.'

It should be noted that whilst the Court of Appeal has firmly rejected the suggestion that discrimination is relevant to the threshold test,[4] there is room for the argument that the court should ensure – through a careful assessment – that the significant harm (or its likelihood) is attributable to

---

[4] See *Re D* [2010] EWCA Civ 1000 at **6.3**.

the care being given by the parent, and not to the fact that the learning disabled parent has not been provided with a reasonable package of parenting support.[5]

**6.5**

## *A Local Authority v A* **[2010] EWHC 1549**

The local authority sought a declaration that a 29-year-old married woman (Mrs A) lacked capacity to decide whether to use contraception, and that it would be in her interests for her to be required to receive it. Mrs A was learning disabled (her cognitive functioning fell in the 'extremely low' category) and was represented by the Official Solicitor (it being accepted by all parties that she did not have litigation capacity). Prior to meeting and marrying Mr A she had had two children removed from her at birth. Mr Justice Bodey held that (a) Mrs A lacked capacity in that she was unable to weigh up the pros and cons of contraception because of the coercive pressure under which Mr A had placed her; and (b) that it was not necessary to make an order as to whether it was in her interests to receive contraception because the local authority did not propose to coerce her to receive it without her consent. In fact, the local authority had accepted that if Mrs A did become pregnant, there would be a pre-birth assessment of their joint parenting abilities before any decisions were made as to whether to initiate care proceedings.

(1) In determining whether or not Mrs A was unable to make a decision on the question of contraception, the court was required to consider under s 3(1) of the Mental Capacity Act 2005 whether she was able to understand, retain, use and weigh the information relevant to the decision. Under s 3(4) of the Act, the 'information relevant to a decision includes information about the reasonably foreseeable consequences of deciding one way or another [whether to use contraception]'. Whilst the local authority argued that the 'reasonably foreseeable consequences' of not using contraception were wide enough to require an understanding of what would actually be involved in caring for and committing to a child, such an approach was impractical in view of the context in which such decisions were made on a day-to-day basis (ie during a short appointment at a health centre). Moreover, this approach would blur the distinction between 'capacity' and 'best interests' in that if it was considered that it would not be in a woman's best interests to have a baby, it would be easy to conclude that she was unable to consider the fact-specific demands of caring for an (as yet unborn) child. As such, there would be a risk of social engineering, which is as impermissible in this context as it is in the context of care proceedings (see *Re L* at **6.1**).
(2) The 'reasonably foreseeable consequences' were therefore limited to requiring an ability to understand and weigh up the immediate medical issues surrounding treatment, such as: the reason for contraception; the

---

[5] See discussion in Chapter 4, at **4.11–4.14**.

types available and how each is used; the advantages and disadvantages of each type; the side-effects; the generally accepted effectiveness. Whilst Bodey J found that Mrs A could sufficiently understand the medical aspects of the issue, he nonetheless found that she was unable to use or weigh that information because of the coercion 'imposed' by Mr A (which was not deliberate but rather a product of their respective personalities and learning disabilities).

(3) This case is included within this section because, as the judgment itself acknowledges, it illustrates the potential discrimination that can prevail in considering whether or not a severely learning disabled parent should be allowed to have children in the first place. The law is clear, however, that an operation to sterilise has to be demonstrated to be in the best interests of the person unable to consent and that whether or not that person will be able to care adequately for a child is not part of the court's consideration at this stage. On the other hand, several of the cases make the (probably realistic) assumption that any such child would be likely to be removed from the mother at birth and that that process would be profoundly upsetting for her. See generally:

- *Re A (Mental Patient: Sterilisation)*,[6] where an application for sterilisation of a man aged 28 with significant to severe learning disabilities was refused on the basis that neither the fact of the birth of any child nor any disapproval of his conduct in abdicating responsibility for any child was likely to impinge on him to any significant degree and that his mother would continue her close supervision of him regardless of whether or not the operation were to take place;
- *Re F (sterilisation: mental patient)*,[7] setting out guidelines for applications for a declaration that a proposed operation can be lawfully carried out despite the patient's inability to consent:
- *Re D (A Minor) (Wardship: Sterilisation)*,[8] where an application to approve the sterilisation of an 11-year-old girl was refused;
- *Re M (Wardship: Sterilisation)*,[9] where the carrying out of the operation on a 17-year-old ward with a mental age of 5 was approved;
- *Re P (A Minor) (Wardship: Sterilisation)*,[10] where Eastham J gave leave in respect of a 17-year-old ward;
- *Re B (A Minor) (Wardship: Sterilisation)*,[11] where the House of Lords approved the sterilisation of a 17-year-old girl with a mental age of 6 who would not be able to understand the causal connection between sexual intercourse and childbirth nor the nature of pregnancy;

---

[6] [2000] 1 FCR 193.
[7] [1989] 2 FLR 376.
[8] [1976] Fam 185.
[9] [1988] 2 FLR 497.
[10] [1989] 1 FLR 182.
[11] [1988] AC 199, [1987] 2 FLR 314.

- *Re W (An Adult: Mental Patient) (Sterilisation)*,[12] where Hollis J approved the operation to sterilise a 20-year-old mentally incapacitated woman with severe epilepsy where there was evidence accepted by the judge of the detrimental effect of pregnancy and the Official Solicitor did not actively oppose the application;
- *Re LC (Medical Treatment: Sterilisation)*,[13] where the local authority's application in respect of a 21-year-old woman with an intellectual age of 3½ living in a specialist residential home was dismissed on the basis of the current high level of supervision and minimal risk for the future; and
- *Re X (Adult Patient: Sterilisation)*,[14] where Holman J granted the declaration in respect of a severely mentally disabled 31-year-old woman on the basis that the process of pregnancy, birth and the subsequent removal of the child would be grossly upsetting and psychologically damaging for her.

## THE ROLE OF THE OFFICIAL SOLICITOR

6.6

### *RP v Nottingham City Council* [2008] EWCA Civ 462

*Test of capacity under the Mental Capacity Act 2005 – fluctuating nature of capacity/incapacity – role of the Official Solicitor towards his or her client – role of the advocate representing the parent via the Official Solicitor*

RP was the mother of KP, who was born in May 2006. KP, who had serious medical conditions and required skilled day-to-day management, remained in hospital after her birth until she was discharged into the care of foster parents in November that year. Care and placement orders were made subsequently in August 2007.

RP was represented in both the care and the placement proceedings by the Official Solicitor, following a recommendation made by the jointly instructed clinical psychologist. The Official Solicitor concluded that the threshold criteria were satisfied, that he could not oppose a care order being made in relation to KP; and that RP was not in a position to consent to or to refuse her consent to the placement order.

RP appealed in person against both orders on the basis that she had been denied a fair trial since the Official Solicitor had not pursued the case she wished him to pursue, namely for the child to return to her care, or to the care of her wider family members; and on the basis that she had not been aware that

---

[12] [1993] 1 FLR 381.
[13] [1997] 2 FLR 258.
[14] [1998] 2 FLR 1124.

she had been represented by the Official Solicitor (a suggestion found by the Court of Appeal on the basis of the waived correspondence files to be 'wholly untenable').

(1) This was the first opportunity for the Court of Appeal to consider the interrelationship between Article 6 of the European Convention on Human Rights and the involvement of the Official Solicitor as the litigation friend of a protected party.

(2) The Practice Direction supplementing Pt 7, r 1 of the Family Procedure (Adoption) Rules 2005[15] stated that the duty of the litigation friend is to 'fairly and competently conduct proceedings on behalf of the non-subject child or protected party' and to have 'no interest adverse to that of the non-subject child or protected party'. It further stated that all steps and decisions the litigation friend takes in the proceedings must be taken 'for the benefit of the non-subject child or protected party'.

(3) Whilst the duty of the Official Solicitor is to put forward any reasonably arguable arguments on behalf of the protected party, there will be cases such as this one where there is a conflict between the wish of the protected party to have the child returned to his or her care (or to the care of the wider family), and the Official Solicitor's view that no reasonably arguable case can be advanced to this end. In these circumstances, however, it will be more consistent with the duty owed to the protected party for the litigation friend not to oppose the application rather than to make explicit concessions on their behalf.

(4) The evidence in this case was overwhelmingly in favour of care and placement orders being made: the teaching methods involved in the local authority's assessment of RP's parenting capacity had been approved as appropriate to her cognitive ability by the jointly instructed consultant clinical psychologist and accordingly had given her the best chance possible to demonstrate her parenting skills. However, her difficulties were such that she would need 24-hour support and supervision from a competent adult in order to play even a limited role in the care of her child. Further, without that support she would pose a high level of risk to the child. It followed that the Official Solicitor – who could not properly have advanced an unarguable case on RP's behalf – had acted entirely appropriately.

(5) The Court of Appeal also clarified that where the local authority in its pre-proceedings work with the family considers that a parent might not have capacity to give instructions in any forthcoming proceedings, it should refer the parent to the local authority's adult learning disability team but was not required to go further than that. Prior to the issue of proceedings there is no difficulty with the parent receiving advice from the adult learning disability team on capacity and representation; however,

---

[15] SI 2005/2795. See now FPR 2010, PD 15A (Protected Parties), para 2.1: 'It is the duty of a litigation friend fairly and competently to conduct proceedings on behalf of a protected party. The litigation friend must have no interest in the proceedings adverse to that of the protected party and all steps and decisions the litigation friend takes in the proceedings must be taken for the benefit of the protected party.'

once proceedings have been instituted the duty to ensure that the parent is properly informed becomes a matter for the parent's legal advisers and the litigation friend if appointed.

**6.7**

## Re M (A Child) (Assessment: Official Solicitor) [2009] EWCA Civ 315

*Parent in care proceedings represented by the Official Solicitor – judge refusing the Official Solicitor's application for the papers to be released to Crown Lodge for purposes of viability assessment – judge also refusing Official Solicitor's application to instruct a further expert*

The mother – who was herself a minor – was represented by the Official Solicitor since she was considered to be incapable of instructing her solicitor directly. At the time that the applications were made by the Official Solicitor, the mother had already undertaken an unsuccessful residential assessment and had had a negative report from a consultant psychologist which stated that without at least 2 years of intensive psychotherapy, she had no chance of providing good enough parenting for her child. The mother applied for leave to appeal against the dismissal of her application to release the case papers to a residential assessment centre for the purposes of a viability assessment; and the dismissal of her application to instruct a child and adolescent psychiatrist.

(1) The Official Solicitor's application for a report from a child and adolescent psychiatrist was made in order to advise on the mother's learning disability and as to how it might impact upon her potential to provide adequate parenting. In allowing the appeal, Lord Justice Thorpe considered that:

> '... if the Official Solicitor, with the responsibility that he holds in the litigation, requires an assessment, a judge should be slow to refuse it. That refusal is all the more extreme if its immediately foreseeable consequence is to deprive the incapacitated litigant of any prospect of averting the care and placement orders sought by the local authority.'

(2) The point was re-iterated by Lord Justice Wall, who allowed the appeal because (a) the Official Solicitor has a duty to explore avenues which are properly open to him in order to ascertain whether or not the mother could parent the child and in order to assist on the issues of contact if appropriate; and (b) the court must also have as much information as can properly be obtained before making a final decision.

(3) The application to release the papers to Crown Lodge for a viability assessment was not an application under s 38(6) of the Children Act 1989 but was simply an attempt to prepare the way for a s 38(6) application. The judge was therefore wrong to consider whether it was fair to the

mother to raise her hopes by releasing the papers in this way, rather than considering whether it was fair to deprive her of a positive case to present at the final hearing.

(4) In refusing the applications for a further assessment and for a viability assessment, the judge at first instance had prevented the mother from accessing a fair forensic process and the approach he had taken smacked of pre-judgment. Of particular importance, however, was the fact that the mother was herself a minor and did not have capacity to conduct the proceedings in her own right.

**6.8**

## *Re B (Children)* [2010] EWCA Civ 363

*Parents in care proceedings represented by the Official Solicitor – Official Solicitor seeking report from a child and family psychiatrist – court should be slow to reject an application from the Official Solicitor for permission to instruct an expert save in exceptional circumstances*

The parents of five children were represented in the care proceedings by the Official Solicitor, following an assessment of the capacity of each of them by a consultant psychologist. A further assessment of both parents by a consultant psychiatrist in learning disabilities recommended that consideration should be given to rehabilitating the family. Sadly, a comprehensive community parenting assessment carried out by Symbol Family Support Services led to the recommendation that all five children should be placed permanently away from their parents, and proposed the instruction of a child and family psychiatrist to report on the children's individual therapeutic needs.

The Official Solicitor's application to instruct such an expert in order to assist with issues such as the combinations of placement and ongoing sibling and parental contact was refused, the judge at first instance considering that the instruction of such an expert would duplicate work which had already been undertaken by the local authority's own therapy assessment team and by Symbol. The Official Solicitor appealed. The appeal was allowed (the Court of Appeal going further than in *Re M* (see **6.7**) by setting out an 'exceptional circumstances' test for refusing the application by the Official Solicitor for a further assessment):

(1) The judge at first instance had misunderstood the point that Symbol considered that its own work was incomplete and that it was recommending the instruction of the consultant psychiatrist. Moreover, the instruction of the expert would not have involved any delay since by the time the report was received there would have been at least 24 clear days until the final hearing.

(2) Furthermore, the judge had failed to acknowledge the overriding principle that the court should be very slow to reject an application from the

Official Solicitor to instruct an expert whose opinion would be pertinent to the discharge of the Official Solicitor's responsibility to the incapacitated litigant.
(3) The Official Solicitor's duty to the incapacitated litigant is to garner all relevant evidence to enable him to make a balanced judgment of the merits of the case of the incapacitated litigant and the likely outcome. Since the Official Solicitor has the power to override the instructions of his client and to decline to pursue the case that his client wishes him to pursue (where, for example, that case is not realistically arguable – see *Re RP v Nottingham* at **6.6**), it is essential that he is able to ensure that he has left no stone unturned in forming this view. It follows that an application by the Official Solicitor to instruct an expert to report is one that, save in the most exceptional situations, should be approved by a judge.

# PROCEDURAL FAIRNESS AND APPROPRIATE ASSESSMENTS

**6.9**

## *Kutzner v Germany* [2003] 1 FCR 249, (2002) 35 EHRR 25

In September 1996 the Osnabruck District Youth Office sought an application to remove parental responsibility from the parents of two children then aged 5 and 3. The court at first instance made an interim order on the basis that the parents 'did not have the intellectual capacity required to bring up their children properly' and the children were placed in separate foster-homes with contact to their parents severely curtailed. Final orders were made in July 1997. The European Court of Human Rights found that there was no doubt that the parents' right to respect for their family life had been interfered with, and that although such interference was 'in accordance with the law' it was not 'necessary in a democratic society'. Further findings were as follows:

(1) The fact that a child could be placed in a more beneficial environment for his or her upbringing will not on its own justify a compulsory measure of removal from the care of the biological parents. Moreover, two of the psychological experts believed that the parents were able both emotionally and intellectually to bring up the children if they were given additional educational support in doing so and it was questionable whether the domestic, administrative and judicial authorities had given sufficient consideration to additional supportive methods rather than removing the children from their parents. The interference was therefore neither proportionate nor necessary for the protection of the children's welfare.
(2) This case is the only reported human rights case dealing with the removal of children from the care of learning disabled parents and is often cited to illustrate the value of supported parenting and the need to avoid making discriminatory assumptions (ie that the parents were not intellectually able to bring up their children).

**6.10**

## *M v Neath Port Talbot CBC* [2010] EWCA Civ 821

*Learning disabled mother with litigation capacity – judge at final hearing refusing her application for an adjournment for the purpose of a specialised parenting assessment – mother's successful application for permission to appeal opposed by neither the local authority nor the guardian*

The respondent mother to care proceedings concerning three children, aged 7, 5 and 3, had learning disabilities although she was not represented by the Official Solicitor. Her full-scale IQ fell on the fifth percentile and was a combination of an extremely low verbal IQ and a considerably higher performance IQ. At a case management conference the guardian had sought a psychological assessment and a specialised parenting assessment of the mother carried out by someone with special training in making assessments of learning disabled parents. Upon the judge ruling that she would give permission for one or other of the proposed assessments but not both, the guardian opted for the psychological assessment and the parenting assessment was carried out by the allocated social worker. At the final hearing, the mother applied for an adjournment of the proceedings for 2–3 months so that a specialised parenting assessment could be undertaken. The judge at first instance made the care and placement orders and the mother appealed:

(1) At the hearing for permission to appeal (with appeal to follow), neither the local authority nor the guardian opposed the proposed appeal, their volte face arising out of (a) further reflection of the evidence given at the final hearing by the psychologist, who had highlighted the prejudice to the mother's position caused by the absence of a specialist learning disabled assessment in what was a 'classic case of neglect'; and (b) a change of counsel.

(2) Whilst allowing the appeal, and referring to the principle that a care plan for adoption should only be undertaken when all avenues towards rehabilitation have been reasonably explored, the Lords Justices nonetheless held that it was still an open question as to what their decision would have been had the local authority and the guardian opposed the appeal.

(3) The Court of Appeal also held that the judge below had in any event fallen into appealable error in rejecting the evidence of two consultant paediatricians on the erroneous basis that neither of them had observed that the anal scar extended to the perianal skin (the judge preferring the opinion of a third consultant paediatrician whose view was that the extension of the scar was diagnostic of sexual abuse).

(4) The case provides an illustration of the benefits of an individualised parenting assessment even where: the learning disabled parent is not represented by the Official Solicitor; the work to be carried out and the

ensuing delay could take between 6 and 12 months; and in the absence of any evidence that the specialist will cast a different light on the mother's learning capacity.

## LITIGATION CAPACITY

6.11

### Re W (Children) (Care Proceedings: Litigation Capacity) [2008] EWHC 1188 (Fam)

*Criminal and care proceedings arising out of injuries to child – stepfather pleading guilty in criminal proceedings but assessed within the care proceedings 2 months later as not having litigation capacity – whether stepfather now has capacity – whether criminal proceedings should be reopened*

The child RH was born in September 2004 and in March 2006 was found have a spiral fracture to his left tibia plus a large number of bruises all over his body. Care proceedings did not begin until November 2006 – after the criminal proceedings had started – and in January 2007 the stepfather pleaded guilty to an offence of causing grievous bodily harm to the child under s 20 of the Offences Against the Person Act 1861.

In March 2007 the stepfather was assessed within the care proceedings as lacking capacity to take part in the litigation and the Official Solicitor agreed to act on his behalf. However, in May 2008, just 2 weeks before the final hearing, he was assessed as now having capacity, following a further assessment by the same psychiatrist.

Two principal issues arose out of those circumstances: first, whether or not the stepfather had had capacity when he pleaded guilty to the criminal charge (it being argued by the stepfather that the court was not estopped from opening up the factual issue of causation since he had lacked litigation capacity at the time he had entered his plea); and secondly, whether or not the stepfather had capacity to litigate now, in the light of the updated assessment.

(1) The case highlights the fluctuating nature of the issue of capacity, particularly where, as in the stepfather's case, his limitations arose not so much from his cognitive functioning (he fell between normal and borderline impaired), but from his variable emotional functioning and degree of suggestibility.
(2) The court's decision on the stepfather's capacity at the time of the guilty plea was left open on the grounds that there were other concerns as to the circumstances in which the plea was made which led to the conclusion that there should be a reopened hearing on the causation of the fracture.
(3) As to the stepfather's current capacity to litigate, the court considered it against the background of the Mental Capacity Act 2005 and took into

consideration the fact that for all of the experts it was a finely balanced issue, varying depending upon his emotional state and the degree of support to which he had access. Whilst expressing concern that the stepfather's capacity depended on an effective support package being put in place, the court concluded that it was a borderline case and that the evidential base for finding that he lacked capacity was only just not there. He further cautioned that the matter of the stepfather's capacity needed to be kept under review.

# Appendix 1

# NATIONAL HEALTH SERVICE AND COMMUNITY CARE ACT 1990, SS 46, 47

A.1

### PART III
### COMMUNITY CARE: ENGLAND AND WALES

\*\*\*\*

*General provisions concerning community care services*

**46 Local authority plans for community care services**

(1) Each local authority –

- (a) shall, within such period after the day appointed for the coming into force of this section as the Secretary of State may direct, prepare and publish a plan for the provision of community care services in their area;
- (b) shall keep the plan prepared by them under paragraph (a) above and any further plans prepared by them under this section under review; and
- (c) shall, at such intervals as the Secretary of State may direct, prepare and publish modifications to the current plan, or if the case requires, a new plan.

(2) In carrying out any of their functions under paragraphs (a) to (c) of subsection (1) above, a local authority shall consult –

- (a) any Health Authority and any Local Health Board the whole or any part of whose area lies within the area of the local authority;
- (b) *(repealed)*
- (c) in so far as any proposed plan, review or modifications of a plan may affect or be affected by the provision or availability of housing and the local authority is not itself a local housing authority, within the meaning of the Housing Act 1985, every such local housing authority whose area is within the area of the local authority;
- (d) such voluntary organisations as appear to the authority to represent the interests of persons who use or are likely to use any community care services within the area of the authority or the interests of private carers who, within that area, provide care to persons for whom, in the exercise of their social services functions, the local authority have a power or a duty to provide a service;

(e) such voluntary housing agencies and other bodies as appear to the local authority to provide housing or community care services in their area; and
(f) such other persons as the Secretary of State may direct.

(3) In this section –

'local authority' means the council of a county, a county borough, a metropolitan district or a London borough or the Common Council of the City of London;
'community care services' means services which a local authority may provide or arrange to be provided under any of the following provisions –
 (a) Part III of the National Assistance Act 1948;
 (b) section 45 of the Health Services and Public Health Act 1968;
 (c) section 254 of, and Schedule 20 to, the National Health Service Act 2006, and section 192 of, and Schedule 15 to, the National Health Service (Wales) Act 2006; and
 (d) section 117 of the Mental Health Act 1983; and

'private carer' means a person who is not employed to provide the care in question by any body in the exercise of its functions under any enactment.

**Amendments** – Health Authorities Act 1995; Local Government (Wales) Act 1994; National Health Service (Consequential Provisions) Act 2006.

## 47 Assessment of needs for community care services

(1) Subject to subsections (5) and (6) below, where it appears to a local authority that any person for whom they may provide or arrange for the provision of community care services may be in need of any such services, the authority –
 (a) shall carry out an assessment of his needs for those services; and
 (b) having regard to the results of that assessment, shall then decide whether his needs call for the provision by them of any such services.

(2) If at any time during the assessment of the needs of any person under subsection (1)(a) above it appears to a local authority that he is a disabled person, the authority –
 (a) shall proceed to make such a decision as to the services he requires as is mentioned in section 4 of the Disabled Persons (Services, Consultation and Representation) Act 1986 without his requesting them to do so under that section; and
 (b) shall inform him that they will be doing so and of his rights under that Act.

(3) If at any time during the assessment of the needs of any person under subsection (1)(a) above, it appears to a local authority –
 (a) that there may be a need for the provision to that person by such Primary Care Trust or Health Authority as may be determined in

accordance with regulations of any services under the National Health Service Act 2006 or the National Health Service (Wales) Act 2006, or

(b) that there may be a need for the provision to him of any services which fall within the functions of a local housing authority (within the meaning of the Housing Act 1985) which is not the local authority carrying out the assessment,

the local authority shall notify that Primary Care Trust, Health Authority or local housing authority and invite them to assist, to such extent as is reasonable in the circumstances, in the making of the assessment; and, in making their decision as to the provision of the services needed for the person in question, the local authority shall take into account any services which are likely to be made available for him by that Primary Care Trust, Health Authority or local housing authority.

(4) The Secretary of State may give directions as to the manner in which an assessment under this section is to be carried out or the form it is to take but, subject to any such directions and to subsection (7) below, it shall be carried out in such manner and take such form as the local authority consider appropriate.

(5) Nothing in this section shall prevent a local authority from temporarily providing or arranging for the provision of community care services for any person without carrying out a prior assessment of his needs in accordance with the preceding provisions of this section if, in the opinion of the authority, the condition of that person is such that he requires those services as a matter of urgency.

(6) If, by virtue of subsection (5) above, community care services have been provided temporarily for any person as a matter of urgency, then, as soon as practicable thereafter, an assessment of his needs shall be made in accordance with the preceding provisions of this section.

(7) This section is without prejudice to section 3 of the Disabled Persons (Services, Consultation and Representation) Act 1986.

(8) In this section –

'disabled person' has the same meaning as in that Act; and
'local authority' and 'community care services' have the same meanings as in section 46 above.

**Amendments** – National Health Service Reform and Health Care Professions Act 2002; Health Authorities Act 1995; National Health Service (Consequential Provisions) Act 2006.

\*\*\*\*

# Appendix 2

# MENTAL CAPACITY ACT 2005, SS 1–3

**A.2**

### PART 1
### PERSONS WHO LACK CAPACITY

*The principles*

**1 The principles**

(1) The following principles apply for the purposes of this Act.

(2) A person must be assumed to have capacity unless it is established that he lacks capacity.

(3) A person is not to be treated as unable to make a decision unless all practicable steps to help him to do so have been taken without success.

(4) A person is not to be treated as unable to make a decision merely because he makes an unwise decision.

(5) An act done, or decision made, under this Act for or on behalf of a person who lacks capacity must be done, or made, in his best interests.

(6) Before the act is done, or the decision is made, regard must be had to whether the purpose for which it is needed can be as effectively achieved in a way that is less restrictive of the person's rights and freedom of action.

*Preliminary*

**2 People who lack capacity**

(1) For the purposes of this Act, a person lacks capacity in relation to a matter if at the material time he is unable to make a decision for himself in relation to the matter because of an impairment of, or a disturbance in the functioning of, the mind or brain.

(2) It does not matter whether the impairment or disturbance is permanent or temporary.

(3) A lack of capacity cannot be established merely by reference to –

　(a)　a person's age or appearance, or
　(b)　a condition of his, or an aspect of his behaviour, which might lead others to make unjustified assumptions about his capacity.

(4) In proceedings under this Act or any other enactment, any question whether a person lacks capacity within the meaning of this Act must be decided on the balance of probabilities.

(5) No power which a person ('D') may exercise under this Act –

    (a)    in relation to a person who lacks capacity, or
    (b)    where D reasonably thinks that a person lacks capacity,

is exercisable in relation to a person under 16.

(6) Subsection (5) is subject to section 18(3).

## 3 Inability to make decisions

For the purposes of section 2, a person is (1) unable to make a decision for himself if he is unable –

    (a)    to understand the information relevant to the decision,
    (b)    to retain that information,
    (c)    to use or weigh that information as part of the process of making the decision, or
    (d)    to communicate his decision (whether by talking, using sign language or any other means).

(2) A person is not to be regarded as unable to understand the information relevant to a decision if he is able to understand an explanation of it given to him in a way that is appropriate to his circumstances (using simple language, visual aids or any other means).

(3) The fact that a person is able to retain the information relevant to a decision for a short period only does not prevent him from being regarded as able to make the decision.

(4) The information relevant to a decision includes information about the reasonably foreseeable consequences of –

    (a)    deciding one way or another, or
    (b)    failing to make the decision.

\*\*\*\*

# Appendix 3

# MENTAL CAPACITY ACT 2005 CODE OF PRACTICE

**A.3**

## 1 WHAT IS THE MENTAL CAPACITY ACT 2005?

1.1 The Mental Capacity Act 2005 (the Act) provides the legal framework for acting and making decisions on behalf of individuals who lack the mental capacity to make particular decisions for themselves. Everyone working with and/or caring for an adult who may lack capacity to make specific decisions must comply with this Act when making decisions or acting for that person, when the person lacks the capacity to make a particular decision for themselves. The same rules apply whether the decisions are life-changing events or everyday matters.

1.2 The Act's starting point is to confirm in legislation that it should be assumed that an adult (aged 16 or over) has full legal capacity to make decisions for themselves (the right to autonomy) unless it can be shown that they lack capacity to make a decision for themselves at the time the decision needs to be made. This is known as the presumption of capacity. The Act also states that people must be given all appropriate help and support to enable them to make their own decisions or to maximise their participation in any decision-making process.

1.3 The underlying philosophy of the Act is to ensure that any decision made, or action taken, on behalf of someone who lacks the capacity to make the decision or act for themselves is made in their best interests.

1.4 The Act is intended to assist and support people who may lack capacity and to discourage anyone who is involved in caring for someone who lacks capacity from being overly restrictive or controlling. But the Act also aims to balance an individual's right to make decisions for themselves with their right to be protected from harm if they lack capacity to make decisions to protect themselves.

1.5 The Act sets out a legal framework of how to act and make decisions on behalf of people who lack capacity to make specific decisions for themselves. It sets out some core principles and methods for making decisions and carrying out actions in relation to personal welfare, healthcare and financial matters affecting people who may lack capacity to make specific decisions about these issues for themselves.

1.6 Many of the provisions in the Act are based upon existing common law principles (i.e. principles that have been established through decisions

made by courts in individual cases). The Act clarifies and improves upon these principles and builds on current good practice which is based on the principles.
1.7 The Act introduces several new roles, bodies and powers, all of which will support the Act's provisions. These include:
- Attorneys appointed under Lasting Powers of Attorney (see chapter 7)
- The new Court of Protection, and court-appointed deputies (see chapter 8)
- Independent Mental Capacity Advocates (see chapter 10).

The roles, bodies and powers are all explained in more depth in the specific chapters of the Code highlighted above.

## What decisions are covered by the Act, and what decisions are excluded?

1.8 The Act covers a wide range of decisions made, or actions taken, on behalf of people who may lack capacity to make specific decisions for themselves. These can be decisions about day-to-day matters – like what to wear, or what to buy when doing the weekly shopping – or decisions about major life-changing events, such as whether the person should move into a care home or undergo a major surgical operation.
1.9 There are certain decisions which can never be made on behalf of a person who lacks capacity to make those specific decisions. This is because they are either so personal to the individual concerned, or governed by other legislation.
1.10 Sections 27–29 and 62 of the Act set out the specific decisions which can never be made or actions which can never be carried out under the Act, whether by family members, carers, professionals, attorneys or the Court of Protection. These are summarised below.

### *Decisions concerning family relationships (section 27)*

Nothing in the Act permits a decision to be made on someone else's behalf on any of the following matters:

- consenting to marriage or a civil partnership
- consenting to have sexual relations
- consenting to a decree of divorce on the basis of two years' separation
- consenting to the dissolution of a civil partnership
- consenting to a child being placed for adoption or the making of an adoption order
- discharging parental responsibility for a child in matters not relating to the child's property, or
- giving consent under the Human Fertilisation and Embryology Act 1990.

## Mental Health Act matters (section 28)

Where a person who lacks capacity to consent is currently detained and being treated under Part 4 of the Mental Health Act 1983, nothing in the Act authorises anyone to:

- give the person treatment for mental disorder, or
- consent to the person being given treatment for mental disorder.

Further guidance is given in chapter 13 of the Code.

## Voting rights (section 29)

Nothing in the Act permits a decision on voting, at an election for any public office or at a referendum, to be made on behalf of a person who lacks capacity to vote.

## Unlawful killing or assisting suicide (section 62)

For the avoidance of doubt, nothing in the Act is to be taken to affect the law relating to murder, manslaughter or assisting suicide.

1.11 Although the Act does not allow anyone to make a decision about these matters on behalf of someone who lacks capacity to make such a decision for themselves (for example, consenting to have sexual relations), this does not prevent action being taken to protect a vulnerable person from abuse or exploitation.

### How does the Act relate to other legislation?

1.12 The Mental Capacity Act 2005 will apply in conjunction with other legislation affecting people who may lack capacity in relation to specific matters. This means that healthcare and social care staff acting under the Act should also be aware of their obligations under other legislation, including (but not limited to) the:
- Care Standards Act 2000
- Data Protection Act 1998
- Disability Discrimination Act 1995
- Human Rights Act 1998
- Mental Health Act 1983
- National Health Service and Community Care Act 1990
- Human Tissue Act 2004.

### What does the Act say about the Code of Practice?

1.13 Section 42 of the Act sets out the purpose of the Code of Practice, which is to provide guidance for specific people in specific circumstances.

Section 43 explains the procedures that had to be followed in preparing the Code and consulting on its contents, and for its consideration by Parliament.

Section 42, subsections (4) and (5), set out the categories of people who are placed under a legal duty to 'have regard to' the Code and gives further information about the status of the Code. More details can be found in the Introduction, which explains the legal status of the Code.

## 2 WHAT ARE THE STATUTORY PRINCIPLES AND HOW SHOULD THEY BE APPLIED?

Section 1 of the Act sets out the five 'statutory principles' – the values that underpin the legal requirements in the Act. The Act is intended to be enabling and supportive of people who lack capacity, not restricting or controlling of their lives. It aims to protect people who lack capacity to make particular decisions, but also to maximise their ability to make decisions, or to participate in decision-making, as far as they are able to do so.

The five statutory principles are:

1. A person must be assumed to have capacity unless it is established that they lack capacity.
2. A person is not to be treated as unable to make a decision unless all practicable steps to help him to do so have been taken without success.
3. A person is not to be treated as unable to make a decision merely because he makes an unwise decision.
4. An act done, or decision made, under this Act for or on behalf of a person who lacks capacity must be done, or made, in his best interests.
5. Before the act is done, or the decision is made, regard must be had to whether the purpose for which it is needed can be as effectively achieved in a way that is less restrictive of the person's rights and freedom of action.

This chapter provides guidance on how people should interpret and apply the statutory principles when using the Act. Following the principles and applying them to the Act's framework for decision-making will help to ensure not only that appropriate action is taken in individual cases, but also to point the way to solutions in difficult or uncertain situations.

> In this chapter, as throughout the Code, a person's capacity (or lack of capacity) refers specifically to their capacity to make a particular decision at the time it needs to be made.

## Quick summary

- Every adult has the right to make their own decisions if they have the capacity to do so. Family carers and healthcare or social care staff must assume that a person has the capacity to make decisions, unless it can be established that the person does not have capacity.
- People should receive support to help them make their own decisions. Before concluding that individuals lack capacity to make a particular decision, it is important to take all possible steps to try to help them reach a decision themselves.
- People have the right to make decisions that others might think are unwise. A person who makes a decision that others think is unwise should not automatically be labelled as lacking the capacity to make a decision.
- Any act done for, or any decision made on behalf of, someone who lacks capacity must be in their best interests.
- Any act done for, or any decision made on behalf of, someone who lacks capacity should be an option that is less restrictive of their basic rights and freedoms – as long as it is still in their best interests.

## What is the role of the statutory principles?

2.1 The statutory principles aim to:
- protect people who lack capacity and
- help them take part, as much as possible, in decisions that affect them.

They aim to assist and support people who may lack capacity to make particular decisions, not to restrict or control their lives.

2.2 The statutory principles apply to any act done or decision made under the Act. When followed and applied to the Act's decision-making framework, they will help people take appropriate action in individual cases. They will also help people find solutions in difficult or uncertain situations.

## How should the statutory principles be applied?

**Principle 1:** *'A person must be assumed to have capacity unless it is established that he lacks capacity.' (section 1(2))*

2.3 This principle states that every adult has the right to make their own decisions – unless there is proof that they lack the capacity to make a particular decision when it needs to be made. This has been a fundamental principle of the common law for many years and it is now set out in the Act.

2.4 It is important to balance people's right to make a decision with their right to safety and protection when they can't make decisions to protect themselves. But the starting assumption must always be that an individual has the capacity, until there is proof that they do not. Chapter 4 explains the Act's definition of 'lack of capacity' and the processes involved in assessing capacity.

> **Scenario:** *Assessing a person's capacity to make decisions*
>
> When planning her retirement, Mrs Arnold made and registered a Lasting Power of Attorney (LPA) – a legal process that would allow her son to manage her property and financial affairs if she ever lacked capacity to manage them herself. She has now been diagnosed with dementia, and her son is worried that she is becoming confused about money.
>
> Her son must assume that his mother has capacity to manage her affairs. Then he must consider each of Mrs Arnold's financial decisions as she makes them, giving her any help and support she needs to make these decisions herself.
>
> Mrs Arnold's son goes shopping with her, and he sees she is quite capable of finding goods and making sure she gets the correct change. But when she needs to make decisions about her investments, Mrs Arnold gets confused – even though she has made such decisions in the past. She still doesn't understand after her son explains the different options.
>
> Her son concludes that she has capacity to deal with everyday financial matters but not more difficult affairs at this time. Therefore, he is able to use the LPA for the difficult financial decisions his mother can't make. But Mrs Arnold can continue to deal with her other affairs for as long as she has capacity to do so.

2.5 Some people may need help to be able to make a decision or to communicate their decision. However, this does not necessarily mean that they cannot make that decision – unless there is proof that they do lack capacity to do so. Anyone who believes that a person lacks capacity should be able to prove their case. Chapter 4 explains the standard of proof required.

**Principle 2:** *'A person is not to be treated as unable to make a decision unless all practicable steps to help him to do so have been taken without success.' (section 1(3))*

2.6 It is important to do everything practical (the Act uses the term 'practicable') to help a person make a decision for themselves before concluding that they lack capacity to do so. People with an illness or disability affecting their ability to make a decision should receive support to help them make as many decisions as they can. This principle aims to stop people being automatically labelled as lacking capacity to make particular decisions. Because it encourages individuals to play as big a role as possible in decision-making, it also helps prevent unnecessary interventions in their lives.

2.7 The kind of support people might need to help them make a decision varies. It depends on personal circumstances, the kind of decision that has to be made and the time available to make the decision. It might include:
- using a different form of communication (for example, non-verbal communication)
- providing information in a more accessible form (for example, photographs, drawings, or tapes)
- treating a medical condition which may be affecting the person's capacity or
- having a structured programme to improve a person's capacity to make particular decisions (for example, helping a person with learning disabilities to learn new skills).

Chapter 3 gives more information on ways to help people make decisions for themselves.

---

*Scenario: Taking steps to help people make decisions for themselves*

Mr Jackson is brought into hospital following a traffic accident. He is conscious but in shock. He cannot speak and is clearly in distress, making noises and gestures.

From his behaviour, hospital staff conclude that Mr Jackson currently lacks capacity to make decisions about treatment for his injuries, and they give him urgent treatment. They hope that after he has recovered from the shock they can use an advocate to help explain things to him.

However, one of the nurses thinks she recognises some of his gestures as sign language, and tries signing to him. Mr Jackson immediately becomes calmer, and the doctors realise that he can communicate in sign language. He can also answer some written questions about his injuries.

The hospital brings in a qualified sign-language interpreter and concludes that Mr Jackson has the capacity to make decisions about any further treatment.

---

2.8 Anyone supporting a person who may lack capacity should not use excessive persuasion or 'undue pressure'.[1] This might include behaving in a manner which is overbearing or dominating, or seeking to influence the

---

[1] Undue influence in relation to consent to medical treatment was considered in *Re T (Adult: Refusal of Treatment)* [1992] 4 All E R 649, 662 and in financial matters in *Royal Bank of Scotland v Etridge* [2001] UKHL 44.

person's decision, and could push a person into making a decision they might not otherwise have made. However, it is important to provide appropriate advice and information.

### Scenario: Giving appropriate advice and support

Sara, a young woman with severe depression, is getting treatment from mental health services. Her psychiatrist determines that she has capacity to make decisions about treatment, if she gets advice and support.

Her mother is trying to persuade Sara to agree to electro-convulsive therapy (ECT), which helped her mother when she had clinical depression in the past. However, a friend has told Sara that ECT is 'barbaric'.

The psychiatrist provides factual information about the different types of treatment available and explains their advantages and disadvantages. She also describes how different people experience different reactions or side effects. Sara is then able to consider what treatment is right for her, based on factual information rather than the personal opinions of her mother and friend.

2.9 In some situations treatment cannot be delayed while a person gets support to make a decision. This can happen in emergency situations or when an urgent decision is required (for example, immediate medical treatment). In these situations, the only practical and appropriate steps might be to keep a person informed of what is happening and why.

**Principle 3:** *'A person is not to be treated as unable to make a decision merely because he makes an unwise decision.' (section 1(4))*

2.10 Everybody has their own values, beliefs, preferences and attitudes. A person should not be assumed to lack the capacity to make a decision just because other people think their decision is unwise. This applies even if family members, friends or healthcare or social care staff are unhappy with a decision.

### Scenario: Allowing people to make decisions that others think are unwise

Mr Garvey is a 40-year-old man with a history of mental health problems. He sees a Community Psychiatric Nurse (CPN) regularly. Mr Garvey decides to spend £2,000 of his savings on a camper van to travel around Scotland for six months. His CPN is concerned that it will be difficult to give Mr Garvey continuous support and treatment while travelling, and that his mental health might deteriorate as a result. ➡

> However, having talked it through with his CPN, it is clear that Mr Garvey is fully aware of these concerns and has the capacity to make this particular decision. He has decided he would like to have a break and thinks this will be good for him.
>
> Just because, in the CPN's opinion, continuity of care might be a wiser option, it should not be assumed that Mr Garvey lacks the capacity to make this decision for himself.

2.11 There may be cause for concern if somebody:
- repeatedly makes unwise decisions that put them at significant risk of harm or exploitation or
- makes a particular unwise decision that is obviously irrational or out of character.

These things do not necessarily mean that somebody lacks capacity. But there might be need for further investigation, taking into account the person's past decisions and choices. For example, have they developed a medical condition or disorder that is affecting their capacity to make particular decisions? Are they easily influenced by undue pressure? Or do they need more information to help them understand the consequences of the decision they are making?

> ***Scenario: Decisions that cause concern***
>
> Cyril, an elderly man with early signs of dementia, spends nearly £300 on fresh fish from a door-to-door salesman. He has always been fond of fish and has previously bought small amounts in this way. Before his dementia, Cyril was always very careful with his money and would never have spent so much on fish in one go.
>
> This decision alone may not automatically mean Cyril lacks capacity to manage all aspects of his property and affairs. But his daughter makes further enquiries and discovers Cyril has overpaid his cleaner on several occasions – something he has never done in the past. He has also made payments from his savings that he cannot account for.
>
> His daughter decides it is time to use the registered Lasting Power of Attorney her father made in the past. This gives her the authority to manage Cyril's property and affairs whenever he lacks the capacity to manage them himself. She takes control of Cyril's chequebook to protect him from possible exploitation, but she can still ensure he has enough money to spend on his everyday needs.

**Principle 4:** *'An act done, or decision made, under this Act for or on behalf of a person who lacks capacity must be done, or made, in his best interests.' (section 1(5))*

2.12 The principle of acting or making a decision in the best interests of a person who lacks capacity to make the decision in question is a well-established principle in the common law.[2] This principle is now set out in the Act, so that a person's best interests must be the basis for all decisions made and actions carried out on their behalf in situations where they lack capacity to make those particular decisions for themselves. The only exceptions to this are around research (see chapter 11) and advance decisions to refuse treatment (see chapter 9) where other safeguards apply.

2.13 It is impossible to give a single description of what 'best interests' are, because they depend on individual circumstances. However, section 4 of the Act sets out a checklist of steps to follow in order to determine what is in the best interests of a person who lacks capacity to make the decision in question each time someone acts or makes a decision on that person's behalf. See chapter 5 for detailed guidance and examples.

**Principle 5:** *'Before the act is done, or the decision is made, regard must be had to whether the purpose for which it is needed can be as effectively achieved in a way that is less restrictive of the person's rights and freedom of action.' (section 1(6))*

2.14 Before somebody makes a decision or acts on behalf of a person who lacks capacity to make that decision or consent to the act, they must always question if they can do something else that would interfere less with the person's basic rights and freedoms. This is called finding the 'less restrictive alternative'. It includes considering whether there is a need to act or make a decision at all.

2.15 Where there is more than one option, it is important to explore ways that would be less restrictive or allow the most freedom for a person who lacks capacity to make the decision in question. However, the final decision must always allow the original purpose of the decision or act to be achieved.

2.16 Any decision or action must still be in the best interests of the person who lacks capacity. So sometimes it may be necessary to choose an option that is not the least restrictive alternative if that option is in the person's best interests. In practice, the process of choosing a less restrictive option and deciding what is in the person's best interests will be combined. But both principles must be applied each time a decision or action may be taken on behalf of a person who lacks capacity to make the relevant decision.

### Scenario: Finding a less restrictive option

Sunil, a young man with severe learning disabilities, also has a very severe and unpredictable form of epilepsy that is associated with drop attacks. This can result in serious injury. A neurologist has advised that, to limit ➡

---

[2] See for example *Re MB (Medical Treatment)* [1997] 2 FLR 426, CA; *Re A (Male Sterilisation)* [2000] 1 FLR 549; *Re S (Sterilisation: Patient's Best Interests)* [2000] 2 FLR 389; *Re F (Adult Patient: Sterilisation)* [2001] Fam 15.

> the harm that might come from these attacks, Sunil should either be under constant close observation, or wear a protective helmet.
>
> After assessment, it is decided that Sunil lacks capacity to decide on the most appropriate course of action for himself. But through his actions and behaviour, Sunil makes it clear he doesn't like to be too closely observed – even though he likes having company.
>
> The staff of the home where he lives consider various options, such as providing a special room for him with soft furnishings, finding ways to keep him under close observation or getting him to wear a helmet. In discussion with Sunil's parents, they agree that the option that is in his best interests, and is less restrictive, will be the helmet – as it will enable him to go out, and prevent further harm.

## 3 HOW SHOULD PEOPLE BE HELPED TO MAKE THEIR OWN DECISIONS?

Before deciding that someone lacks capacity to make a particular decision, it is important to take all practical and appropriate steps to enable them to make that decision themselves (statutory principle 2, see chapter 2). In addition, as section 3(2) of the Act underlines, these steps (such as helping individuals to communicate) must be taken in a way which reflects the person's individual circumstances and meets their particular needs. This chapter provides practical guidance on how to support people to make decisions for themselves, or play as big a role as possible in decision-making.

> In this chapter, as throughout the Code, a person's capacity (or lack of capacity) refers specifically to their capacity to make a particular decision at the time it needs to be made.

### Quick summary

To help someone make a decision for themselves, check the following points:

Providing relevant information

- Does the person have all the relevant information they need to make a particular decision?
- If they have a choice, have they been given information on all the alternatives?

Communicating in an appropriate way

- Could information be explained or presented in a way that is easier for the person to understand (for example, by using simple language or visual aids)?
- Have different methods of communication been explored if required, including non-verbal communication?
- Could anyone else help with communication (for example, a family member, support worker, interpreter, speech and language therapist or advocate)?

Making the person feel at ease

- Are there particular times of day when the person's understanding is better?
- Are there particular locations where they may feel more at ease?
- Could the decision be put off to see whether the person can make the decision at a later time when circumstances are right for them?

Supporting the person

- Can anyone else help or support the person to make choices or express a view?

## How can someone be helped to make a decision?

3.1  There are several ways in which people can be helped and supported to enable them to make a decision for themselves. These will vary depending on the decision to be made, the time-scale for making the decision and the individual circumstances of the person making it.

3.2  The Act applies to a wide range of people with different conditions that may affect their capacity to make particular decisions. So, the appropriate steps to take will depend on:
   - a person's individual circumstances (for example, somebody with learning difficulties may need a different approach to somebody with dementia)
   - the decision the person has to make and
   - the length of time they have to make it.

3.3  Significant, one-off decisions (such as moving house) will require different considerations from day-to-day decisions about a person's care and welfare. However, the same general processes should apply to each decision.

3.4  In most cases, only some of the steps described in this chapter will be relevant or appropriate, and the list included here is not exhaustive. It is up to the people (whether family carers, paid carers, healthcare staff or anyone else) caring for or supporting an individual to consider what is possible and appropriate in individual cases. In all cases it is extremely important to find the most effective way of communicating with the person concerned. Good communication is essential for explaining relevant information in an appropriate way and for ensuring that the steps being taken meet an individual's needs.

3.5 Providing appropriate help with decision-making should form part of care planning processes for people receiving health or social care services. Examples include:
- Person Centred Planning for people with learning disabilities
- the Care Programme Approach for people with mental disorders
- the Single Assessment Process for older people in England, and
- the Unified Assessment Process in Wales.

## What happens in emergency situations?

3.6 Clearly, in emergency medical situations (for example, where a person collapses with a heart attack or for some unknown reason and is brought unconscious into a hospital), urgent decisions will have to be made and immediate action taken in the person's best interests. In these situations, it may not be practical or appropriate to delay the treatment while trying to help the person make their own decisions, or to consult with any known attorneys or deputies. However, even in emergency situations, healthcare staff should try to communicate with the person and keep them informed of what is happening.

## What information should be provided to people and how should it be provided?

3.7 Providing relevant information is essential in all decision-making. For example, to make a choice about what they want for breakfast, people need to know what food is available. If the decision concerns medical treatment, the doctor must explain the purpose and effect of the course of treatment and the likely consequences of accepting or refusing treatment.

3.8 All practical and appropriate steps must be taken to help people to make a decision for themselves. Information must be tailored to an individual's needs and abilities. It must also be in the easiest and most appropriate form of communication for the person concerned.

### *What information is relevant?*

3.9 The Act cannot state exactly what information will be relevant in each case. Anyone helping someone to make a decision for themselves should therefore follow these steps.
- Take time to explain anything that might help the person make a decision. It is important that they have access to all the information they need to make an informed decision.
- Try not to give more detail than the person needs – this might confuse them. In some cases, a simple, broad explanation will be enough. But it must not miss out important information.

- What are the risks and benefits? Describe any foreseeable consequences of making the decision, and of not making any decision at all.
- Explain the effects the decision might have on the person and those close to them – including the people involved in their care.
- If they have a choice, give them the same information in a balanced way for all the options.
- For some types of decisions, it may be important to give access to advice from elsewhere. This may be independent or specialist advice (for example, from a medical practitioner or a financial or legal adviser). But it might simply be advice from trusted friends or relatives.

## *Communication – general guidance*

3.10 To help someone make a decision for themselves, all possible and appropriate means of communication should be tried.
- Ask people who know the person well about the best form of communication (try speaking to family members, carers, day centre staff or support workers). They may also know somebody the person can communicate with easily, or the time when it is best to communicate with them.
- Use simple language. Where appropriate, use pictures, objects or illustrations to demonstrate ideas.
- Speak at the right volume and speed, with appropriate words and sentence structure. It may be helpful to pause to check understanding or show that a choice is available.
- Break down difficult information into smaller points that are easy to understand. Allow the person time to consider and understand each point before continuing.
- It may be necessary to repeat information or go back over a point several times.
- Is help available from people the person trusts (relatives, friends, GP, social worker, religious or community leaders)? If so, make sure the person's right to confidentiality is respected.
- Be aware of cultural, ethnic or religious factors that shape a person's way of thinking, behaviour or communication. For example, in some cultures it is important to involve the community in decision-making. Some religious beliefs (for example, those of Jehovah's Witnesses or Christian Scientists) may influence the person's approach to medical treatment and information about treatment decisions.
- If necessary, consider using a professional language interpreter. Even if a person communicated in English or Welsh in the past, they may have lost some verbal skills (for example, because of dementia). They may now prefer to communicate in their first language. It is often more appropriate to use a professional interpreter rather than to use family members.

- If using pictures to help communication, make sure they are relevant and the person can understand them easily. For example, a red bus may represent a form of transport to one person but a day trip to another.
- Would an advocate (someone who can support and represent the person) improve communication in the current situation? (See chapters 10 and 15 for more information about advocates.)

---

### Scenario: *Providing relevant information*

Mrs Thomas has Alzheimer's disease and lives in a care home. She enjoys taking part in the activities provided at the home. Today there is a choice between going to a flower show, attending her usual pottery class or watching a DVD. Although she has the capacity to choose, having to decide is making her anxious.

The care assistant carefully explains the different options. She tells Mrs Thomas about the DVD she could watch, but Mrs Thomas doesn't like the sound of it. The care assistant shows her a leaflet about the flower show. She explains the plans for the day, where the show is being held and how long it will take to get there in the mini-van. She has to repeat this information several times, as Mrs Thomas keeps asking whether they will be back in time for supper. She also tells Mrs Thomas that one of her friends is going on the trip.

At first, Mrs Thomas is reluctant to disturb her usual routine. But the care assistant reassures her she will not lose her place at pottery if she misses a class. With this information, Mrs Thomas can therefore choose whether or not to go on the day trip.

---

## Helping people with specific communication or cognitive problems

3.11 Where people have specific communication or cognitive problems, the following steps can help:
- Find out how the person is used to communicating. Do they use picture boards or Makaton (signs and symbols for people with communication or learning difficulties)? Or do they have a way of communicating that is only known to those close to them?
- If the person has hearing difficulties, use their preferred method of communication (for example, visual aids, written messages or sign language). Where possible, use a qualified interpreter.
- Are mechanical devices such as voice synthesisers, keyboards or other computer equipment available to help?
- If the person does not use verbal communication skills, allow more time to learn how to communicate effectively.

- For people who use non-verbal methods of communication, their behaviour (in particular, changes in behaviour) can provide indications of their feelings.
- Some people may prefer to use non-verbal means of communication and can communicate most effectively in written form using computers or other communication technologies. This is particularly true for those with autistic spectrum disorders.
- For people with specific communication difficulties, consider other types of professional help (for example, a speech and language therapist or an expert in clinical neuropsychology).

> ### Scenario: Helping people with specific communication difficulties
>
> David is a deafblind man with learning disabilities who has no formal communication. He lives in a specialist home. He begins to bang his head against the wall and repeats this behaviour throughout the day. He has not done this before.
>
> The staff in the home are worried and discuss ways to reduce the risk of injury. They come up with a range of possible interventions, aimed at engaging him with activities and keeping him away from objects that could injure him. They assess these as less restrictive ways to ensure he is safe. But David lacks the capacity to make a decision about which would be the best option.
>
> The staff call in a specialist in challenging behaviour, who says that David's behaviour is communicative. After investigating this further, staff discover he is in pain because of tooth decay. They consult a dentist about how to resolve this, and the dentist decides it is in David's best interests to get treatment for the tooth decay. After treatment, David's head-banging stops.

## What steps should be taken to put a person at ease?

3.12 To help put someone at ease and so improve their ability to make a decision, careful consideration should be given to both location and timing.

### Location

3.13 In terms of location, consider the following:
- Where possible, choose a location where the person feels most at ease. For example, people are usually more comfortable in their own home than at a doctor's surgery.

- Would the person find it easier to make their decision in a relevant location? For example, could you help them decide about medical treatment by taking them to hospital to see what is involved?
- Choose a quiet location where the discussion can't be easily interrupted.
- Try to eliminate any background noise or distractions (for example, the television or radio, or people talking).
- Choose a location where the person's privacy and dignity can be properly respected.

## *Timing*

3.14 In terms of timing, consider the following:
- Try to choose the time of day when the person is most alert – some people are better in the mornings, others are more lively in the afternoon or early evening. It may be necessary to try several times before a decision can be made.
- If the person's capacity is likely to improve in the foreseeable future, wait until it has done so – if practical and appropriate. For example, this might be the case after treatment for depression or a psychotic episode. Obviously, this may not be practical and appropriate if the decision is urgent.
- Some medication could affect a person's capacity (for example, medication which causes drowsiness or affects memory). Can the decision be delayed until side effects have subsided?
- Take one decision at a time – be careful to avoid making the person tired or confused.
- Don't rush – allow the person time to think things over or ask for clarification, where that is possible and appropriate.
- Avoid or challenge time limits that are unnecessary if the decision is not urgent. Delaying the decision may enable further steps to be taken to assist people to make the decision for themselves.

### Scenario: *Getting the location and timing right*

Luke, a young man, was seriously injured in a road traffic accident and suffered permanent brain damage. He has been in hospital several months, and has made good progress, but he gets very frustrated at his inability to concentrate or do things for himself.

Luke now needs surgical treatment on his leg. During the early morning ward round, the surgeon tries to explain what is involved in the operation. She asks Luke to sign a consent form, but he gets angry and says he doesn't want to talk about it.

His key nurse knows that Luke becomes more alert and capable later in the day. After lunch, she asks him if he would like to discuss the

> operation again. She also knows that he responds better one-to-one than in a group. So she takes Luke into a private room and repeats the information that the surgeon gave him earlier. He understands why the treatment is needed, what is involved and the likely consequences. Therefore, Luke has the capacity to make a decision about the operation.

## *Support from other people*

3.15 In some circumstances, individuals will be more comfortable making decisions when someone else is there to support them.
- Might the person benefit from having another person present? Sometimes having a relative or friend nearby can provide helpful support and reduce anxiety. However, some people might find this intrusive, and it could increase their anxiety or affect their ability to make a free choice. Find ways of getting the person's views on this, for example, by watching their behaviour towards other people.
- Always respect a person's right to confidentiality.

> ### *Scenario: Getting help from other people*
>
> Jane has a learning disability. She expresses herself using some words, facial expressions and body language. She has lived in her current community home all her life, but now needs to move to a new group home. She finds it difficult to discuss abstract ideas or things she hasn't experienced. Staff conclude that she lacks the capacity to decide for herself which new group home she should move to.
>
> The staff involve an advocate to help Jane express her views. Jane's advocate spends time with her in different environments. The advocate uses pictures, symbols and Makaton to find out the things that are important to Jane, and speaks to people who know Jane to find out what they think she likes. She then supports Jane to show their work to her care manager, and checks that the new homes suggested for her are able to meet Jane's needs and preferences.
>
> When the care manager has found some suitable places, Jane's advocate visits the homes with Jane. They take photos of the houses to help her distinguish between them. The advocate then uses the photos to help Jane work out which home she prefers. Jane's own feelings can now play an important part in deciding what is in her best interests – and so in the final decision about where she will live.

## **What other ways are there to enable decision-making?**

3.16 There are other ways to help someone make a decision for themselves.

- Many people find it helpful to talk things over with people they trust – or people who have been in a similar situation or faced similar dilemmas. For example, people with learning difficulties may benefit from the help of a designated support worker or being part of a support network.
- If someone is very distressed (for example, following a death of someone close) or where there are long-standing problems that affect someone's ability to understand an issue, it may be possible to delay a decision so that the person can have psychological therapy, if needed.
- Some organisations have produced materials to help people who need support to make decisions and for those who support them. Some of this material is designed to help people with specific conditions, such as Alzheimer's disease or profound learning disability.
- It may be important to provide access to technology. For example, some people who appear not to communicate well verbally can do so very well using computers.

---

*Scenario: Making the most of technology*

Ms Patel has an autistic spectrum disorder. Her family and care staff find it difficult to communicate with her. She refuses to make eye contact, and gets very upset and angry when her carers try to encourage her to speak.

One member of staff notices that Ms Patel is interested in the computer equipment. He shows her how to use the keyboard, and they are able to have a conversation using the computer. An IT specialist works with her to make sure she can make the most of her computing skills to communicate her feelings and decisions.

---

# 4 HOW DOES THE ACT DEFINE A PERSON'S CAPACITY TO MAKE A DECISION AND HOW SHOULD CAPACITY BE ASSESSED?

This chapter explains what the Act means by 'capacity' and 'lack of capacity'. It provides guidance on how to assess whether someone has the capacity to make a decision, and suggests when professionals should be involved in the assessment.

---

In this chapter, as throughout the Code, a person's capacity (or lack of capacity) refers specifically to their capacity to make a particular decision at the time it needs to be made

## Quick summary

This checklist is a summary of points to consider when assessing a person's capacity to make a specific decision. Readers should also refer to the more detailed guidance in this chapter and chapters 2 and 3.

Presuming someone has capacity

- The starting assumption must always be that a person has the capacity to make a decision, unless it can be established that they lack capacity.

Understanding what is meant by capacity and lack of capacity

- A person's capacity must be assessed specifically in terms of their capacity to make a particular decision at the time it needs to be made.

Treating everyone equally

- A person's capacity must not be judged simply on the basis of their age, appearance, condition or an aspect of their behaviour.

Supporting the person to make the decision for themselves

- It is important to take all possible steps to try to help people make a decision for themselves (see chapter 2, principle 2, and chapter 3).

Assessing capacity

Anyone assessing someone's capacity to make a decision for themselves should use the two-stage test of capacity.

- Does the person have an impairment of the mind or brain, or is there some sort of disturbance affecting the way their mind or brain works? (It doesn't matter whether the impairment or disturbance is temporary or permanent.)
- If so, does that impairment or disturbance mean that the person is unable to make the decision in question at the time it needs to be made?

Assessing ability to make a decision

- Does the person have a general understanding of what decision they need to make and why they need to make it?
- Does the person have a general understanding of the likely consequences of making, or not making, this decision?
- Is the person able to understand, retain, use and weigh up the information relevant to this decision?

- Can the person communicate their decision (by talking, using sign language or any other means)? Would the services of a professional (such as a speech and language therapist) be helpful?

Assessing capacity to make more complex or serious decisions

- Is there a need for a more thorough assessment (perhaps by involving a doctor or other professional expert)?

## What is mental capacity?

4.1 Mental capacity is the ability to make a decision.
- This includes the ability to make a decision that affects daily life – such as when to get up, what to wear or whether to go to the doctor when feeling ill – as well as more serious or significant decisions.
- It also refers to a person's ability to make a decision that may have legal consequences – for them or others. Examples include agreeing to have medical treatment, buying goods or making a will.

4.2 The starting point must always be to assume that a person has the capacity to make a specific decision (see chapter 2, principle 1). Some people may need help to be able to make or communicate a decision (see chapter 3). But this does not necessarily mean that they lack capacity to do so. What matters is their ability to carry out the processes involved in making the decision – and not the outcome.

## What does the Act mean by 'lack of capacity'?

4.3 Section 2(1) of the Act states:

> 'For the purposes of this Act, a person lacks capacity in relation to a matter if at the material time he is unable to make a decision for himself in relation to the matter because of an impairment of, or a disturbance in the functioning of, the mind or brain.'

This means that a person lacks capacity if:
- they have an impairment or disturbance (for example, a disability, condition or trauma) that affects the way their mind or brain works, and
- the impairment or disturbance means that they are unable to make a specific decision at the time it needs to be made.

4.4 An assessment of a person's capacity must be based on their ability to make a specific decision at the time it needs to be made, and not their ability to make decisions in general. Section 3 of the Act defines what it means to be unable to make a decision (this is explained in paragraph 4.14 below).

4.5 Section 2(2) states that the impairment or disturbance does not have to be permanent. A person can lack capacity to make a decision at the time it needs to be made even if:
- the loss of capacity is partial
- the loss of capacity is temporary
- their capacity changes over time.

A person may also lack capacity to make a decision about one issue but not about others.

4.6 The Act generally applies to people who are aged 16 or older. Chapter 12 explains how the Act affects children and young people – in particular those aged 16 and 17 years.

## What safeguards does the Act provide around assessing someone's capacity?

4.7 An assessment that a person lacks capacity to make a decision must never be based simply on:
- their age
- their appearance
- assumptions about their condition, or
- any aspect of their behaviour. (section 2(3))

4.8 The Act deliberately uses the word 'appearance', because it covers all aspects of the way people look. So for example, it includes the physical characteristics of certain conditions (for example, scars, features linked to Down's syndrome or muscle spasms caused by cerebral palsy) as well as aspects of appearance like skin colour, tattoos and body piercings, or the way people dress (including religious dress).

4.9 The word 'condition' is also wide-ranging. It includes physical disabilities, learning difficulties and disabilities, illness related to age, and temporary conditions (for example, drunkenness or unconsciousness). Aspects of behaviour might include extrovert (for example, shouting or gesticulating) and withdrawn behaviour (for example, talking to yourself or avoiding eye contact).

---

### Scenario: Treating everybody equally

Tom, a man with cerebral palsy, has slurred speech. Sometimes he also falls over for no obvious reason

One day Tom falls in the supermarket. Staff call an ambulance, even though he says he is fine. They think he may need treatment after his fall.

When the ambulance comes, the ambulance crew know they must not make assumptions about Tom's capacity to decide about treatment, based simply on his condition and the effects of his disability. They talk to him and find that he is capable of making healthcare decisions for himself.

## What proof of lack of capacity does the Act require?

4.10 Anybody who claims that an individual lacks capacity should be able to provide proof. They need to be able to show, on the balance of probabilities, that the individual lacks capacity to make a particular decision, at the time it needs to be made (section 2(4)). This means being able to show that it is more likely than not that the person lacks capacity to make the decision in question.

## What is the test of capacity?

To help determine if a person lacks capacity to make particular decisions, the Act sets out a two-stage test of capacity.

### *Stage 1: Does the person have an impairment of, or a disturbance in the functioning of, their mind or brain?*

4.11 Stage 1 requires proof that the person has an impairment of the mind or brain, or some sort of or disturbance that affects the way their mind or brain works. If a person does not have such an impairment or disturbance of the mind or brain, they will not lack capacity under the Act.

4.12 Examples of an impairment or disturbance in the functioning of the mind or brain may include the following:
- conditions associated with some forms of mental illness
- dementia
- significant learning disabilities
- the long-term effects of brain damage
- physical or medical conditions that cause confusion, drowsiness or loss of consciousness
- delirium
- concussion following a head injury, and
- the symptoms of alcohol or drug use.

---

### *Scenario: Assessing whether an impairment or disturbance is affecting someone's ability to make a decision*

Mrs Collins is 82 and has had a stroke. This has weakened the left-hand side of her body. She is living in a house that has been the family home for years. Her son wants her to sell the house and live with him.

Mrs Collins likes the idea, but her daughter does not. She thinks her mother will lose independence and her condition will get worse. She talks to her mother's consultant to get information that will help stop the sale. But he says that although Mrs Collins is anxious about the physical effects the stroke has had on her body, it has not caused any mental ➔

> impairment or affected her brain, so she still has capacity to make her own decision about selling her house.

## Stage 2: Does the impairment or disturbance mean that the person is unable to make a specific decision when they need to?

4.13 For a person to lack capacity to make a decision, the Act says their impairment or disturbance must affect their ability to make the specific decision when they need to. But first people must be given all practical and appropriate support to help them make the decision for themselves (see chapter 2, principle 2). Stage 2 can only apply if all practical and appropriate support to help the person make the decision has failed. See chapter 3 for guidance on ways of helping people to make their own decisions.

### What does the Act mean by 'inability to make a decision'?

4.14 A person is unable to make a decision if they cannot:
1. understand information about the decision to be made (the Act calls this 'relevant information')
2. retain that information in their mind
3. use or weigh that information as part of the decision-making process, or
4. communicate their decision (by talking, using sign language or any other means). See section 3(1).

4.15 These four points are explained in more detail below. The first three should be applied together. If a person cannot do any of these three things, they will be treated as unable to make the decision. The fourth only applies in situations where people cannot communicate their decision in any way.

### Understanding information about the decision to be made

4.16 It is important not to assess someone's understanding before they have been given relevant information about a decision. Every effort must be made to provide information in a way that is most appropriate to help the person to understand. Quick or inadequate explanations are not acceptable unless the situation is urgent (see chapter 3 for some practical steps). Relevant information includes:
- the nature of the decision
- the reason why the decision is needed, and
- the likely effects of deciding one way or another, or making no decision at all.

4.17 Section 3(2) outlines the need to present information in a way that is appropriate to meet the individual's needs and circumstances. It also stresses the importance of explaining information using the most effective form of communication for that person (such as simple language, sign language, visual representations, computer support or any other means).

4.18 For example:
- a person with a learning disability may need somebody to read information to them. They might also need illustrations to help them to understand what is happening. Or they might stop the reader to ask what things mean. It might also be helpful for them to discuss information with an advocate.
- a person with anxiety or depression may find it difficult to reach a decision about treatment in a group meeting with professionals. They may prefer to read the relevant documents in private. This way they can come to a conclusion alone, and ask for help if necessary.
- someone who has a brain injury might need to be given information several times. It will be necessary to check that the person understands the information. If they have difficulty understanding, it might be useful to present information in a different way (for example, different forms of words, pictures or diagrams). Written information, audiotapes, videos and posters can help people remember important facts.

4.19 Relevant information must include what the likely consequences of a decision would be (the possible effects of deciding one way or another) – and also the likely consequences of making no decision at all (section 3(4)). In some cases, it may be enough to give a broad explanation using simple language. But a person might need more detailed information or access to advice, depending on the decision that needs to be made. If a decision could have serious or grave consequences, it is even more important that a person understands the information relevant to that decision.

---

### Scenario: *Providing relevant information in an appropriate format*

Mr Leslie has learning disabilities and has developed an irregular heartbeat. He has been prescribed medication for this, but is anxious about having regular blood tests to check his medication levels. His doctor gives him a leaflet to explain:

- the reason for the tests
- what a blood test involves
- the risks in having or not having the tests, and
- that he has the right to decide whether or not to have the test.

The leaflet uses simple language and photographs to explain these things. Mr Leslie's carer helps him read the leaflet over the next few days, and checks that he understands it.

Mr Leslie goes back to tell the doctor that, even though he is scared of needles, he will agree to the blood tests so that he can get the right

> medication. He is able to pick out the equipment needed to do the blood test. So the doctor concludes that Mr Leslie can understand, retain and use the relevant information and therefore has the capacity to make the decision to have the test.

## Retaining information

4.20 The person must be able to hold the information in their mind long enough to use it to make an effective decision. But section 3(3) states that people who can only retain information for a short while must not automatically be assumed to lack the capacity to decide – it depends on what is necessary for the decision in question. Items such as notebooks, photographs, posters, videos and voice recorders can help people record and retain information.

> ### Scenario: Assessing a person's ability to retain information
>
> Walter, an elderly man, is diagnosed with dementia and has problems remembering things in the short term. He can't always remember his great-grandchildren's names, but he recognises them when they come to visit. He can also pick them out on photographs.
>
> Walter would like to buy premium bonds (a type of financial investment) for each of his great-grandchildren. He asks his solicitor to make the arrangements. After assessing his capacity to make financial decisions, the solicitor is satisfied that Walter has capacity to make this decision, despite his short-term memory problems.

## Using or weighing information as part of the decision-making process

4.21 For someone to have capacity, they must have the ability to weigh up information and use it to arrive at a decision. Sometimes people can understand information but an impairment or disturbance stops them using it. In other cases, the impairment or disturbance leads to a person making a specific decision without understanding or using the information they have been given.[3]

4.22 For example, a person with the eating disorder anorexia nervosa may understand information about the consequences of not eating. But their compulsion not to eat might be too strong for them to ignore. Some people who have serious brain damage might make impulsive decisions regardless of information they have been given or their understanding of it.

---

[3] This issue has been considered in a number of court cases, including *Re MB* [1997] 2 FLR 426; *R v Collins and Ashworth Hospital Authority ex parte Brady* [2001] 58 BMLR 173.

## *Inability to communicate a decision in any way*

4.23 Sometimes there is no way for a person to communicate. This will apply to very few people, but it does include:
- people who are unconscious or in a coma, or
- those with the very rare condition sometimes known as 'locked-in syndrome', who are conscious but cannot speak or move at all.

If a person cannot communicate their decision in any way at all, the Act says they should be treated as if they are unable to make that decision.

4.24 Before deciding that someone falls into this category, it is important to make all practical and appropriate efforts to help them communicate. This might call for the involvement of speech and language therapists, specialists in non-verbal communication or other professionals. Chapter 3 gives advice for communicating with people who have specific disabilities or cognitive problems.

4.25 Communication by simple muscle movements can show that somebody can communicate and may have capacity to make a decision.[4] For example, a person might blink an eye or squeeze a hand to say 'yes' or 'no'. In these cases, assessment must use the first three points listed in paragraph 4.14, which are explained in more depth in paragraphs 4.16–4.22.

## What other issues might affect capacity?

### *People with fluctuating or temporary capacity*

4.26 Some people have fluctuating capacity – they have a problem or condition that gets worse occasionally and affects their ability to make decisions. For example, someone who has manic depression may have a temporary manic phase which causes them to lack capacity to make financial decisions, leading them to get into debt even though at other times they are perfectly able to manage their money. A person with a psychotic illness may have delusions that affect their capacity to make decisions at certain times but disappear at others. Temporary factors may also affect someone's ability to make decisions. Examples include acute illness, severe pain, the effect of medication, or distress after a death or shock. More guidance on how to support someone with fluctuating or temporary capacity to make a decision can be found in chapter 3, particularly paragraphs 3.12–3.16. More information about factors that may indicate that a person may regain or develop capacity in the future can be found at paragraph 5.28.

4.27 As in any other situation, an assessment must only examine a person's capacity to make a particular decision when it needs to be made. It may be possible to put off the decision until the person has the capacity to make it (see also guidance on best interests in chapter 5).

---

[4] This was demonstrated in the case *Re AK (Adult Patient) (Medical Treatment: Consent)* [2001] 1 FLR 129.

## Ongoing conditions that may affect capacity

4.28 Generally, capacity assessments should be related to a specific decision. But there may be people with an ongoing condition that affects their ability to make certain decisions or that may affect other decisions in their life. One decision on its own may make sense, but may give cause for concern when considered alongside others.

4.29 Again, it is important to review capacity from time to time, as people can improve their decision-making capabilities. In particular, someone with an ongoing condition may become able to make some, if not all, decisions. Some people (for example, people with learning disabilities) will learn new skills throughout their life, improving their capacity to make certain decisions. So assessments should be reviewed from time to time. Capacity should always be reviewed:
- whenever a care plan is being developed or reviewed
- at other relevant stages of the care planning process, and
- as particular decisions need to be made.

4.30 It is important to acknowledge the difference between:
- unwise decisions, which a person has the right to make (chapter 2, principle 3), and
- decisions based on a lack of understanding of risks or inability to weigh up the information about a decision.

Information about decisions the person has made based on a lack of understanding of risks or inability to weigh up the information can form part of a capacity assessment – particularly if someone repeatedly makes decisions that put them at risk or result in harm to them or someone else.

> ### Scenario: Ongoing conditions
>
> Paul had an accident at work and suffered severe head injuries. He was awarded compensation to pay for care he will need throughout his life as a result of his head injury. An application was made to the Court of Protection to consider how the award of compensation should be managed, including whether to appoint a deputy to manage Paul's financial affairs. Paul objected as he believed he could manage his life and should be able to spend his money however he liked.
>
> He wrote a list of what he intended to spend his money on. This included fully-staffed luxury properties and holiday villas, cars with chauffeurs, jewellery and various other items for himself and his family. But spending money on all these luxury items would not leave enough money to cover the costs of his care in future years.
>
> The court judged that Paul had capacity to make day-to-day financial decisions, but he did not understand why he had received compensation and what the money was supposed to be used for. Nor did he understand how buying luxuries now could affect his future care. The court therefore decided Paul lacked capacity to manage large amounts of money and ➡

> appointed a deputy to make ongoing financial decisions relating to his care. But it gave him access to enough funds to cover everyday needs and occasional treats.

## *What other legal tests of capacity are there?*

4.31 The Act makes clear that the definition of 'lack of capacity' and the two-stage test for capacity set out in the Act are 'for the purposes of this Act'. This means that the definition and test are to be used in situations covered by this Act. Schedule 6 of the Act also amends existing laws to ensure that the definition and test are used in other areas of law not covered directly by this Act.

For example, Schedule 6, paragraph 20 allows a person to be disqualified from jury service if they lack the capacity (using this Act's definition) to carry out a juror's tasks.

4.32 There are several tests of capacity that have been produced following judgments in court cases (known as common law tests).[5] These cover:
- capacity to make a will[6]
- capacity to make a gift[7]
- capacity to enter into a contract[8]
- capacity to litigate (take part in legal cases),[9] and
- capacity to enter into marriage.[10]

4.33 The Act's new definition of capacity is in line with the existing common law tests, and the Act does not replace them. When cases come before the court on the above issues, judges can adopt the new definition if they think it is appropriate. The Act will apply to all other cases relating to financial, healthcare or welfare decisions.

## When should capacity be assessed?

4.34 Assessing capacity correctly is vitally important to everyone affected by the Act. Someone who is assessed as lacking capacity may be denied their right to make a specific decision – particularly if others think that the decision would not be in their best interests or could cause harm. Also, if a person lacks capacity to make specific decisions, that person might make decisions they do not really understand. Again, this could cause harm or put the person at risk. So it is important to carry out an assessment when a person's capacity is in doubt. It is also important that the person who

---

[5] For details, see British Medical Association & Law Society, *Assessment of Mental Capacity: Guidance for Doctors and Lawyers* (BMA, 1995; BMJ Books, 2nd edn, 2004; Law Society Publishing, 3rd edn, 2009).
[6] *Banks v Goodfellow* (1870) LR 5 QB 549.
[7] *Re Beaney (deceased)* [1978] 2 All ER 595.
[8] *Boughton v Knight* (1873) LR 3 PD 64.
[9] *Masterman-Lister v Brutton & Co and Jewell & Home Counties Dairies* [2003] 3 All ER 162, CA.
[10] *E (an Alleged Patient), Re; Sheffield City Council v E & S* [2005] 1 FLR 965.

does an assessment can justify their conclusions. Many organisations will provide specific professional guidance for members of their profession.[11]

4.35 There are a number of reasons why people may question a person's capacity to make a specific decision:
- the person's behaviour or circumstances cause doubt as to whether they have the capacity to make a decision
- somebody else says they are concerned about the person's capacity, or
- the person has previously been diagnosed with an impairment or disturbance that affects the way their mind or brain works (see paragraphs 4.11–4.12 above), and it has already been shown they lack capacity to make other decisions in their life.

4.36 The starting assumption must be that the person has the capacity to make the specific decision. If, however, anyone thinks a person lacks capacity, it is important to then ask the following questions:
- Does the person have all the relevant information they need to make the decision?
- If they are making a decision that involves choosing between alternatives, do they have information on all the different options?
- Would the person have a better understanding if information was explained or presented in another way?
- Are there times of day when the person's understanding is better?
- Are there locations where they may feel more at ease?
- Can the decision be put off until the circumstances are different and the person concerned may be able to make the decision?
- Can anyone else help the person to make choices or express a view (for example, a family member or carer, an advocate or someone to help with communication)?

4.37 Chapter 3 describes ways to deal with these questions and suggest steps which may help people make their own decisions. If all practical and appropriate steps fail, an assessment will then be needed of the person's capacity to make the decision that now needs to be made.

## Who should assess capacity?

4.38 The person who assesses an individual's capacity to make a decision will usually be the person who is directly concerned with the individual at the time the decision needs to be made. This means that different people will be involved in assessing someone's capacity to make different decisions at different times.

For most day-to-day decisions, this will be the person caring for them at the time a decision must be made. For example, a care worker might need

---

[11] See for example, British Medical Association & Law Society, *Assessment of Mental Capacity: Guidance for Doctors and Lawyers* (BMA, 1995; BMJ Books, 2nd edn, 2004; Law Society Publishing, 3rd edn, 2009); the Joint Royal Colleges Ambulance Service Liaison Committee Clinical Practice Guidelines (JRCALC, available online at www2.warwick.ac.uk/fac/med/research/hsri/ emergencycare/jrcalc_2006/clinical_guidelines_2006.pdf) and British Psychological Society, *Guidelines on assessing capacity* (BPS, 2006 available online at www.bps.org.uk).

to assess if the person can agree to being bathed. Then a district nurse might assess if the person can consent to have a dressing changed.

4.39 For acts of care or treatment (see chapter 6), the assessor must have a 'reasonable belief' that the person lacks capacity to agree to the action or decision to be taken (see paragraphs 4.44–4.45 for a description of reasonable belief).

4.40 If a doctor or healthcare professional proposes treatment or an examination, they must assess the person's capacity to consent. In settings such as a hospital, this can involve the multi-disciplinary team (a team of people from different professional backgrounds who share responsibility for a patient). But ultimately, it is up to the professional responsible for the person's treatment to make sure that capacity has been assessed.

4.41 For a legal transaction (for example, making a will), a solicitor or legal practitioner must assess the client's capacity to instruct them. They must assess whether the client has the capacity to satisfy any relevant legal test. In cases of doubt, they should get an opinion from a doctor or other professional expert.

4.42 More complex decisions are likely to need more formal assessments (see paragraph 4.54 below). A professional opinion on the person's capacity might be necessary. This could be, for example, from a psychiatrist, psychologist, a speech and language therapist, occupational therapist or social worker. But the final decision about a person's capacity must be made by the person intending to make the decision or carry out the action on behalf of the person who lacks capacity – not the professional, who is there to advise.

4.43 Any assessor should have the skills and ability to communicate effectively with the person (see chapter 3). If necessary, they should get professional help to communicate with the person.

### Scenario: *Getting help with assessing capacity*

Ms Dodd suffered brain damage in a road accident and is unable to speak. At first, her family thought she was not able to make decisions. But they soon discovered that she could choose by pointing at things, such as the clothes she wants to wear or the food she prefers. Her behaviour also indicates that she enjoys attending a day centre, but she refuses to go swimming. Her carers have assessed her as having capacity to make these decisions.

Ms Dodd needs hospital treatment but she gets distressed when away from home. Her mother feels that Ms Dodd is refusing treatment by her behaviour, but her father thinks she lacks capacity to say no to treatment that could improve her condition.

The clinician who is proposing the treatment will have to assess Ms Dodd's capacity to consent. He gets help from a member of staff at the day centre who knows Ms Dodd's communication well and also discusses things with her parents. Over several meetings the clinician

> explains the treatment options to Ms Dodd with the help of the staff member. The final decision about Ms Dodd's capacity rests with the clinician, but he will need to use information from the staff member and others who know Ms Dodd well to make this assessment.

## What is 'reasonable belief' of lack of capacity?

4.44 Carers (whether family carers or other carers) and care workers do not have to be experts in assessing capacity. But to have protection from liability when providing care or treatment (see chapter 6), they must have a 'reasonable belief' that the person they care for lacks capacity to make relevant decisions about their care or treatment (section 5(1)). To have this reasonable belief, they must have taken 'reasonable' steps to establish that that the person lacks capacity to make a decision or consent to an act at the time the decision or consent is needed. They must also establish that the act or decision is in the person's best interests (see chapter 5).

They do not usually need to follow formal processes, such as involving a professional to make an assessment. However, if somebody challenges their assessment (see paragraph 4.63 below), they must be able to describe the steps they have taken. They must also have objective reasons for believing the person lacks capacity to make the decision in question.

4.45 The steps that are accepted as 'reasonable' will depend on individual circumstances and the urgency of the decision. Professionals, who are qualified in their particular field, are normally expected to undertake a fuller assessment, reflecting their higher degree of knowledge and experience, than family members or other carers who have no formal qualifications. See paragraph 4.36 for a list of points to consider when assessing someone's capacity. The following may also be helpful:
- Start by assuming the person has capacity to make the specific decision. Is there anything to prove otherwise?
- Does the person have a previous diagnosis of disability or mental disorder? Does that condition now affect their capacity to make this decision? If there has been no previous diagnosis, it may be best to get a medical opinion.
- Make every effort to communicate with the person to explain what is happening.
- Make every effort to try to help the person make the decision in question.
- See if there is a way to explain or present information about the decision in a way that makes it easier to understand. If the person has a choice, do they have information about all the options?
- Can the decision be delayed to take time to help the person make the decision, or to give the person time to regain the capacity to make the decision for themselves?
- Does the person understand what decision they need to make and why they need to make it?

- Can they understand information about the decision? Can they retain it, use it and weigh it to make the decision?
- Be aware that the fact that a person agrees with you or assents to what is proposed does not necessarily mean that they have capacity to make the decision.

## What other factors might affect an assessment of capacity?

4.46 It is important to assess people when they are in the best state to make the decision, if possible. Whether this is possible will depend on the nature and urgency of the decision to be made. Many of the practical steps suggested in chapter 3 will help to create the best environment for assessing capacity. The assessor must then carry out the two stages of the test of capacity (see paragraphs 4.11–4.25 above).

4.47 In many cases, it may be clear that the person has an impairment or disturbance in the functioning of their mind or brain which could affect their ability to make a decision. For example, there might be a past diagnosis of a disability or mental disorder, or there may be signs that an illness is returning. Old assumptions about an illness or condition should be reviewed. Sometimes an illness develops gradually (for example, dementia), and it is hard to know when it starts to affect capacity. Anyone assessing someone's capacity may need to ask for a medical opinion as to whether a person has an illness or condition that could affect their capacity to make a decision in this specific case.

> ### Scenario: *Getting a professional opinion*
>
> Mr Elliott is 87 years old and lives alone. He has poor short-term memory, and he often forgets to eat. He also sometimes neglects his personal hygiene. His daughter talks to him about the possibility of moving into residential care. She decides that he understands the reasons for her concerns as well as the risks of continuing to live alone and, having weighed these up, he has the capacity to decide to stay at home and accept the consequences.
>
> Two months later, Mr Elliott has a fall and breaks his leg. While being treated in hospital, he becomes confused and depressed. He says he wants to go home, but the staff think that the deterioration in his mental health has affected his capacity to make this decision at this time. They think he cannot understand the consequences or weigh up the risks he faces if he goes home. They refer him to a specialist in old age psychiatry, who assesses whether his mental health is affecting his capacity to make this decision. The staff will then use the specialist's opinion to help their assessment of Mr Elliott's capacity.

4.48 Anyone assessing someone's capacity must not assume that a person lacks capacity simply because they have a particular diagnosis or condition.

There must be proof that the diagnosed illness or condition affects the ability to make a decision when it needs to be made. The person assessing capacity should ask the following questions:
- Does the person have a general understanding of what decision they need to make and why they need to make it?
- Do they understand the likely consequences of making, or not making, this decision?
- Can they understand and process information about the decision? And can they use it to help them make a decision?

In borderline cases, or where there is doubt, the assessor must be able to show that it is more likely than not that the answer to these questions is 'no'.

## What practical steps should be taken when assessing capacity?

4.49 Anyone assessing someone's capacity will need to decide which of these steps are relevant to their situation.
- They should make sure that they understand the nature and effect of the decision to be made themselves. They may need access to relevant documents and background information (for example, details of the person's finances if assessing capacity to manage affairs). See chapter 16 for details on access to information.
- They may need other relevant information to support the assessment (for example, healthcare records or the views of staff involved in the person's care).
- Family members and close friends may be able to provide valuable background information (for example, the person's past behaviour and abilities and the types of decisions they can currently make). But their personal views and wishes about what they would want for the person must not influence the assessment.
- They should again explain to the person all the information relevant to the decision. The explanation must be in the most appropriate and effective form of communication for that person.
- Check the person's understanding after a few minutes. The person should be able to give a rough explanation of the information that was explained. There are different methods for people who use nonverbal means of communication (for example, observing behaviour or their ability to recognise objects or pictures).
- Avoid questions that need only a 'yes' or 'no' answer (for example, did you understand what I just said?). They are not enough to assess the person's capacity to make a decision. But there may be no alternative in cases where there are major communication difficulties. In these cases, check the response by asking questions again in a different way.
- Skills and behaviour do not necessarily reflect the person's capacity to make specific decisions. The fact that someone has good social or language skills, polite behaviour or good manners doesn't necessarily mean they understand the information or are able to weigh it up.

- Repeating these steps can help confirm the result.
4.50 For certain kinds of complex decisions (for example, making a will), there are specific legal tests (see paragraph 4.32 above) in addition to the two-stage test for capacity. In some cases, medical or psychometric tests may also be helpful tools (for example, for assessing cognitive skills) in assessing a person's capacity to make particular decisions, but the relevant legal test of capacity must still be fulfilled.

## When should professionals be involved?

4.51 Anyone assessing someone's capacity may need to get a professional opinion when assessing a person's capacity to make complex or major decisions. In some cases this will simply involve contacting the person's general practitioner (GP) or family doctor. If the person has a particular condition or disorder, it may be appropriate to contact a specialist (for example, consultant psychiatrist, psychologist or other professional with experience of caring for patients with that condition). A speech and language therapist might be able to help if there are communication difficulties. In some cases, a multi-disciplinary approach is best. This means combining the skills and expertise of different professionals.

4.52 Professionals should never express an opinion without carrying out a proper examination and assessment of the person's capacity to make the decision. They must apply the appropriate test of capacity. In some cases, they will need to meet the person more than once – particularly if the person has communication difficulties. Professionals can get background information from a person's family and carers. But the personal views of these people about what they want for the person who lacks capacity must not influence the outcome of that assessment.

4.53 Professional involvement might be needed if:
- the decision that needs to be made is complicated or has serious consequences
- an assessor concludes a person lacks capacity, and the person challenges the finding
- family members, carers and/or professionals disagree about a person's capacity
- there is a conflict of interest between the assessor and the person being assessed
- the person being assessed is expressing different views to different people – they may be trying to please everyone or telling people what they think they want to hear
- somebody might challenge the person's capacity to make the decision – either at the time of the decision or later (for example, a family member might challenge a will after a person has died on the basis that the person lacked capacity when they made the will)
- somebody has been accused of abusing a vulnerable adult who may lack capacity to make decisions that protect them
- a person repeatedly makes decisions that put them at risk or could result in suffering or damage.

> **Scenario: Involving professional opinion**
>
> Ms Ledger is a young woman with learning disabilities and some autistic spectrum disorders. Recently she began a sexual relationship with a much older man, who is trying to persuade her to move in with him and come off the pill. There are rumours that he has been violent towards her and has taken her bankbook.
>
> Ms Ledger boasts about the relationship to her friends. But she has admitted to her key worker that she is sometimes afraid of the man. Staff at her sheltered accommodation decide to make a referral under the local adult protection procedures. They arrange for a clinical psychologist to assess Ms Ledger's understanding of the relationship and her capacity to consent to it.

4.54 In some cases, it may be a legal requirement, or good professional practice, to undertake a formal assessment of capacity. These cases include:
- where a person's capacity to sign a legal document (for example, a will), could later be challenged, in which case an expert should be asked for an opinion[12]
- to establish whether a person who might be involved in a legal case needs the assistance of the Official Solicitor or other litigation friend (somebody to represent their views to a court and give instructions to their legal representative) and there is doubt about the person's capacity to instruct a solicitor or take part in the case[13]
- whenever the Court of Protection has to decide if a person lacks capacity in a certain matter
- if the courts are required to make a decision about a person's capacity in other legal proceedings[14]
- if there may be legal consequences of a finding of capacity (for example, deciding on financial compensation following a claim for personal injury).

## Are assessment processes confidential?

4.55 People involved in assessing capacity will need to share information about a person's circumstances. But there are ethical codes and laws that require professionals to keep personal information confidential. As a general rule, professionals must ask their patients or clients if they can reveal information to somebody else – even close relatives. But sometimes

---

[12] *Kenward v Adams* (1975) *The Times*, 29 November.
[13] Civil Procedure Rules 1998, r 21.1
[14] *Masterman-Lister v Brutton & Co and Jewell & Home Counties Dairies* [2002] EWCA Civ 1889, CA at 54.

information may be disclosed without the consent of the person who the information concerns (for example, to protect the person or prevent harm to other people).[15]

4.56 Anyone assessing someone's capacity needs accurate information concerning the person being assessed that is relevant to the decision the person has to make. So professionals should, where possible, make relevant information available. They should make every effort to get the person's permission to reveal relevant information. They should give a full explanation of why this is necessary, and they should tell the person about the risks and consequences of revealing, and not revealing information. If the person is unable to give permission, the professional might still be allowed to provide information that will help make an accurate assessment of the person's capacity to make the specific decision. Chapter 16 has more detail on how to access information.

## What if someone refuses to be assessed?

4.57 There may be circumstances in which a person whose capacity is in doubt refuses to undergo an assessment of capacity or refuses to be examined by a doctor or other professional. In these circumstances, it might help to explain to someone refusing an assessment why it is needed and what the consequences of refusal are. But threats or attempts to force the person to agree to an assessment are not acceptable.

4.58 If the person lacks capacity to agree or refuse, the assessment can normally go ahead, as long as the person does not object to the assessment, and it is in their best interests (see chapter 5).

4.59 Nobody can be forced to undergo an assessment of capacity. If someone refuses to open the door to their home, it cannot be forced. If there are serious worries about the person's mental health, it may be possible to get a warrant to force entry and assess the person for treatment in hospital – but the situation must meet the requirements of the Mental Health Act 1983 (section 135). But simply refusing an assessment of capacity is in no way sufficient grounds for an assessment under the Mental Health Act 1983 (see chapter 13).

## Who should keep a record of assessments?

4.60 Assessments of capacity to take day-to-day decisions or consent to care require no formal assessment procedures or recorded documentation. Paragraphs 4.44–4.45 above explain the steps to take to reach a 'reasonable belief' that someone lacks capacity to make a particular decision. It is good practice for paid care workers to keep a record of the steps they take when caring for the person concerned.

---

[15] For example, in the circumstances discussed in *W v Egdell and others* [1990] 1 All ER 835 at 848; *R (S) v Plymouth City Council and C* [2002] EWCA Civ 388 at 49.

## Professional records

4.61 It is good practice for professionals to carry out a proper assessment of a person's capacity to make particular decisions and to record the findings in the relevant professional records.
- A doctor or healthcare professional proposing treatment should carry out an assessment of the person's capacity to consent (with a multi-disciplinary team, if appropriate) and record it in the patient's clinical notes.
- Solicitors should assess a client's capacity to give instructions or carry out a legal transaction (obtaining a medical or other professional opinion, if necessary) and record it on the client's file.
- An assessment of a person's capacity to consent or agree to the provision of services will be part of the care planning processes for health and social care needs, and should be recorded in the relevant documentation. This includes:
- Person Centred Planning for people with learning disabilities
- the Care Programme Approach for people with mental illness
- the Single Assessment Process for older people in England, and
- the Unified Assessment Process in Wales.

## Formal reports or certificates of capacity

4.62 In some cases, a more detailed report or certificate of capacity may be required, for example,
- for use in court or other legal processes
- as required by Regulations, Rules or Orders made under the Act.

## How can someone challenge a finding of lack of capacity?

4.63 There are likely to be occasions when someone may wish to challenge the results of an assessment of capacity. The first step is to raise the matter with the person who carried out the assessment. If the challenge comes from the individual who is said to lack capacity, they might need support from family, friends or an advocate. Ask the assessor to:
- give reasons why they believe the person lacks capacity to make the decision, and
- provide objective evidence to support that belief.

4.64 The assessor must show they have applied the principles of the Mental Capacity Act (see chapter 2). Attorneys, deputies and professionals will need to show that they have also followed guidance in this chapter.

4.65 It might be possible to get a second opinion from an independent professional or another expert in assessing capacity. Chapter 15 has other suggestions for dealing with disagreements. But if a disagreement cannot be resolved, the person who is challenging the assessment may be able to apply to the Court of Protection. The Court of Protection can rule on whether a person has capacity to make the decision covered by the assessment (see chapter 8).

\*\*\*\*

# Appendix 4

# PRACTICE NOTE
# 2 APRIL 2001

### CITATION: [2001] 2 FLR 155

**A.4**

#### Official Solicitor: Appointment in Family Proceedings

1 This Practice Note supersedes *Practice Note (Official Solicitor: Appointment in Family Proceedings)* (4 December 1998) [1999] 1 FLR 310 issued by the Official Solicitor in relation to his appointment in family proceedings. It is issued in conjunction with a Practice Note dealing with the appointment of officers of CAFCASS Legal Services and Special Casework in family proceedings. This Practice Note is intended to be helpful guidance, but always subject to Practice Directions, decisions of the court and other legal guidance.

2 The Children and Family Court Advisory and Support Service (CAFCASS) has responsibilities in relation to children in family proceedings in which their welfare is or may be in question (Criminal Justice and Court Services Act 2000, s 12). From 1 April 2001, the Official Solicitor will no longer represent children who are the subject of family proceedings (other than in very exceptional circumstances and after liaison with CAFCASS).

3 This Practice Note summarises the continuing role of the Official Solicitor in family proceedings. Since there are no provisions for parties under disability in the Family Proceedings Courts (Children Act 1989) Rules 1991, the Official Solicitor can only act in the High Court or in a county court, pursuant to Part IX of the Family Proceedings Rules 1991. The Official Solicitor will shortly issue an updated Practice Note about his role for adults under disability who are the subject of declaratory proceedings in relation to their medical treatment or welfare.

**Adults under disability**

4 The Official Solicitor will, in the absence of any other willing and suitable person, act as next friend or guardian ad litem of an adult party under disability, a "patient". "Patient" means someone who is incapable by reason of mental disorder of managing and administering his property and affairs (Family Proceedings Rules 1991, r 9.1). Medical evidence will usually be required before the Official Solicitor can consent to act and his staff can

provide a standard form of medical certificate. Where there are practical difficulties in obtaining such medical evidence, the Official Solicitor should be consulted.

**Non-subject children**

5 Again in the absence of any other willing and suitable person, the Official Solicitor will act as next friend or guardian ad litem of a child party whose own welfare is not the subject of family proceedings (Family Proceedings Rules 1991, r 2.57, r 9.2 and r 9.5). The most common examples will be:

(a) a child who is also the parent of a child, and who is a respondent to a Children Act 1989 or Adoption Act 1976 application. If a child respondent is already represented by a CAFCASS officer in pending proceedings of which he or she is the subject, then the Official Solicitor will liaise with CAFCASS to agree the most appropriate arrangements;

(b) a child who wishes to make an application for a Children Act 1989 order naming another child (typically a contact order naming a sibling). The Official Solicitor will need to satisfy himself that the proposed proceedings would benefit the child applicant before proceeding;

(c) a child witness to some disputed factual issue in a children case and who may require intervener status. In such circumstances the need for party status and legal representation should be weighed in the light of *Re H (Care Proceedings: Intervener)* [2000] 1 FLR 775;

(d) a child party to a petition for a declaration of status under Part III of the Family Law Act 1986;

(e) a child intervener in divorce or ancillary relief proceedings (r 2.57 or r 9.5);

(f) a child applicant for, or respondent to, an application for an order under Part IV of the Family Law Act 1996. In the case of a child applicant, the Official Solicitor will need to satisfy himself that the proposed proceedings would benefit the child before pursuing them, with leave under Family Law Act 1996, s 43 if required.

6 Any children who are parties to Children Act 1989 or inherent jurisdiction proceedings may rely on the provisions of Family Proceedings Rules 1991, r 9.2A if they wish to instruct a solicitor without the intervention of a next friend or guardian ad litem. Rule 9.2A does not apply to Adoption Act 1976, Family Law Act 1986/1996 or Matrimonial Causes Act 1973 proceedings.

**Older children who are also patients**

7 Officers of CAFCASS will not be able to represent anyone who is over the age of 18. The Official Solicitor may therefore be the more appropriate next friend or guardian ad litem of a child who is also a patient and whose disability will persist beyond his or her eighteenth birthday, especially in non-emergency cases where the substantive hearing is unlikely to take place before the child's eighteenth birthday. The Official Solicitor may also be the more appropriate

next friend or guardian ad litem in medical treatment cases such as sterilisation or vegetative state cases, in which his staff have particular expertise deriving from their continuing role for adult patients.

**Advising the court**

8 The Official Solicitor may be invited to act or instruct counsel as a friend of the court (amicus) if it appears to the court that such an invitation is more appropriately addressed to him rather than (or in addition to) CAFCASS Legal Services and Special Casework.

**Liaison with CAFCASS**

9 In cases of doubt or difficulty, staff of the Official Solicitor's office will liaise with staff of CAFCASS Legal Services and Special Casework to avoid duplication and ensure the most suitable arrangements are made.

**Invitations to act in new cases**

10 Solicitors who have been consulted by a child or an adult under disability (or by someone acting on their behalf, or concerned about their interests) should write to the Official Solicitor setting out the background to the proposed case and explaining why there is no other willing and suitable person to act as next friend or guardian ad litem. Where the person concerned is an adult, medical evidence in the standard form of the Official Solicitor's medical certificate should be provided.

**Invitations to act in pending proceedings**

11 Where a case is already before the court, an order appointing the Official Solicitor should be expressed as being made subject to his consent. The Official Solicitor aims to provide a response to any invitation within 10 working days. He will be unable to consent to act for an adult until satisfied that the party is a "patient". A further directions appointment after 28 days may therefore be helpful. If he accepts appointment the Official Solicitor will need time to prepare the case on behalf of the child or patient and may wish to make submissions about any substantive hearing date. The following documents should be forwarded to the Official Solicitor without delay:

(*a*) a copy of the order inviting him to act (with a note of the reasons approved by the judge if appropriate);
(*b*) the court file;
(*c*) if available, a bundle with summary, statement of issues and chronology (as required by *President's Direction (Family Proceedings: Court Bundles)* (10 March 2000) [2000] 1 FLR 536).

**Contacting the Official Solicitor**

12 It is often helpful to discuss the question of appointment with the Official Solicitor or one of his staff by telephoning 020 7911 7127. Enquiries about family proceedings should be addressed to the Team Manager, Family Litigation.

The Official Solicitor's address is:

81 Chancery Lane
London WC2A 1DD
DX 0012 London Chancery Lane
Fax: 020 7911 7105
Email: officialsolicitor@offsol.gsi.gov.uk

Laurence Oates
Official Solicitor

# Appendix 5

# PRESIDENT'S JOINT GUIDANCE DECEMBER 2010

**A.5**

**Guidance in cases involving protected parties in which the Official Solicitor is being invited to act as guardian ad litem or litigation friend**

**Public and private law children's cases**

1 Many practitioners and judges will know of the Official Solicitor's recent difficulties in accepting requests to act as guardian ad litem/litigation friend for protected parties in proceedings relating to children. Although, currently, there are unallocated cases, the backlog has reduced significantly in recent months.

2 The Official Solicitor is subject to severe budgetary constraints – a situation which is unlikely to ameliorate in the medium term.

3 In all cases, the Official Solicitor will need to be satisfied of the following criteria before accepting a case, and parties may need reminding of the need to provide confirmation of these matters immediately on approaching the Official Solicitor's office:

- satisfactory evidence or a finding by the court that the party lacks capacity to conduct the proceedings and is therefore a protected party;
- confirmation that there is security for the costs of legal representation;
- there is no other person who is suitable and willing to act as guardian ad litem/litigation friend.

4 In order to assist the Official Solicitor in the decisions he makes about allocating case workers, in certain cases, judges should consider whether it may be appropriate to indicate with as much particularity as possible the relative urgency of the proceedings and the likely effect upon the child (and family) of delay. The Official Solicitor will very carefully consider giving priority to such cases.

5 It is and remains the judge's duty in children's cases, so far as he is able, to eradicate delay.

**Court of Protection welfare cases (including medical cases)**

6 The number of welfare cases brought under the provisions of the Mental Capacity Act 2005 is rising exponentially with concomitant resource implications for the Official Solicitor.

7 Judges should be alert to the problems the Official Solicitor may have in attending at each and every preliminary hearing. Consideration should be given, in appropriate cases, to dispensing with the requirement that he should be present at a time when he is unable to contribute meaningfully to the process. In circumstances where his position has been/will be communicated in writing it may be particularly appropriate for the judge to indicate that the Official Solicitor's attendance at the next directions' hearing is unnecessary.

8 The Court of Protection Rules make clear that the judge is under a duty to restrict expert evidence to that which is reasonably required to resolve the proceedings. The explanatory note to r.121 states that the court will consider what 'added value' expert evidence will give to the case. Unnecessary expert assessments must be avoided. It will be rare indeed for the court to sanction the instruction of more than one expert to advise in relation to the same issue.

9 The Practice Direction – Experts (PD15A) specifies that the expert should assist by "providing objective, unbiased opinion on matters within his expertise, and should not assume the role of advocate". The form and content of the expert's report are prescribed, in detail, by paragraph 9 of the Practice Direction. It is no part of the expert's function to analyse or summarise the evidence. Focused brevity in report writing is to be preferred over discussion.

*Mrs Justice Pauffley*

# Appendix 6

# LETTER TO INDEPENDENT EXPERT

**A.6**

Dear ...

**[*name of person concerned*] (DOB....)**

[*name of person concerned*] is a party to court proceedings concerning his/her child[ren] which are continuing in the ........................ court.

I am the solicitor for ........................ and the lead solicitor for these instructions.

## 1   THE PARTIES AND THEIR REPRESENTATIVES

In this case:

1. The local authority, ........... is represented by ...........
   Address:
   T:
   F:
   Email:
2. The mother, ........... is represented by ...........
   Address:
   T:
   F:
   Email:
3. The father, ........... is represented by ...........
   Address:
   T:
   F:
   Email:
4. The child, ........... is represented by ...........
   Address:
   T:
   F:
   Email:

The child's guardian is .........

## 2 BACKGROUND

The court is concerned that [*name of person concerned*] may be suffering from an impairment of, or a disturbance in the functioning of, the mind or brain, to the extent that [he/she] lacks capacity, within the meaning of the Mental Capacity Act 2005 ('the MCA'), to conduct the proceedings and is therefore a 'protected party' in the proceedings.

Where a person is a 'protected party' the law provides that [he/she] may defend family proceedings only by a litigation friend.

The role of the litigation friend is to supplement the protected party's lack of capacity and to take necessary action in the proceedings in their best interests. It is, therefore, the litigation friend, rather than the protected party, who is responsible for making the decisions about the conduct of the proceedings and who instructs the solicitor in place of, and on behalf of, the protected party.

You should be aware that capacity is issue specific so that whether or not [*name of person concerned*] either has, or lacks, capacity for other purposes is not determinative of whether or not [*name of person concerned*] has capacity to conduct these proceedings. Please note that the question of capacity to conduct the proceedings is to be considered by reference to the proceedings in question and *"not by reference to each step in the process of litigation"* (Lord Justice Kennedy at paragraph 27 in the case of *Masterman-Lister* referred to below).

The purpose of your instruction is to assist the court in deciding whether this is a case in which a litigation friend should be appointed for [*name of person concerned*].

To assist you when considering the information relevant to [*name of person concerned*]'s capacity to conduct the proceedings I have set out below the legal framework for assessment of capacity to conduct proceedings and the context within which capacity to conduct the proceedings falls to be considered in this case.

## 3 LEGAL FRAMEWORK

Whilst the principles in section 1 of the MCA are expressed to apply only for the purposes of the MCA I would nonetheless invite you have to regard to those principles when carrying out your assessment. They include the following: a person must be assumed to have capacity unless it is established that he lacks capacity; a person is not to be treated as unable to make a decision unless all practicable steps to help him to do so have been taken without success; and a person is not to be treated as unable to make a decision merely because he makes an unwise decision.

Sections 2 and 3 of the MCA define what is meant by lack of capacity.

Section 2 and 3 provide (insofar as is material):

### Section 2 – People who lack capacity

(1) For the purposes of this Act, a person lacks capacity in relation to a matter if at the material time he is unable to make a decision for himself in relation to the matter because of an impairment of, or a disturbance in the functioning of, the mind or brain.
(2) It does not matter whether the impairment or disturbance is permanent or temporary.
(3) A lack of capacity cannot be established merely by reference to—
   (a) a person's age or appearance, or
   (b) a condition of his, or an aspect of his behaviour, which might lead others to make unjustified assumptions about his capacity.
(4) In proceedings under this Act or any other enactment, any question whether a person lacks capacity within the meaning of this Act must be decided on the balance of probabilities ...

### Section 3 – Inability to make decisions

(1) For the purposes of section 2, a person is unable to make a decision for himself if he is unable—
   (a) to understand the information relevant to the decision,
   (b) to retain that information,
   (c) to use or weigh that information as part of the process of making the decision, or
   (d) to communicate his decision (whether by talking, using sign language or any other means).
(2) A person is not to be regarded as unable to understand the information relevant to a decision if he is able to understand an explanation of it given to him in a way that is appropriate to his circumstances (using simple language, visual aids or any other means).
(3) The fact that a person is able to retain the information relevant to a decision for a short period only does not prevent him from being regarded as able to make the decision.
(4) The information relevant to a decision includes information about the reasonably foreseeable consequences of—
   (a) deciding one way or another, or
   (b) failing to make the decision.

The Code of Practice ("the Code") which supports the MCA 2005 refers to a two-stage capacity test comprising:

(i) Stage 1 (the "diagnostic test"): Does the person have an impairment of, or a disturbance in the functioning of, their mind or brain?
(ii) Stage 2 (the "functional test"): Does the impairment or disturbance mean that the person is unable to make a specific decision when they need to?

Please note that the Code also expressly confirms (at paragraph 4.32) that common law tests of capacity have survived the enactment of the MCA.

The leading case on the common law approach to capacity to conduct proceedings is that of *Masterman-Lister v Brutton & Co* [2003] 3 All ER 162 in which Lord Justice Chadwick stated the following:

> "... the test to be applied ... is whether the party to legal proceedings is capable of understanding, with the assistance of such proper explanation from legal advisors and experts in other disciplines as the case may require, the issues on which his consent or decision is likely to be necessary in the course of those proceedings ...

(paragraph 75)

and

> ... a person should not be held unable to understand the information relevant to a decision if he can understand an explanation of that information in broad terms and simple language; and that he should not be regarded as unable to make a rational decision merely because the decision which he does in fact make is a decision which would not be made by a person of ordinary prudence ...

(paragraph 79)

In the same case Lord Justice Kennedy commented as follows (at paragraph 26):

> "... the mental abilities required include the ability to recognise a problem, obtain and receive, understand and retain relevant information, including advice; the ability to weigh the information (including that derived from advice) in the balance in reaching a decision, and the ability to communicate that decision ..."

and (at paragraph 27):

> "... Of course, as Boreham J said in White's case, capacity must be approached in a common sense way, not by reference to each step in the process of litigation, but bearing in mind the basic right of any person to manage his property and affairs for himself, a right with which no lawyer and no court should rush to interfere ...

## 4 THESE PROCEEDINGS

### Legal context for the proceedings

I set out below the context within which **[name of the person concerned]** will need to be advised and give instructions.

The application before the court is an application for a care order under section 31 Children Act 1989.

Before a care order is made the court must be satisfied that the child concerned is suffering or is likely to suffer significant harm and that the harm or likelihood of harm is attributable to the care given to the child, or likely to be given to the child if the order were not made, not being what it would be reasonable to expect a parent to give to him; or that the child is beyond parental control. If a care order is made the child is placed in the care of the local authority, the local authority shares parental responsibility for the child with the child's parents, and has the power to determine the extent to which a parent or other person with parental responsibility for the child may meet their parental responsibility for the child.

You should be aware that a range of other possible orders may come up for consideration during the course of care proceedings including:

i) a special guardianship order
(an order appointing one or more individuals as special guardian(s) for the child – a special guardian has parental responsibility for the child and is entitled to exercise parental responsibility to the exclusion of any other person with parental responsibility for the child)
ii) a residence order
(an order settling the arrangements to be made as to the person with whom the child is to live)
iii) a supervision order
(an order which puts the supervisor under a duty to advise, assist and befriend the supervised child, to take such steps as may be reasonably necessary to give effect to the order and where the order is not wholly complied with or the supervisor considers that the order may no longer be necessary to consider whether or not to apply to the court for its variation or discharge).
iv) a contact order
(an order requiring the person with whom a child lives or is to live to allow the child to visit or stay with the person named in the order or for that person and the child otherwise to have contact with each other).

You should also be aware that pursuant to section 22(2) of the Adoption and Children Act 2002 if an application has been made (and has not been disposed of) on which a care order might be made in respect of a child, or a child is subject to a care order and the appropriate local authority are not authorised to place the child for adoption the appropriate local authority must apply to the court for a placement order if they are satisfied that the child ought to be placed for adoption.

This means that during the course of the care proceedings an application may (although not necessarily will) also be issued for a placement order. In such event the placement application will run concurrently with the care application and the hearing may follow immediately after the hearing on the care order (if a care order is made).

A placement order authorises a local authority to place a child for adoption with any prospective adopters who may be chosen by the local authority.

## The facts of this case

*[insert:*

- *brief summary of the proceedings;*
- *if it appears to you or you are being told that the proceedings are particularly complex, then you should say so and set out the reasons;*
- *if it is the view of the solicitors for the person concerned, or the view of others involved in the proceedings that the person concerned is unable to make decisions about the conduct of the proceedings, you should say so and give their reasons;*
- *you should also say if the person concerned asserts their own capacity].*

## 5 DOCUMENTS

I enclose:

1. An indexed bundle of all documents filed in the case so far;
2. Practice Direction: Experts in Family Proceedings Relating to Children, 13 February 2008;
3. Certificate of capacity to conduct the proceedings;
4. [Medical notes of the person concerned];
5. [Any other assessments of the person concerned outside of the proceedings].

As the lead solicitor I will also send you copies of any relevant documents filed after the date of this letter.

## 6 CONTACT WITH OTHERS

Pursuant to an order dated, you are being instructed by ............... but on the basis that you will provide an expert opinion independent of the person(s) from whom you have received your instructions or by whom you are paid.

It is expected that you will have one or more meetings with *[name of person concerned]* in order to carry out your assessment. If you believe that it would assist you to meet with, or speak to any other person as part of your assessment, please notify me and I will make the necessary arrangements.

It is essential both to your role as an independent expert and to the parties' perception of your independent status that there are no informal unrecorded discussions or correspondence with any of the professionals or the lay parties involved in the case.

**[I set out below the details of:**

**insert details of any other relevant person whom the expert may need to contact, for example, treating psychiatrist or other clinician, adult social worker, community psychiatric nurse, keyworker for the person concerned, lay advocate etc]**

If you need further information, please contact me and I will provide it after consultation with the other legal representatives. If documents are exchanged with one party, please copy them to all the others. Where possible, communication is best achieved by fax or letter.

## 7 FACTUAL ISSUES AND YOUR REPORT

Unless you have been specifically asked to do so, you should avoid expressing a view regarding the factual disputes as this is, of course, the task of the Court at the final hearing. Where appropriate, it will be of assistance if you are able to express your opinion on the basis of alternative findings regarding the factual disputes.

I am under a duty to disclose your report to the court and to the other parties and we will circulate your report on receipt. If you believe, as a rare exception to the general rule, that it should not be disclosed to any party (including [*name of person concerned*]), please let me know and I will seek the court's directions.

Your report may be subject to challenge including by [*name of person concerned*]. It is possible that one or more of the parties may put written questions to you following receipt of your report or that you may be asked to make an addendum report addressed to other issues during the course of this case.

## 8 YOUR INSTRUCTIONS

1. Does [*name of person concerned*] lack capacity within the meaning of the Mental Capacity Act 2005 to conduct the proceedings?
2. If so, I shall be grateful if, in addition to your report, you would complete the enclosed certificate of capacity to conduct the proceedings and return it to me.
    Please ensure when completing the certificate that you set out:
    - your own qualifications and your experience in assessing capacity;
    - your degree of familiarity with [*name of person concerned*];
    - reference to the particular factors which impact on, or restrict capacity to conduct the proceedings;
    - any particular tests carried out;
    - whether capacity has fluctuated in the past, and/or if [*name of the person concerned*] may recover capacity to conduct the proceedings in

a reasonable time frame, and if so, what that time frame may be and what support, assistance or other practicable steps which could be offered to that end.

I also refer you to the guidance notes attached to the certificate which you should read before completing the certificate.

3. Please include within your report a record of any views expressed by [*name of person concerned*] regarding:
   i) his/her capacity to conduct the proceedings.
   ii) support, assistance or other practicable steps which would be helpful in enhancing his/her involvement in the proceedings.

[4. If [*name of person concerned*] has capacity to conduct the proceedings please comment on:
   i) whether there are particular factors which (whilst not causing a lack of capacity to conduct the proceedings) impact on, or restrict [*name of person concerned*]'s his/her ability to conduct the proceedings; and on
   ii) whether any support, assistance or other practicable steps should be offered to [*name of person concerned*] in order to assist in overcoming the difficulties identified at (i) above.

5. Please include in your report a full cognitive assessment of [*name of person concerned*] and comment on [*name of person concerned*]'s present level of functioning.]

The certificate may be returned in advance of your substantive report, and should be returned as soon as possible, if it is your finding that [*name of person concerned*] does lack capacity to conduct the proceedings.

If, during the course of your assessment, other issues appear to you to become relevant, please immediately contact me as lead solicitor. After consultation with the other legal representatives, I will inform you if the scope of your instructions should be amended.

## 9 EXPERT'S DUTIES

I draw your attention to paragraphs 3.1–3.3 of the Practice Direction in particular which set out the duties of an expert and the matters which must be included within an expert's report.

## 10 TIMESCALE

[insert]

It is important that you comply with this time limit as the issue of [*name of person concerned*] must be resolved as soon as possible having regard to the fact that delay in the progression of these proceedings is likely to prejudice the welfare of the child/ren.

## 11 YOUR FEES

**[insert]**

Please do not hesitate to contact me if you wish to discuss this request, or if you need any further clarification or assistance.

Yours sincerely

AB
X, Y, Z & Co

# Appendix 7

# FAMILY PROCEDURE RULES 2010, PT 15

**A.7**

\*\*\*\*

## PART 15
## REPRESENTATION OF PROTECTED PARTIES

### 15.1 Application of this Part

This Part contains special provisions which apply in proceedings involving protected parties.

### 15.2 Requirement for litigation friend in proceedings

A protected party must have a litigation friend to conduct proceedings on that party's behalf.

### 15.3 Stage of proceedings at which a litigation friend becomes necessary

(1) A person may not without the permission of the court take any step in proceedings except –

    (*a*)   filing an application form; or
    (*b*)   applying for the appointment of a litigation friend under rule 15.6,

until the protected party has a litigation friend.

(2) If during proceedings a party lacks capacity (within the meaning of the 2005 Act) to continue to conduct proceedings, no party may take any step in proceedings without the permission of the court until the protected party has a litigation friend.

(3) Any step taken before a protected party has a litigation friend has no effect unless the court orders otherwise.

### 15.4 Who may be a litigation friend for a protected party without a court order

(1) This rule does not apply if the court has appointed a person to be a litigation friend.

(2) A person with authority as a deputy to conduct the proceedings in the name of a protected party or on that party's behalf is entitled to be the litigation friend of the protected party in any proceedings to which that person's authority extends.

(3) If there is no person with authority as a deputy to conduct the proceedings in the name of a protected party or on that party's behalf, a person may act as a litigation friend if that person –

    (a) can fairly and competently conduct proceedings on behalf of the protected party;
    (b) has no interest adverse to that of the protected party; and
    (c) subject to paragraph (4), undertakes to pay any costs which the protected party may be ordered to pay in relation to the proceedings, subject to any right that person may have to be repaid from the assets of the protected party.

(4) Paragraph (3)(c) does not apply to the Official Solicitor.

    ('deputy' is defined in rule 2.3.)

### 15.5 How a person becomes a litigation friend without a court order

(1) If the court has not appointed a litigation friend, a person who wishes to act as a litigation friend must follow the procedure set out in this rule.

(2) A person with authority as a deputy to conduct the proceedings in the name of a protected party or on that party's behalf must file an official copy$^{(GL)}$ of the order, declaration or other document which confers that person's authority to act.

(3) Any other person must file a certificate of suitability stating that that person satisfies the conditions specified in rule 15.4(3).

(4) A person who is to act as a litigation friend must file –

    (a) the document conferring that person's authority to act; or
    (b) the certificate of suitability,

at the time when that person first takes a step in the proceedings on behalf of the protected party.

(5) A court officer will send the certificate of suitability to every person on whom, in accordance with rule 6.28, the application form should be served.

(6) This rule does not apply to the Official Solicitor.

### 15.6 How a person becomes a litigation friend by court order

(1) The court may, if the person to be appointed so consents, make an order appointing –

    (a) a person other than the Official Solicitor; or
    (b) the Official Solicitor,

as a litigation friend.

(2) An order appointing a litigation friend may be made by the court of its own initiative or on the application of –

    (a) a person who wishes to be a litigation friend; or

(b) a party to the proceedings.

(3) The court may at any time direct that a party make an application for an order under paragraph (2).

(4) An application for an order appointing a litigation friend must be supported by evidence.

(5) Unless the court directs otherwise, a person appointed under this rule to be a litigation friend for a protected party will be treated as a party for the purpose of any provision in these Rules requiring a document to be served on, or sent to, or notice to be given to, a party to the proceedings.

(6) Subject to rule 15.4(4), the court may not appoint a litigation friend under this rule unless it is satisfied that the person to be appointed complies with the conditions specified in rule 15.4(3).

### 15.7 Court's power to change litigation friend and to prevent person acting as litigation friend

(1) The court may –

    (a)    direct that a person may not act as a litigation friend;
    (b)    terminate a litigation friend's appointment; or
    (c)    appoint a new litigation friend in substitution for an existing one.

(2) An application for an order or direction under paragraph (1) must be supported by evidence.

(3) Subject to rule 15.4(4), the court may not appoint a litigation friend under this rule unless it is satisfied that the person to be appointed complies with the conditions specified in rule 15.4(3).

### 15.8 Appointment of litigation friend by court order – supplementary

(1) A copy of the application for an order under rule 15.6 or 15.7 must be sent by a court officer to –

    (a)    every person on whom, in accordance with rule 6.28, the application form should be served; and
    (b)    unless the court directs otherwise, the protected party.

(2) A copy of an application for an order under rule 15.7 must also be sent to –

    (a)    the person who is the litigation friend, or who is purporting to act as the litigation friend, when the application is made; and
    (b)    the person, if not the applicant, who it is proposed should be the litigation friend.

### 15.9 Procedure where appointment of litigation friend comes to an end

(1) When a party ceases to be a protected party, the litigation friend's appointment continues until it is brought to an end by a court order.

(2) An application for an order under paragraph (1) may be made by –

(a) the former protected party;
(b) the litigation friend; or
(c) a party.

(3) On the making of an order under paragraph (1), the court officer will send a notice to the other parties stating that the appointment of the protected party's litigation friend to act has ended.

\*\*\*\*

## PRACTICE DIRECTION 15A – PROTECTED PARTIES

This Practice Direction supplements FPR Part 15

### General

1.1 A protected party must have a litigation friend to conduct proceedings on the protected party's behalf.

1.2 In the proceedings the protected party should be referred to in the title as 'A.B. (by C.D. his/her litigation friend)'.

### Duties of the Litigation Friend

2.1 It is the duty of a litigation friend fairly and competently to conduct proceedings on behalf of a protected party. The litigation friend must have no interest in the proceedings adverse to that of the protected party and all steps and decisions the litigation friend takes in the proceedings must be taken for the benefit of the protected party.

### Becoming a Litigation Friend without a court order

3.1 In order to become a litigation friend without a court order the person who wishes to act as litigation friend must –

(a) file an official copy of the order, declaration or other document which confers the litigation friend's authority as a deputy to conduct the proceedings in the name of a protected party or on his/her behalf; or
(b) file a certificate of suitability –
    (i) stating that the litigation friend consents to act;
    (ii) stating that the litigation friend knows or believes that the [applicant][respondent] lacks capacity (within the meaning of the 2005 Act) to conduct proceedings;
    (iii) stating the grounds of that belief and if the belief is based upon medical opinion attaching any relevant document to the certificate;
    (iv) stating that the litigation friend can fairly and competently conduct proceedings on behalf of the protected party and has no interest adverse to that of the protected party;

(v) undertaking to pay any costs which the protected party may be ordered to pay in relation to the proceedings, subject to any right the litigation friend may have to be repaid from the assets of the protected party; and

(vi) which the litigation friend has verified by a statement of truth.

3.2 Paragraph 3.1 does not apply to the Official Solicitor.

3.3 The court officer will send the certificate of suitability to the person who is the attorney of a registered enduring power of attorney, donee of a lasting power of attorney or deputy or, if there is no such person, to the person with whom the protected party resides or in whose care the protected party is.

3.4 The court officer is not required to send the documents referred to in paragraph 3.1(*b*)(iii) when sending the certificate of suitability to the person to be served under paragraph 3.3.

3.5 The litigation friend must file either the certificate of suitability or the authority referred to in paragraph 3.1(*a*) at a time when the litigation friend first takes a step in the proceedings on behalf of the protected party.

### Application for a court order appointing a litigation friend

4.1 An application for a court order appointing a litigation friend should be made in accordance with Part 18 and must be supported by evidence.

4.2 The court officer must serve the application notice –

(*a*) on the persons referred to in paragraph 3.3; and
(*b*) on the protected party unless the court directs otherwise.

4.3 The evidence in support must satisfy the court that the proposed litigation friend –

(*a*) consents to act;
(*b*) can fairly and competently conduct proceedings on behalf of the protected party;
(*c*) has no interest adverse to that of the protected party; and
(*d*) undertakes to pay any costs which the protected party may be ordered to pay in relation to the proceedings, subject to any right the litigation friend may have to be repaid from the assets of the protected party.

4.4 Paragraph 4.3(*d*) does not apply to the Official Solicitor.

4.5 The proposed litigation friend may be one of the persons referred to in paragraph 3.3 where appropriate, or otherwise may be the Official Solicitor. Where it is sought to appoint the Official Solicitor, provision must be made for payment of his charges.

### Change of litigation friend and prevention of person acting as litigation friend.

5.1 Where an application is made for an order under rule 15.7, the application must set out the reasons for seeking it and must be supported by evidence.

5.2 Subject to paragraph 4.4, if the order sought is substitution of a new litigation friend for an existing one, the evidence must satisfy the court of the matters set out in paragraph 4.3.

5.3 The court officer will serve the application notice on –

(*a*)   the persons referred to in paragraph 3.3; and
(*b*)   the litigation friend or person purporting to act as litigation friend.

**Procedure where the need for a litigation friend has come to an end**

6.1 Where a person who was a protected party regains or acquires capacity (within the meaning of the 2005 Act) to conduct the proceedings, an application under rule 15.9(2) must be made for an order under rule 15.9(1) that the litigation friend's appointment has ceased.

6.2 The application must be supported by the following evidence –

(*a*)   a medical report or other suitably qualified expert's report indicating that the protected party has regained or acquired capacity (within the meaning of the 2005 Act) to conduct the proceedings; and
(*b*)   a copy of any relevant order or declaration of the Court of Protection.

# Appendix 8

# LEARNING DISABILITY: DEFINITIONS AND CONTEXTS

**Professional Affairs Board of The British Psychological Society, 2000**

## A.8

## INTRODUCTION

Following the introduction of new and revised mental health and local government legislation in the 1980s,[1] the British Psychological Society published a guidance document, *Mental Impairment and Severe Mental Impairment: A Search for Definitions* (BPS, 1991). This document highlighted the different definitions used within the respective Acts, and offered guidelines on operational criteria. The document was generally well received within the profession and was followed, in 1995, by a similar paper relating specifically to the Mental Health (N. Ireland) Order 1986.[2]

The original documents focused on specific pieces of legislation which used the terms *'(severe) mental impairment'* and *'(severe) mental handicap'*. This led to some debate regarding the need for a broader document with respect to 'learning disability' and its relation to other legislation in a wider context. As a result, the Society's Professional Affairs Board invited the Special Interest Group (Learning Disabilities) of the Division of Clinical Psychology to look again at these documents, with a view to updating and, where appropriate, amending them to cover a broader field. This document is the result of that review.

The guidelines presented in this document are not intended to be sufficient for a full psychological assessment for adults with learning disabilities. The nature of any such assessment would obviously depend on individual circumstances but, within most contexts, reliance solely on overall figures derived from assessments of intellectual functioning and/or other norm-based assessments would have limited value.[3] Indeed, presenting an overall figure derived from

---

[1] The Mental Health Act 1983, the Mental Health (Scotland) Act 1984, the Abolition of Domestic Rates (Scotland) Act 1987 and the Local Government Finance Act 1988.
[2] British Psychological Society (1995). *Mental Handicap, Severe Mental Handicap and Severe Mental Impairment: The Mental Health (N.Ireland) Order 1986. Definitions and Operational Guidelines.*
[3] It is accepted that the use of such instruments to profile abilities, particularly within a neurological context, does have value and, used in this way, such, well chosen, assessments

such assessments may be misleading and potentially damaging, particularly if used in any predictive sense.[4] Psychologists should be sensitive to the issues related to labelling[5] – particularly in terms of test scores alone – and should resist simplistic interpretations of an individual's need based on broad classifications.

There has been a welcome trend away from assessments based exclusively on psychometric test results which lead solely to simple classification and categorisation of 'learning disability', to one which seeks to assess individual need and to identify the necessary supports to meet that need.[6]

To be valid, a psychological assessment needs to be based on a comprehensive analysis, including reference to biological, psychological and interactional factors, within the broader social/cultural and environmental context.

As the concept of learning disabilities may be seen as a social construction[7] – even when the biological/neurological basis is known – the idea of any permanency of the concept must be questioned, as the phenomenon of IQ drift, and its changing criteria, clearly illustrate.

However, *given* its social construction, and whatever one's views are on its theoretical basis, it has to be acknowledged that the concept is enshrined within our social and legal systems. As such, the concept affects peoples' legal and civil rights.

Some psychologists may find that the concept of classification presents some personal difficulties, particularly as it may have lasting implications on an individual's life. Over time many injustices have been done to people labelled as *different*. However, there are situations in which an opinion on classification can assist a person to gain access to civil and legal rights and protections. For example, to prove discrimination, to argue against denial of an 'appropriate adult' during police questioning,[8] to consider a case under the Sexual Offences

---

afford people with learning disabilities access to the same type of service provided for people with disorders of neurological functioning but who do not have learning disabilities. However, within this context, it would be the interpretation of the range of scores that would be of importance, not the overall figure *per se*.

[4] This point is relevant in all areas but particularly so for children and young adults.

[5] Labelling can be socially devaluing. Equally, it can be argued that it is not the labelling *per se* which is of prime significance but the *social consequence* of the labelling. Construed in this way, meaningful change for individuals would include change within the wider social and political systems (see Bell, 1989; Szivos, 1992; Brown & Smith, 1992, for general discussion).

[6] The American Association on Mental Retardation (AAMR, 1992) avoids reliance on IQ scores to assign a level of disability by suggesting a framework which relates the person's needs to the intensities of '... *the supports necessary to enhance their independence/interdependence, productivity and community integration.*' However, even under this system, there is an agreed definition of Mental Retardation which does rely on assessments of intellectual and social functioning.

[7] See Clements (1998) for discussion.

[8] Under the Police and Criminal Evidence Act 1984 (PACE).

Acts 1956[9]/1967, at some point it may be appropriate to consider whether a person could be seen to have a *(severe)* learning disability. Without acknowledgement of the disability a person might be denied rights to justice and/or equality.

This document was proposed in response to an expressed need for guidance on how the concept of learning disabilities, as used within a health and personal social services setting, relates to its use in civil, legal and medico-legal contexts.

Much of the content of the Society's original documents has been retained. The Society wishes to reaffirm its view that the guidance offered should be used both with caution and in full knowledge of the limitations of classification within specific contexts.

## SCOPE OF THE CURRENT GUIDELINES

The functions of this document are to outline the features that make up the definition of 'learning disability', as used within a health and social care context, and to introduce the complexities of the use of that term in a variety of other contexts. Recommendations regarding good practice are also included.

There are a number of areas *not* covered by these guidelines, one of which is 'mental (in)capacity'. This is a legal concept, involving a person's ability to make informed decisions (e.g. about medical treatments, financial matters, contracts, wills, etc.). Clearly, there is a relationship between intellectual ability and mental capacity. However, 'learning disability' and 'mental incapacity' are *not* synonymous, and it is possible for someone to have a 'learning disability' and yet also to be deemed as 'mentally capable'.[10] Further, mental incapacity may arise for reasons other than learning disability (e.g. dementia, mental illness, acquired brain damage in adulthood, etc.). Any assessment relating to mental incapacity or consent should not rely on generalised inferences relating to the broad categorisation of people. Assessments for this purpose should always be conducted within the context of the particular issue in question and of the particular individual concerned.[11]

Equally, even if an assessment is made with respect to classification, it is unlikely – except in certain instances[12] – that this will be sufficiently comprehensive or meaningful. Further work would be required to assess exactly how the learning disability might affect a person's performance within

---

[9] For Scotland, Mental Health (Scotland) Act 1984 (s 106).
[10] Williams (1995) notes that there '... *should be an assumption that witnesses with learning disabilities are competent, both in law and in practice, and that the burden of proof for determining otherwise should be put on the party challenging competence*'.
[11] Command Paper Cm 3803 (1997); Command Paper Cm 4465 (1999); Cohen (1998); Gelsthorpe (1998).
[12] Perhaps within the context of the Sexual Offences Acts 1956/1967.

the relevant setting, and what additional supports he/she might need.[13] Again, discussion on the range of assessment required within this context falls outside the scope of these guidelines.

This document deals only with *adults* with learning disabilities, and as such specifically excludes discussion on legislation and assessment relating to children. Guidance on the assessment of children is available elsewhere within the Society.[14]

Owing to the different legislative systems, some difficulties are encountered when producing one document that is relevant for use throughout the UK. Because of this, Part 2 of this document, *Associated Contexts,* makes some compromises and, thus, focuses on commonalities (whilst *highlighting* differences) between the respective UK legislation. Readers requiring specific detail on a particular piece of legislation should refer to the appropriate Statute.

# PART 1: DEFINING 'LEARNING DISABILITY'[15]

People with learning disabilities do not constitute an homogeneous group. However, in terms of diagnosis and classification there are a number of features of learning disability which have gained widespread acceptance across professional boundaries within the UK and America.[16] Irrespective of the precise terminology, or the wording in the various definitions, there are three core criteria for learning disability:

- **Significant impairment of intellectual functioning;**
- **Significant impairment of adaptive/social functioning;**
- **Age of onset before adulthood.**

All three criteria must be met for a person to be considered to have a learning disability (see Appendix I for further details of the main clinical conditions).

Difficulties in assessing adaptive/social functioning have contributed, in the past, to a tendency amongst clinicians to concentrate on assessment of

---

[13] For example, as a witness in court (see Sanders *et al.*, 1996).
[14] Contact the Division of Educational and Child Psychology and the Division of Clinical Psychology, Special Interest Group – Children and Young People.
[15] At present, within the UK, *learning disability/disabilities* is the terminology with the greatest currency and, within the context of health and social care, has largely replaced the term *mental handicap* – although *mental handicap* is still used in the Mental Health (N Ireland) Order, 1986. *Intellectual disabilities* is favoured by some authorities – but using this terminology, there is a danger that the concept could be construed solely as one relating to intellectual impairment (i.e. excluding the aspect of adaptive/social functioning). The term *mental retardation* is in common usage in North America.
[16] American Association on Mental Retardation, 1992; World Health Organisation, 1992 (ICD-10); American Psychiatric Association, 1994 (DSM-IV); Department of Health, 1998.

intellectual functioning only. The assumption has been that, provided a significant impairment of intellectual functioning has been demonstrated, similar deficits in adaptive/social functioning are likely. However, this is not always the case.

**The Society recommends that, in accordance with the various definitions, classification of learning disability should only be made on the basis of assessed impairments of both intellectual and adaptive/social functioning which have been acquired before adulthood.**

## 1.1 ASSESSMENT OF IMPAIRMENT OF INTELLECTUAL FUNCTIONING

The principal method for determining levels of intellectual functioning still remains psychometric assessment. Assessments which are based on an explicit model of normal distribution of general intelligence are the procedures of choice.

Assessment of general intellectual functioning, for clinical, medico-legal and other purposes, should be obtained through the use of an individually administered test which is recognised as being reliable, valid and properly standardised. The test employed in any given case must be appropriate for the person's age, cultural, linguistic and social background.

Using tests based on a normal distribution of general intelligence, significant impairment of intellectual functioning has, by convention, become defined as a performance more than two standard deviations below the population mean. On the Wechsler Adult Intelligence Scale – Revised (WAIS-R) (Wechsler, 1981; Lea, 1986), the most commonly used measure of general intellectual functioning for the adult population, and the more recently published WAIS-III[UK] (Wechsler, 1999), the mean is 100 and the standard deviation is 15. More than two standard deviations below the mean thus corresponds to an Intelligence Quotient (IQ) of 69 or less.[17]

IQ scores for individual cases should always be quoted with explicit confidence limits. Confidence limits represent the probable extent of measurement error for scores derived from a particular test. On the Wechsler scales, the 95 per cent confidence limits vary with age group and measured IQ level (see Appendix III).

---

[17] The 'cut-off' for 'learning disability' of an IQ of 69 is in line with both ICD-10 and DSM-IV (see Appendix I): the former states that *'an IQ of 69 or below is indicative of mental retardation'*, while the latter notes that the *'disorder is characterised by significantly sub average intellectual functioning (an IQ of approximately 70 or below)'*. It should be noted, however, that any overly strict cut-off criterion would not fully reflect the limitations inherent within each test. Informed clinical judgement would be required especially around transitional cut-off points.

When conducting psychometric assessments of intellectual functioning, careful consideration should be given to differentiating between performance which is due to learning disability and performance which is impaired by other factors. For example, the presence of emotional/psychological distress (or other psychological/psychiatric factors), medication, alcohol or other drugs, may have consequences in terms of (perhaps, temporary) diminution in performance. Similarly, caution will need to be exercised regarding the assessment of individuals with cognitive impairments acquired during adulthood as a consequence of neurological trauma or disease. These acquired impairments may exhibit through generalised flattening of scores, or extreme variability in IQ or test Index or sub-test scores, or through specific deficits.

The findings from these assessments should always be interpreted in the light of knowledge of the individual's personal, cultural circumstances, clinical status and other assessment information, and with a sound knowledge of the uses and limitations of such assessment methods.

**The Society notes that psychometric test results, in particular, are open to misrepresentation or inappropriate usage. In order to achieve the best possible understanding of the technical information given, and to avoid misuse, non-psychologist readers of this document are encouraged to make use of available help from a qualified psychologist whose credentials are recognised by the profession, i.e. a Chartered Psychologist.**

## 1.2 IMPAIRMENT OF ADAPTIVE/SOCIAL FUNCTIONING

### 1.2.1 DEFINITION OF ADAPTIVE/SOCIAL FUNCTIONING

The concept of adaptive/social functioning is very broad and relates to a person's performance in coping on a day-to-day basis with the demands of his/her environment. It is, therefore, very much related to a person's age and the socio-cultural expectancies associated with his/her environment at any given time. It is concerned with what a person *does* (i.e. actual behaviour/ performance).

The concept of *'adaptive functioning'* has been further refined by reference to its component parts. Both the American Association on Mental Retardation (AAMR, 1992) and DSM-IV[18] adopt a criterion of impairments in 'at least two' of the following areas: *communication, self-care, home living, social/ interpersonal skills, use of community resources, self direction, functional academic skills, work, leisure, health and safety.* The use of *'at least two'* impairments as a criterion may, however, produce some anomalies, with little

---

[18] *Diagnostic and Statistical Manual of Mental Disorders* – 4th Edition (American Psychiatric Association, 1994).

face validity. For example, in the case where, perhaps, only *work* and *leisure* are impaired (with other skills intact), the extent of the overall impairment of adaptive skills may be questioned. Additionally, the DSM-IV gives no guidance concerning the *severity* of impairment within the respective areas.

Within the context of 'mental impairment', the BPS document (1991) focused on the concept of *'social functioning'*, which included only those skills that may be considered as *personal life survival skills* – other skills, related more to interpersonal/cultural/social aspects of day-to-day living, and alluded to in other definitions, were omitted.[19,20,21] By excluding wider aspects of social/community adaptation, it is now considered that the previous BPS definition (1991) is unduly restrictive. By broadening the criteria, it is accepted that the tightness of the previous definition has been lost. Nevertheless the following is recommended:

***Impairment of Adaptive/Social Functioning*** – **The individual requires significant assistance to provide for his/her own survival (eating and drinking needs and to keep himself/herself clean, warm and clothed), and/or with his/her social/ community adaptation (e.g. social problem solving, and social reasoning).**

The degree of assistance required may vary in terms of intensity (e.g. physical or verbal prompting) and frequency (e.g. daily or less often than daily), but the required assistance should always be outside the range of that expected within the individual's particular culture/community.

## 1.2.2 ASSESSMENT OF ADAPTIVE/SOCIAL FUNCTIONING

Despite the difficulties in defining adaptive/social functioning, there exists a variety of scales purporting to measure it. These are completed usually by direct observation and/or in conjunction with at least one informant who knows the person well (for example, a parent, carer or friend).

Assessments of adaptive/social functioning may be norm-referenced, criterion-referenced and those of the skills checklist variety.[22,23] The use of any

---

[19] Gunn (1996) notes that, from a legal perspective, *'social functioning ... includes such matters as: ability to care for oneself; personal hygiene; personal and social (perhaps sexual) relationships with others'*.

[20] Nunkoosing (1995) cites two components: *'personal independence'* (being able to sustain oneself in everyday living activities) and *'social responsibility'* (being able to conduct oneself appropriately in social situations).

[21] AAMR (1992) refers to two facets of social functioning: *'practical intelligence'* and *'social intelligence'*.

[22] For information about the validity and reliability of the tests available, Hogg and Raynes (1987) remains a useful text although some assessments have had subsequent revisions.

[23] Those scales that list some psychometric properties and/or normative data include the *AAMR Adaptive Behaviour Scale – Residential and Community* (Nihira, Leland & Lambert, 1993); the *Vineland Adaptive Behaviour Scales* (Sparrow, Balla & Chichetti, 1984) and the *Hampshire Assessment for Living with Others (*Shackleton Bailey *et al.,* 1982).

one such assessment should be considered only after some scrutiny, and with reference to the specific item content, as some scales consist of items that may extend the definition of adaptive/social functioning beyond that given above.[24]

An assessment of adaptive/social functioning must be made with reference to the person's age, gender, socio-cultural background, religion and community setting. To be relevant, within the context of learning disability, any impairment of adaptive/social functioning must not *solely* be a consequence of other disabilities (e.g. physical illness, mental health problems or sensory impairment).

**Despite the inherent difficulties with many such instruments, the use of a formal assessment of adaptive/social functioning should be seen as good practice. At least one assessment (preferably completed with more than one informant, and on more than one occasion) should be carried out.**

**The Society believes that there is not, as yet, sufficient consensus within the area for one single assessment to be recommended. Judgement will need to be made based on item analysis of the assessment and on the significance of any impairment (see Section 1.4.2).**

## 1.3 AGE OF ONSET

For a person to be considered to have a learning disability, significant impairments of intellectual and adaptive/social functioning must have been acquired during the developmental period. There is some consensus that the Age of Onset criterion is *below 18 years*.[25,26] However, there is some concern, shared by many clinicians, that people acquiring learning disabilities later in childhood (but before the age of 18 years) as a consequence of cerebral trauma may face different challenges than a person showing learning disabilities from infancy.

This issue may not be significant if individualised assessments are undertaken with the intention of identifying a person's support needs. However, if such assessments are simply used to serve a 'gate-keeping' function, for example (see

---

[24] Analysis of some assessments of adaptive/social functioning reveal sub-tests of a *descriptive* nature (e.g. *Physical Disability, Posture*) rather than having an *operational* criteria – the former may have an *influence* on adaptive functioning but do not *measure* actual behaviour/performance.

[25] Whilst both the DSM-IV and the AAMR (1992) recommend an age criterion for *Age of Onset* of before 18 years, the ICD-10 (WHO, 1992) makes no specific criterion other than '... *during the developmental period*'. Hatton (1998) draws attention to the cultural nature of this age criterion.

[26] Given its cultural nature, and with reference to Sexual Offences legislation, theoretically there may be some advantage to linking this age of onset criterion to the 'age of consent' for sexual relationships. However, this would also lead to major discrepancies, particularly with respect to the variable ages of consent in different countries (even within the UK) and/or where age of consent is dependent on gender and/or type (heterosexual or other) of sexual relationship.

Section 2.5 below), such a person may be disadvantaged if this results in exclusion from a more appropriate service (e.g. one designed for people with acquired brain damage).

In order to determine the most appropriate service support, it is recommended that the effect of acquired impairment on a previously higher, non-impaired level of functioning is taken into account. Particular reference should be made to any profile of psychometric sub-test scores that would indicate, clinically, that the person's abilities would be more appropriately construed as specific brain/neurological damage.

**The Society recommends that in all cases where a medical condition or trauma is present, the age this occurred should be documented, whether before birth, at birth or during childhood.**

Age of onset before adulthood may be demonstrated by historical evidence from medical records (e.g. developmental milestones), educational records such as a Statement of Educational Need, or records of previous use of specialist health and social services. However, it is always possible for an individual to have 'slipped through the net'. Any historical information needs to be interpreted with care as functioning can change over time and the results of different psychometric assessments are usually not directly comparable.

## 1.4 SYSTEMS OF SUB-CLASSIFICATION

Within the clinical context, sub-classifications of *mild, moderate, severe and profound* 'mental retardation' are used in two main classification/diagnostic manuals.[27] Although these systems employ the same descriptive categories, the quoted IQ ranges do not correspond exactly.

It is notable that the AAMR (1992) no longer uses these four clinical sub-categories, favouring instead a classification system of 'mental retardation' which specifies *the level of support required within respective areas of functioning*. Such a system is seen by the Association as being '... more *functional, relevant, and orientated to service delivery and outcomes than the labelling system currently in use.*'

Traditionally, in the UK, two (occasionally three) categories of learning disability have been favoured.[28][29] However, more recently, the Department of Health (1999) has referred to *mild, moderate, severe* and *profound* learning disabilities, reflecting the categorisations in the classification/diagnostic manuals.[30]

---

[27] ICD-10 (1992) and DSM-IV (1994)
[28] DHSS/Welsh Office (1971); National Development Group (1977); DHSS (1980); Audit Commission (1988); DoH, (1992).
[29] For more recent discussion see Dodd & Webb (1998).
[30] See also Evers & Hill (1999) and, in contrast, Dodd & Webb (1998).

The operational guidance issued by the Society in 1991 did not comment on sub-classification of learning disability *per se* but made a two-category subdivision into *significant* and *severe* impairments of intelligence and social functioning in the context of mental health legislation categories of 'mental impairment' and 'severe mental impairment'.

**The Society recommends that decisions involving sub-classification of 'learning disability' should make reference to both intellectual and to adaptive/social functioning using the criteria below as guidance. Furthermore, it is considered good practice to make reference to the levels of supports required.**

## 1.4.1 SUB-CLASSIFICATION OF IMPAIRMENT OF INTELLECTUAL FUNCTIONING

In line with the previous BPS document (1991), *significant* impairment of intellectual functioning is considered to be represented by an IQ between two and three standard deviations below the population mean, and *severe* impairment of intellectual functioning is considered to be represented by an IQ of more than three standard deviations below the mean. On the most commonly used measures of intellectual functioning (the Wechsler scales), with a standard deviation of 15 points, these cut-off points correspond to IQs of <70 and <55 respectively:

**Significant Impairment of Intellectual Functioning:**      IQ 55-69
**Severe Impairment of Intellectual Functioning:**      IQ <55

Again, it is noted that owing to errors of measurement[31] there is some flexibility around these transition points (see Appendix III).

Whether based on standard deviations (as in DSM-IV) or arbitrary cut-offs (as in ICD-10) the use of fine-grained sub-divisions below an IQ of approximately 55, in the case of adults, depends on IQ figures which are hypothetical or extrapolated. There seem to be no reliable or valid psychometric instruments, for the adult population, to enable the clinician to arrive at the IQ figures needed to make these distinctions. Thus sub-classification on the basis of IQ scores from directly administered IQ tests cannot be carried out reliably for the lowest levels of intellectual functioning.

In practice, some clinicians are known to use child development scales or children's intelligence tests to profile aspects of intellectual functioning of very disabled adults. Whilst, clinically, this may have some use in assessing performance on specific tasks, attempts to derive extrapolated IQ scores from the use of developmental scales or child intelligence tests constitutes extremely dubious practice and is not recommended. Likewise, the practice of referring to 'mental age' when reporting on the level of intellectual or social functioning of adults should be avoided.

---

[31] Approximately ± 5 IQ points on the Full Scale scores of the WAIS-R (Wechsler, 1981).

> **Note:** In early versions of the WAIS-III$^{UK}$ manual, the section on *'Diagnosing Severe Learning Disability'* quotes the criteria for *significant* (i.e. not *severe*) learning disability. This is an error.

## 1.4.2 SUB-CLASSIFICATION OF IMPAIRMENT OF ADAPTIVE/SOCIAL FUNCTIONING

The operational guidance issued by the Society in 1991 distinguished between requiring 'partial help' (a *significant* impairment) and 'continued assistance' (a *severe* impairment). However, this guidance did not define the difference between these two levels of help. How the degree of adaptive/social impairment is associated with *level* of learning disability has led to some debate. Dodd and Webb (1998) suggest using certain score profiles on the HALO (Shackleton Bailey *et al.*, 1982) to distinguish between *significant* and *severe* impairment of social functioning. The Vineland Adaptive Behaviour Scales (Sparrow *et al.*, 1984) classifies 'adaptive' levels into 'mild, moderate, severe and profound deficit' on the basis of standard scores.

Given the presented definition of adaptive/social functioning and the item content of the many scales which profess to measure the concept, no one particular assessment can, at this stage, be recommended for determining levels of adaptive/social functioning. However, when making a judgement as to the degree of impairment of adaptive/social functioning, the following levels of support (AAMR, 1992) are considered useful as a guide:[32]

| | |
|---|---|
| Intermittent | Supports on an 'as needed basis'. Characterised by episodic nature, person not always needing the support(s), or short-term supports needed during life-span transition (e.g. job loss or an acute medical crisis). Intermittent supports may be high or low intensity when provided. |
| Limited | ... supports characterised by consistency over time, time-limited but not of an intermittent nature, may require fewer ... [resources] than more intense levels of support ... |
| Extensive | Supports characterised by regular involvement (e.g. daily) in at least some environments (such as work or home) and not time-limited ... |
| Pervasive | Supports characterised by their consistency, high intensity; provided across environments; potential life-sustaining nature ... |

---

[32] For the complete tabulated descriptions refer to Mental Retardation: *Definition, Classification, and System of Supports – 9th Edition* (AAMR, 1992).

When determining level of impairment of adaptive/social functioning, the following may be used as a guide:

- **Intermittent and Limited** support indicate a sig*nificant im*pairment of adaptive/social functioning;
- **Extensive and Pervasive** support indicate a se*vere im*pairment of adaptive/social functioning.

It should be stressed that the above is presented as a *guide*.[33] The judgement will rest on both the intensity of the assistance (e.g. verbal or physical prompting, or carrying out tasks on the individual's behalf) and on its frequency (e.g. daily or less often than daily); the required assistance should always be outside that range of that expected within the individual's particular culture/community.

## 1.4.3 REQUIREMENT FOR CONCURRENCE OF THE TWO IMPAIRMENTS

Learning disability requires that significant impairments of intellectual and adaptive/social functioning coexist. This means that a person with a *significant* (or even *severe*) impairment in one of the two domains only, and with no significant impairment in the other, may not be adjudged to have a learning disability.[34]

Similarly, for *severe* learning disability, severe impairments of *both* intellectual and adaptive/social functioning must be evident.

For some individuals, levels of intellectual functioning and adaptive/social functioning will be relatively consistent. For others this may not be the case.

When there is large discrepancy between intellectual functioning and adaptive/social functioning, great care must be taken during assessment – particularly when the extent of a person's impairment in intellectual and/or adaptive/social functioning is near the boundary between *severe* and *significant*, or between *significant* and *non-significant*. Bearing in mind the limits in rigour of, especially, adaptive/social functioning assessments, it is in these circumstances that such judgements need to be approached with appropriate caution.

---

[33] The categories of support defined by AAMR (1992) generally reflect both the *frequency* and *intensity* of support – although not consistently so. With respect to intensity, the *Intermittent* and *Pervasive* categories contain relatively clear operational criteria; the *Limited* category contains some reference, whereas the *Extensive* category contains no reference. Particularly with these latter two categories, a judgement will have to be made based on the criteria which appear in the other categories. The criteria for frequency is more consistent, ranging from an 'as needed basis' for *Intermittent* to their 'constancy' for Pervasive support.

[34] DSM-IV (1994) notes that: *'Mental retardation would not be diagnosed in an individual with an IQ lower than 70 if there are no significant deficits or impairments in adaptive functioning.'*

# PART 2: ASSOCIATED CONTEXTS

Learning disability, or associated terminology, appears in a wide range of contexts:

- Mental Health Legislation;
- Criminal Justice System;
- Local Government/Benefits Legislation;
- Miscellaneous.

It should be noted that within these contexts, similar terminology is often used with *different definitions* (see Appendix II). For instance, the term *severe mental impairment* under the Mental Health Act 1983 has a different definition from the same term used within local government legislation. Thus, it is important to ensure that the specific context in which any classification occurs is made explicit, and that classification in one particular context does not imply classification in any other.

In addition, many legal classifications, whilst appearing similar, should not be confused with clinical or psychological classification. It must be accepted that the context is different. However, within a legal context, clinical or psychological terminology may justifiably be used to assist the Court to make its judgement.

Within contexts other than the purely clinical it is important that the psychologist should first identify the appropriate clinical classification, and then judge how this relates to the specific definition used within the applied context.

Above, we have argued that classifications used by psychologists can be valid and justified within certain contexts. Equally we would argue that, in certain contexts, classification *per se* has no valid role – it would be important to recognise other factors that are more significant than inferences drawn from broad classifications.

As was mentioned above (page 3), owing to the complexities of relating the different legislative systems to each other, some compromises have been necessary in order to produce one document which is equally relevant throughout the UK. Thus, in this section, the document draws mainly on the commonalities between the respective UK legislation. Where significant differences occur, these are highlighted, but readers requiring more specific detail on a particular piece of legislation should refer to the appropriate Statute.

## 2.1 MENTAL HEALTH LEGISLATION

This part of the document relates to those categories that appear within the respective Mental Health Acts/Orders, throughout the UK, and which pertain to Admission for Assessment and for Treatment under the Acts/Orders.

With respect to the Assessment and Treatment sections that are potentially relevant to people with learning disability there is much similarity between the Mental Heath Act, 1983 (England & Wales) and the Mental Health (Scotland) Act 1984.[35]

There are, however, differences between these Acts, specifically relating to crimes *against* the person who is subject to the Act. For instance, in addition to the sections relating to Assessment and Treatment, the Mental Health (Scotland) Act 1984 includes a range of legislation relating to unlawful sexual intercourse with women with 'mental handicap'.[36][37] Sections relating to aspects other than Admission for Assessment and Treatment are further discussed in Section 2.2 of this present document.

The categories in the Mental Health (N.Ireland) Order 1986 differ from the above Acts. These are discussed in Section 2.1.3 below.

The 'conduct' criterion (i.e. abnormally aggressive and/or seriously irresponsible conduct) which appears in the definitions of *mental impairment* and *severe mental impairment* appears in certain categories in all the Acts/Orders, and is further discussed in Section 2.1.4 below.

### 2.1.1 MENTAL HEALTH LEGISLATION – ENGLAND AND WALES

The Mental Health Act 1983 uses the term mental disorder which is defined as:

> *mental illness, arrested or incomplete development of mind, psychopathic disorder and any other disorder or disability of mind.*

Although the phrase *arrested* or *incomplete development of mind* is relevant to people with learning disabilities, for many purposes of the Act it is not sufficient that a person is suffering from mental disorder *per se* but from one of the four *specific* categories of mental disorder specified in the Act. The main two categories that are potentially relevant to people with learning disabilities are *mental impairment* and *severe mental impairment*.

---

[35] Under the definition of 'mental disorder', the Mental Health (Scotland) Act 1984 does not contain specific reference to 'psychopathic disorder' or to 'any other disorder or disability of mind' which appears in the Mental Health Act 1983.
[36] Reference to homosexual acts appears in the Criminal Justice (Scotland) Act 1980.
[37] Similar, but not directly comparable, legislation appears, in England, in the Sexual Offences Acts.

Although related, the terms *mental impairment* and *severe mental impairment* are not synonymous with 'learning disability'. Under this Act these terms are defined as follows:

- Mental Impairment:

    *... a state of arrested or incomplete development of mind not amounting to severe mental impairment which includes significant impairment of intelligence and social functioning and is associated with abnormally aggressive or seriously irresponsible conduct on the part of the person concerned.* [s 1(2)]

- Severe Mental Impairment:

    *... a state of arrested or incomplete development of mind which includes severe impairment of intelligence and social functioning and is associated with abnormally aggressive or seriously irresponsible conduct on the part of the person concerned.* [s 1(2)]

These definitions of *mental impairment* and *severe mental impairment* make reference to two of the three 'core' criteria for learning disability (i.e. *significant/severe impairment of intelligence* and *social functioning*) but also include a criterion of *'abnormally aggressive or seriously irresponsible conduct'*.

Again, it should be emphasised that these terms are legal classifications, to be used for the purposes of the Act, and as such are distinct from medical/clinical terminology.[38] As the criteria specified in the Act are not further defined, the importance of clinical judgement is acknowledged. The Mental Health Act 1983 Memorandum[39] notes that:

*The distinction between 'severe mental impairment' and 'mental impairment' is one of degree: the impairment of intelligence and social functioning is 'severe' in the former and only 'significant' in the latter. Slight impairment cannot fall within either definition. The assessment of level of impairment is a matter for clinical judgement.*[40]

Whilst the above guidance states that the assessment of degree of impairment is a matter for clinical judgement, it is the view of the Society that such a judgement should be based on a full assessment as outlined in Part 1 above (in addition to the 'conduct' criteria' see Section 2.1.4 below).

---

[38] Gostin (1983) *A Practical Guide to Mental Health Law*. London: MIND.
[39] Department of Health and Welsh Office (1998) *The Mental Health Act 1983, Memorandum on Parts I to VI, VIII and X*. See also Department of Health and Welsh Office (1999) *Mental Health Act 1983 Code of Practice Mental Health Act*.
[40] Department of Health and Welsh Office (1999) The Mental Health Act 1983 Code of Practice adds that this clinical judgement should be '*... guided by current professional practice and subject to the relevant legal requirements*'.

It should be noted that the *level* of mental impairment (i.e. significant or severe) is of some consequence under the Act, as different legal consequences may ensue from the respective classifications. The Mental Health Act 1983 Memorandum states:

> *This distinction between the two degrees of mental impairment is important because there are differences in the grounds on which patients can be detained, or have their detention renewed if they suffer from severe mental impairment as opposed to mental impairment.* [s.10]

With regard to assessment, the Mental Health Act 1983 Code of Practice gives the following guidance:

> *No patient should be classified under the Act as mentally impaired or severely mentally impaired without an assessment by a consultant psychiatrist in learning disabilities and a formal psychological assessment. This assessment should be part of a complete appraisal by medical, nursing, social work and psychology professionals with experience in learning disabilities...* [s.30.4]

### 2.1.2 MENTAL HEALTH LEGISLATION – SCOTLAND

The Mental Health (Scotland) Act 1984 also uses the term *mental disorder*, albeit defined slightly differently from the Mental Health Act 1983

> *Mental illness, or mental handicap however caused or manifested.*

As with the Mental Health Act 1983, for most purposes of the Act it is not sufficient that a person is suffering from mental disorder *per se* but from one of the four *specific* categories of mental disorder specified in the Act. Again, the main two categories that are relevant to people with learning disabilities are *mental impairment* and *severe mental impairment*.

The definitions of *mental impairment* and *severe mental impairment* are identical to the definition appearing in the Mental Health Act 1983 (see above).

### 2.1.3 MENTAL HEALTH LEGISLATION – NORTHERN IRELAND

The Mental Health (N. Ireland) Order 1986 defines Mental Disorder as:

> *Mental illness, mental handicap and any other disorder or disability of mind.*

The following terms, further defined in the Act, are relevant to people with learning disabilities:

- **Mental Handicap:** *a state of arrested or incomplete development of mind which includes significant impairment of intelligence and social functioning.*

- **Severe Mental Handicap:** *a state of arrested or incomplete development of mind which includes severe impairment of intelligence and social functioning.*
- **Severe Mental Impairment:** *a state of arrested or incomplete development of mind which includes severe impairment of intelligence and social functioning and is associated with abnormally aggressive or seriously irresponsible conduct on the part of the person concerned.*

Within this Order it should be noted that the definition of *severe mental impairment* is identical to that of *severe mental handicap*, save for an additional 'conduct' criterion.

The definition of *severe mental impairment* is identical to that of *severe mental impairment* in both the Mental Health Act 1983 and the Mental Health (Scotland) Act 1984 but unlike these two Acts, the Northern Ireland Order does not contain a category of *mental impairment*.

Since a Treatment Order in Northern Ireland can be invoked only in a case of *severe mental impairment* (with its attendant severe impairments of both intelligence and social functioning), this makes it crucial for accurate operational distinctions between *significant* and *severe* impairments to be agreed in that particular context.

## 2.1.4 ABNORMALLY AGGRESSIVE OR SERIOUSLY IRRESPONSIBLE CONDUCT

*Abnormally aggressive or seriously irresponsible conduct* are behaviours which must be associated with 'a state of arrested or incomplete development of mind' in order to meet the criteria for categorisation as *mental impairment* under the Mental Health Act 1983 and the Mental Health (Scotland) Act 1984, or in order to meet the criteria for categorisation as *severe mental impairment* under the Mental Health Act 1983, the Mental Health (Scotland) Act 1984 and the Mental Health (Northern Ireland) Order 1986.

These behaviours are not further defined within the Acts or the Order, but the Mental Health Act 1983 Memorandum[41] comments that they were included in the formulation of *mental impairment* and *severe mental impairment* so as:

> to ensure that people with learning disabilities are not subject to long-term compulsory powers unless the behaviour which is part of their condition in that particular case justifies the use of those powers. [s.9]

In seeking to operationalise these terms, therefore, it is appropriate to bear in mind that they should constrain, rather than maximise, the extent to which people with learning disabilities can be compulsorily detained.

---

[41] Department of Health and Welsh Office (1998).

The Mental Health Act 1983, Code of Practice (1999) gives the following guidance on how to assess these behaviours:

- **Abnormally aggressive behaviour:** *Any assessment of this category should be based on observations of behaviour which lead to a conclusion that the actions are outside the usual range of aggressive behaviour, and which cause actual damage and/or real distress occurring recently or persistently or with excessive severity.* [s.30.5]
- **Irresponsible conduct:** *The assessment of this characteristic should be based on an observation of behaviour which shows a lack of responsibility, a disregard of the consequences of action taken, and where the results cause actual damage or real distress, either recently or persistently or with excessive severity.* [s.30.5]

Thus, the assessment of *'abnormally aggressive or seriously irresponsible conduct'* can be seen to have both observational (i.e. the actual behaviour) and judgement (i.e. the abnormality and/or seriousness) components. In this connection the previous recommendations (BPS, 1991) are developed here.

For both abnormally aggressive and seriously irresponsible conduct there should be direct observation of actual conduct/behaviour, or reported observation by at least two reliable witnesses (although in some instances no second person may be present, when this criterion for reliability cannot be met), and there should be recording of this conduct/behaviour in behavioural terms.

Abnormally aggressive conduct must be judged to be 'outside the usual range of aggressive behaviour' – unpredictability or unreasonableness *under the circumstances* will be factors which may establish the criterion.

Irresponsible conduct is that which shows a lack of responsibility and/or a disregard of the consequences of the action – it does not necessarily require the person to be capable of judging these consequences. In certain circumstances, *failure to act* can also be evidence of irresponsibility.

To met the criteria for each, abnormally aggressive and seriously irresponsible conduct should result in actual damage and/or real distress (in some cases to the self), and should occur *'either recently or persistently or with excessive severity'*.

There is a lack of official guidance on how to decide when abnormally aggressive or seriously irresponsible conduct have ceased, although the importance of being able to do so is clear. It would not be appropriate to continue to regard a person who has a learning disability as being mentally impaired, if remission or treatment have eliminated their abnormally aggressive or seriously irresponsible conduct. In most circumstances, observed cessation of key behaviours, or clinically significant reductions in their frequency, will provide adequate evidence of change. In evaluating this, however, account must be taken of the extent to which characteristics of detention or a treatment regime are serving to render the problematical conduct temporarily impossible of execution. There may be similar difficulty in deciding whether infrequently occurring irresponsible conduct of extreme severity has ceased. Judgement in these circumstances is likely to be most readily optimised by drawing upon clinical experience of similar profiles.

## 2.2 CRIMINAL JUSTICE SYSTEM[42]

There are a number of Statutes that are specifically relevant to people with learning disabilities, and for which psychological assessment and opinion may have some applicability. The following is not intended as an exhaustive list, but does include some legislative areas in which a psychologist's opinion or advice may be sought (see also Appendix II):

- **Sexual Offences Act 1956**[43] – includes reference to unlawful (i.e. outside marriage) sexual intercourse with a woman who is a *'defective'*, and reference to indecent assault on a man or woman who is a *'defective'*.
- **Mental Health Act 1959** – Section 128 deals with unlawful sexual intercourse between a male employee and a woman being treated for *'mental disorder'*. The Act defines *'mental disorder'*.
- **Sexual Offences Act 1967** – deals with male homosexuality, and includes reference to males with *'severe mental handicap'*.
- **Mental Health (Amendment) Act 1982** – updated parts of the Sexual Offences Acts 1956 and 1967, amended the definition of *'defective'* and *'severe mental handicap'*.
- **Police and Criminal Evidence Act 1984 (PACE) and the Codes of Practice** – concerning the requirement for an *'appropriate adult'* to be present at interviews related to suspects who have a *'mental handicap'*.
- **Mental Health (Scotland) Act 1984** – Section 106 relates to unlawful sexual intercourse with a woman who has a *'mental handicap'*.[44]
- **Mental Health (Scotland) Act 1984** – Section 107 relates to unlawful sexual intercourse between a male employee and a woman being treated for *'mental disorder'*.

Again, it is important to re-emphasise that clinical diagnoses/classifications are not the same as *legal* classifications. Gunn (1996) notes: *'It is important to understand the definitions used in each Act and to remember that these terms have a specific legal meaning which may not be the same as the meanings given to them in general or professional conversation.'*[45]

---

[42] Some legislation across England and Wales, Scotland and Northern Ireland will differ.
[43] An 'unlawful sexual intercourse' clause appears, in Scotland, in the Mental Health (Scotland) Act 1984. [s.106] However, it is important to note that the *level* of disability criterion differs.
[44] This is a similar clause to that in the Sexual Offences Act 1956 under English Law. However, it should be noted, again, that the *level* of disability criterion, under the respective legislation, differs.
[45] Gunn (1996) cites a case in which the Court of Appeal decided that the words defining

However, within a legal context, clinical terminology may justifiably be used to assist the Court to make a judgement, with respect to legal classifications. The relationship between the clinical and the legal context has to be carefully considered. For instance, in drawing conclusions from one legal case, Gudjonsson and Haward (1998) note that '... *successful submissions under PACE might involve borderline IQ scores*', i.e. IQ scores of 70 to 79 (Wechsler, 1981). In the same case, trial judges were '... *not attracted to the concept that the judicial approach to submissions under... the Police and Criminal Evidence Act 1984 (PACE) should be governed by which side of an arbitrary line, whether 69/70 or elsewhere, the IQ falls.*' Equally the same authors stress the difficulties of generalising, even within the legal system, noting a case in which '*the Court of Appeal decided it was wrong to take the IQ scores from one case and apply them slavishly to another.*'

Finally, it is important to note that although, within English law, individuals identified as 'defective'/'severely mentally handicapped' within the Sexual Offences legislation are considered, in law, as not being able to consent to unlawful sexual relationships,[46] this should not be used as a generalised criterion for determining the ability to consent with respect to other issues, choices or situations. Again, any assessment addressing mental incapacity/ capacity and issues of consent should not rely on generalised inferences relating to broad classification but should be conducted in the context of the particular issues in question and of the individual being assessed.[47]

## 2.3 LOCAL GOVERNMENT/BENEFITS LEGISLATION

Classifications that are relevant to people with learning disabilities appear in local government/benefits legislation. Examples of associated definitions are given in Appendix II.

Benefits legislation is quite complex, and subject to frequent change, so in those instances when an opinion of a psychologist is sought, the psychologist should be fully aware of the context of the assessment, and of any recent changes within the legislation. It should also be noted that interpretations of the Regulations are subject to Commissioners' decisions. As within the criminal justice system, the clinical diagnoses/classifications are not the same as the classifications within the specific Act/Regulation the latter will have their specific own meanings.[48]

---

'defective' were '*words of the ordinary English language*' and that whether someone is a 'defective' is to be measured by the '*standards of normal persons*' and is to be decided by the jury.

[46] Again, it should be noted that the *level* of disability criterion differs for Scotland. See the Mental Health (Scotland) Act 1984 (s.106). See also McKay (1994).

[47] For further discussion on issues of incapacity and consent see Wong, J. (1997); British Medical Association and the Law Society (1995); Law Commission (1995); Command Papers Cm 3803 (1997) & Cm 4465 (1999).

[48] In the context of the Disability Living Allowance (higher rate mobility component) a

However, again, as within the criminal justice system, an expert opinion may be requested in order to make a judgement in any one particular case.

## 2.4 MISCELLANEOUS

Classifications with respect to people with learning disabilities occur in a variety of other contexts. Examples of associated definitions are given in Appendix II.

## 2.5 'GATE-KEEPING' – ACCESS TO SERVICES

There has been some debate regarding requests for psychological assessment which relate to a person's suitability or eligibility for access to learning disability services (i.e. a 'gate-keeping' function). Although the Society cannot be prescriptive regarding local responses, it is important to note that access to services will not depend solely on the characteristics of the individual service user but also on the extent and configuration of local service provision.[49]

It is important to recognise that whilst some of these requests may be presented in terms of *assisting access* to specialist services, this may also imply *restricted* access to or *exclusion* from appropriate generic/mainstream services. Psychologists should be aware of this risk and should avoid making a recommendation that, by implication or inference, might be used to restrict or exclude people from the most appropriate services available.

In responding to requests to classify people for service/administrative purposes, there is a danger that the unique characteristics of the individual will be lost. In such circumstances it is essential not simply to apply labels, but to focus the

---

Commissioner's decision (CDLA/6219/97) has defined 'severe impairment of intelligence' as an IQ of 55 or less. However, as with other medico-legal judgements, it has also been argued that 'intelligence' is used in the ordinary sense of the word and has no *technical* meaning (Commissioner's decision CDLA/12148/96) (cited in Paterson, 1999). Either way, a judgement should not be based on severe impairment of intelligence alone, but should take into account impairment of social functioning and, in this case, other aspects. The Court of Appeal Judgement – *Megarry v CoA* gives support for this. Additionally this same judgement (relating to a person with autism) concluded that whilst the claimant's IQ is likely to be *'the essential starting point for considering impairment of intelligence'* and that it was *'reasonable to take an IQ of 55 or less'* as being severe impairment of intelligence, the IQ score would not necessarily prove decisive. Thus (certainly in the case of people with autism), where the IQ is over 55, all the available evidence should be considered when deciding if the severe impairment of intelligence is satisfied.

[49] Fox & Lamb (1998) have invited comments on the use of psychological assessments for potential administrative service functions. This issue has been considered by a number of clinical psychologists on behalf of local services e.g. Burton (1997), Dodd & Webb (1998) and Evers & Hill (1999).

assessment on specific individual need, and to make recommendations on the type of service and supports that would best meet that need.[50,51,52]

# PART 3: APPENDICES

## APPENDIX I: CLINICAL DEFINITIONS

| Organisation | Terminology | Definition/Criteria |
|---|---|---|
| **ICD-10**[53]<br>The ICD10 Classification of Mental and Behavioural Disorders[54] | Mental Retardation | *... a condition of arrested or incomplete development of the mind, which is especially characterised by impairment of skills manifested during the developmental period, which contribute to the overall level of intelligence, i.e. cognitive, language, motor and social abilities.*<br><br>*... Adaptive behaviour is always impaired ...* |

---

[50] Within some areas, people with a learning disability receive high quality psychological primary care services like any other person. Unfortunately, however, there is also evidence that people with a learning disability may be marginalised, having little access to mainstream services (DoH, 1998; Band, 1998).

[51] The AAMR (1992) avoids sub-classification, and emphasises a process which relates a person's needs with respect to '... *the intensities of supports necessary to enhance the person's independence/interdependence, productivity, and community integration.*'

[52] Schalock *et al.* (1994).

[53] At the time of writing, *The International Classification of Impairments, Activities and Participation: a Manual of Dimensions of Disablement and Functioning* ICIDH-20 is being developed. The intellectual disability part of this manual is being trialed in Australia (Cooper, 1997).

[54] World Health Organisation (1992).

| Organisation | Terminology | Definition/Criteria |
|---|---|---|
| **AAMR** The American Association on Mental Retardation (1992) | Mental Retardation | *... substantial limitations in present functioning. It is characterised by significantly sub-average intellectual functioning, existing concurrently with related limitations in two or more of the following applicable adaptive skill areas: communication, self-care, home-living, social skills, community use, self-direction, health and safety, functional academics, leisure and work. Mental retardation manifests before age 18.* |
| **DSM-IV** Diagnostic and Statistical Manual of Mental Disorders[55] | Mental Retardation | *(a) Significantly sub-average intellectual functioning: an IQ of approximately 70 or below on an individually administered IQ test.*<br><br>*(b) Concurrent deficits or impairments in present adaptive functioning (i.e. the person's effectiveness in meeting the standards expected for his or her age by his or her cultural group) in at least two of the following areas: communication, self-care, home-living, social/interpersonal skills, use of community resources, self-direction, functional academic skills, work, leisure, health, and safety.*<br><br>*(c) The onset is before age 18 years.* |
| **Department of Health (1998)**[56] | Learning Disability | *... usually described as a significant impairment of intelligence and social functioning acquired before adulthood.* |

---

[55] American Psychiatric Association (1994).
[56] Department of Health (1998): *Signposts for Success...*

# APPENDIX II: SAMPLE OF RELATED DEFINITIONS MENTAL HEALTH LEGISLATION

| Act/Regulation | Terminology | Definition/Criteria |
| --- | --- | --- |
| **Mental Health Act 1983** | Mental Disorder | *Mental illness, arrested or incomplete development of mind, psychopathic disorder and any other disorder or disability of mind.* |
| | Arrested or incomplete development of mind | Not defined. |
| | Mental Impairment | *A state of arrested or incomplete development of mind ... which includes significant impairment of intelligence and social functioning and is associated with abnormally aggressive or seriously irresponsible conduct on the part of the person concerned.* |
| | Severe Mental Impairment | *A state of arrested or incomplete development of mind which includes severe impairment of intelligence and social functioning and is associated with abnormally aggressive or seriously irresponsible conduct on the part of the person concerned.* |

| Act/Regulation | Terminology | Definition/Criteria |
|---|---|---|
| **Mental Health (Scotland) Act 1984** | Mental Disorder | *Mental illness or mental handicap however caused or manifested.* |
| | Mental Impairment/ Severe Mental Impairment | As for Mental Health Act 1983. |
| | Mental Handicap | *A state of arrested or incomplete development of mind which includes significant impairment of intelligence and social functioning.* |
| | Mental Disorder | *Mental illness, mental handicap and any other disorder or disability of mind.* |
| **Mental Health (N.Ireland) Order 1986** | Mental Handicap | *A state of arrested or incomplete development of mind which includes significant impairment of intelligence and social functioning.* |
| | Severe Mental Handicap | *A state of arrested or incomplete development of mind which includes severe impairment of intelligence and social functioning.* |
| | Severe Mental Impairment | *A state of arrested or incomplete development of mind which includes severe impairment of intelligence and social functioning and is associated with abnormally aggressive or seriously irresponsible conduct on the part of the person concerned.* |

# LOCAL GOVERNMENT/BENEFITS LEGISLATION

| Act/Regulation | Terminology | Definition/Criteria |
| --- | --- | --- |
| **Local Government Finance Act 1992** (Relates to Council Tax) | Severely Mentally Impaired | *Severe impairment of intelligence and social functioning (however caused) which appears to be permanent. This includes people who are severely mentally impaired as a result of a degenerative brain disorder such as Alzheimer's Disease, a stroke or other forms of dementia.* |
| **Social Security (Disability Living Allowance) Regulations 1991; Social Security Contributions and Benefits Act 1992 sec. 73** (Relates to the higher rate mobility component of the Disability Living Allowance) | Severely Mentally Impaired | *A state of arrested development or incomplete physical development of the brain, which results in severe impairment of intelligence and social functioning.*[57] *'Arrested development or incomplete physical development of the brain' must take place before the brain is fully developed. In most cases this will be by the late twenties, and invariably before age 30. (R(DLA)2/96).* |
|  |  | Note: Degenerative diseases such as Alzheimer's Disease that begin after the brain is fully developed do not satisfy the severely mentally impaired criteria. |
|  |  | Criteria for higher rate mobility component of Disability Living Allowance includes a *'severe behavioural problem'* criteria which includes *(extreme) disruptive behaviour ... regularly requires another person to intervene and physically restrain ... so unpredictable that another person [must] be present and watching over him whenever he is awake. Reg 12(5), (6) DLA Regs.* |

---

[57] For further discussion, see footnote 48, page 18.

| Act/Regulation | Terminology | Definition/Criteria |
|---|---|---|
| **Social Security (Incapacity for Work) General Regulations 1995; Social Security (Incapacity Benefit) (Transitional) Regulations 1995** | Severe Learning Disability | *A condition which results from the arrested or incomplete physical development of the brain, or severe damage to the brain, and which involves severe impairment of intelligence and social functioning.* (This is less restrictive than 'severely mentally impaired' as defined in some Regulations in that it includes conditions that arise later in life, e.g. a later head injury.) |
| **Disability Discrimination Act 1995** | Disability | *A physical or mental impairment which has a substantial and long-term adverse effect on a person's ability to carry out normal day-to-day activities. 'Mental impairment' includes learning disabilities and mental illness (if recognised by a respected body of medical opinion).* |

## CRIMINAL JUSTICE SYSTEM[58]

| Act/Regulation | Terminology | Definition/Criteria |
|---|---|---|
| **Police and Criminal Evidence Act 1984; Police and Criminal Evidence (N Ireland) Order 1989** | Mentally Handicapped (person) | *A state of arrested or incomplete development of mind which includes significant impairment of intelligence and social functioning.* |

---

[58] The section refers to legislation in England and Wales. Although comparable legislation in Scotland may exist, this may appear in different Statues. The difference in the level of disability criterion for unlawful sexual intercourse between Sexual Offences Act 1956 [England] and Mental Health (Scotland) Act 1984 (s. 106) is particularly important. A useful reference on Scottish law relevant to personal relationships is McKay (1994).

| Act/Regulation | Terminology | Definition/Criteria |
|---|---|---|
| **Sexual Offences Act 1956** | Defective | *A state of arrested or incomplete development of mind which includes severe impairment of intelligence and social functioning.* [As amended by the Mental Health (Amendment) Act 1982]. |
| **Sexual Offences Act 1967** | Severe Mental Handicap (males) | *A state of arrested or incomplete development of mind which includes severe impairment of intelligence and social functioning.* [As amended by the Mental Health (Amendment) Act 1982]. |

## MISCELLANEOUS

| Act/Regulation | Terminology | Definition/Criteria |
|---|---|---|
| **Registered Homes Act 1984** | Mental Handicap | *A state of arrested or incomplete development of mind which includes significant impairment of intelligence and social functioning.* |
| **Residential Care Homes Regulations 1984** | Mental Handicap | *A state of arrested or incomplete development of mind which includes significant impairment of intelligence and social functioning.* |
| **Road Traffic Act 1988** | Mild to Moderate Mental Handicap | *If stable, it may be possible to hold a licence but he/she will need to demonstrate functional ability at the wheel and be otherwise stable [No other definition is given].* |
| | Severe Mental Handicap | *A state of arrested or incomplete development of mind which includes severe impairment of intelligence and social functioning.* |

## APPENDIX III: CONFIDENCE LIMITS IN PSYCHOMETRIC ASSESSMENT

Confidence intervals for any score can be calculated from the standard error of measurement (SEM) statistic. This indicates the probable extent of error in any score in the set to which it applies. The range of error depends on test reliability, so the higher the reliability, the narrower the range of error. Most test manuals should provide either the SEM statistic directly or, at the very least, reliability figures from which it can be calculated. Where such information is not available for a particular test, the use of results from that test is severely constrained.

If a particular test does provide this statistic, it is possible to derive the 95 per cent probability of the limits (i.e. the confidence limits) within which a particular score might be expected to lie. Assuming that the test has been standardised on a large sample, this can be done by multiplying the SEM by 1.96.

The WAIS-R (Wechsler, 1981), which can be used with persons over 16 years of age, gives SEM figures for IQ scores which vary depending on the age group concerned. For *Full Scale* IQ scores, SEM figures range from 2.20 to 2.96, with an average of 2.53.[59] This latter figure gives confidence limits of ± 4.96 (i.e. approximately ± 5).

The WAIS-III$^{UK}$ (Wechsler, 1999) provides 90 per cent and 95 per cent confidence intervals for each level of observed score for IQ and Index scores. These have been calculated slightly differently – being based on the estimated true score and standard error of estimation for each observed score level.

Figures for other tests will obviously vary and it should be noted that, as a general rule, intelligence tests are least reliable at their extremes, and the SEM figures published in the test manuals may contain an underestimate of the size of measurement error in the case of those with greater intellectual disability.

At transition points of classification (e.g. between significant and severe impairment of intellectual functioning) it will be necessary to treat IQ figures with caution. To make allowance for the possibility of measurement error, the limits within which the IQ score probably lies should be stated. The chartered psychologist will be guided by proper use of psychometric information in determining whether or not a particular individual is functioning above, at, or below a given transition point.

There has been some debate about the interpretation of scores around the transition points for the age bands of particular tests (Murray & McKenzie, 1999).[60] Some caution is needed when the age of the person being assessed is close to the age transition points.

---

[59] Figures for Verbal IQ and Performance IQ differ.
[60] See also Collerton (1999) and Leyin (2000).

# REFERENCES

American Association on Mental Retardation (1992). *Mental retardation: Definitions, classification and systems of supports* (9th ed.). Washington, DC: American Association on Mental Retardation.

American Psychiatric Association (1994). *Diagnostic and statistical manual of mental disorders* (4th ed.). Washington DC: APA.

Audit Commission (1988). *Personal social services for people with a mental handicap – audit guide supplement.* Audit Commission.

Band, R. (1998). *The NHS – health for All? People with learning disabilities and healthcare.* London: Mencap.

Bell, L. (1989). The politics of clinical psychology in adult mental handicap. *Clinical Psychology Forum, 20,* 3–5.

British Medical Association and the Law Society (1995). *Assessment of mental capacity.* London: British Medical Association.

British Psychological Society (1991). *Mental impairment and severe mental impairment: A search for definitions.* Leicester: British Psychological Society.

British Psychological Society (1995). *Mental handicap, severe mental handicap and severe mental impairment: The Mental Health (N Ireland) Order 1986. Definitions and operational guidelines.* Leicester: British Psychological Society.

Brown, H. & Smith, H. (Eds.) (1992). *Normalisation: A reader for the nineties.* London: Routledge.

Burton, M. (1997). Intellectual disability: developing a definition. *Journal of Learning Disabilities for Nursing Health and Social Care, 1*(1), 37–43.

Clements, J. (1998). Development, cognition and performance. In E. Emerson, C. Hatton, J. Bromley & A. Caine (Eds.), *Clinical psychology and people with intellectual disabilities.* Chichester: Wiley.

Cohen, L. (1998). The BPS Response to the Green Paper *Who decides?* (Communication to the Department of Health).

Collerton, D. (1999). Response to Murray & McKenzie (1999) (correspondence). *Clinical Psychology Forum, 132,* 4–5.

Command Paper Cm 3803 (1997). *Who decides? Making decisions on behalf of mentally incapacitated adults.* London: HMSO.

Command Paper Cm 4465 (1999). *Making decisions. The government's proposals for making decisions on behalf of mentally incapacitated adults.* London: HMSO.

Cooper, J. (1997). *A brief guide to the ICIDH (June 1997 Beta-1 Draft).* Unpublished.

Department of Health and Social Security/Welsh Office (1971). *Better services for the mentally handicapped.* London: HSMO.

Department of Health and Social Security (1980). *Mental handicap: Progress, problems and priorities. A review of mental handicap services in England since the 1971 White Paper 'Better services for the mentally handicapped'.* London: HSMO.

Department of Health (1992). *Social care for adults with learning disabilities (mental handicap)*. Local Authority Circular, LAC (92) 15, Lancs: Health Publications Unit.

Department of Health (1998). *Signposts for success in commissioning and providing health services for people with learning disabilities*. NHS Executive

Department of Health and Welsh Office (1998). *Mental Health Act 1983 Memorandum on Parts I to VI, VIII and X*. London: HMSO.

Department of Health and Welsh Office (1999). *Code of Practice Mental Health Act 1983*. London: HMSO.

Department of Health (1999). *Once a day*. NHS Executive.

Dodd, K. & Webb, Z. (1998). Defining and classifying learning disabilities in practice. *Clinical Psychology Forum, 111*, 12–15.

Evers, C. & Hill, J. (1999). Identifying and classifying learning disabilities. *Clinical Psychology Forum, 129*, 9–13.

Fox, P. & Lamb, I. (1998). Suitability to receive learning disability services (Correspondence). *Clinical Psychology Forum, 114*, 2–3.

Gelsthorpe, S. (1998). A beginners guide to mental incapacity: A summary of LC231 and the Green Paper Who Decides? *Clinical Psychology Forum, 119*, 39–42.

Gostin, L. (1983). *A practical guide to mental health law*. London: MIND.

Gudjonsson, G.H. & Haward, L.R.C. (1998). *Forensic psychology: A guide to practice*. London: Routledge.

Gunn, M.J. (1996). *Sex and the Law* (4th ed.). London: Family Planning Association.

Hatton, C. (1998). Intellectual disabilities – epidemiology and causes. In E. Emerson, C. Hatton, J. Bromley & A. Caine (Eds.), *Clinical psychology and people with intellectual disabilities*. Chichester: Wiley.

Hogg, J. & Raynes, V. (1987). *Assessment in mental handicap: A guide to assessment practices, tests and checklists*. Beckenham: Croom Helm.

Jones, R. (1996). *Mental Health Act Manual* (5th ed.). London: Sweet & Maxwell.

Law Commission (1995). *Mental Incapacity* (Law Com No. 231). London: HMSO.

Lea, M. (1986). *WAIS-R UK – A British supplement to the manual of the WAIS-R*. The Psychological Corporation/NFER-Nelson.

Leyin, A. (2000). Psychometric assessment, learning disabilities and the law – Response to Murray & McKenzie (1999) (correspondence). *Clinical Psychology Forum, 135*, 3–4.

Murray, G.C., & McKenzie K. (1999). What a difference a day makes: A cautionary tale in the use of the WAIS-R in assessing mental impairment. *Clinical Psychology Forum, 130*, 27–28.

McKay, C. (1994). *Sex, laws and red tape: Scots law, personal relationships and people with learning difficulties*. ENABLE (formerly Scottish Society for the Mentally Handicapped).

National Development Group (1977). *Day services for mentally handicapped adults*. London: HMSO.

Nihira, K., Leland, H. & Lambert, N. (1993). *AAMR Adaptive Behaviour Scale – Residential and Community* (2nd ed.). Austin Texas: American Association on Mental Retardation.

Nunkoosing, K. (1995). Learning disability: Psychology's contribution to diagnosis, assessment and treatment. In R. Bull & D. Carson (Eds.), *Handbook of psychology in legal contexts.* Chichester: Wiley.

Paterson, J. (1999). *Disability rights handbook* (24th ed.). London: Disability Alliance Educational and Research Association.

Sanders, A., Creaton, J., Bird, S. & Weber, L. (1996). Witnesses with learning disabilities. Research Finding No. 44. Home Office Research and Statistical Directorate.

Sacks, O. (1985). *The man who mistook his wife for a hat.* London: Duckworth.

Schalock, R.L., Stark, A.J., Snell, N.E., Coulter, D.L., Polloway, E.W., Luckasson, R., Reiss, S. & Spitalnik, M. (1994). The changing conception of mental retardation: Implications for the field. *Mental Retardation, 32*(3), 81–193.

Scottish Home and Health Department (1984). Mental Health (Scotland) Act 1984. Notes on the Act. Scotland: HMSO.

Shackleton Bailey, M., Pidock, B. & Hampshire Social Services (1982). *Hampshire assessment for living with others. Users manual.* Winchester: Hampshire Social Services.

Sparrow, S.S., Balla, D.A. & Chichetti, D.V. (1984). *Vineland adaptive behaviour scales.* Minnesota: American Guidance Service.

Szivos, S. (1992). The limits to integration? In H. Brown & H. Smith (Eds.), *Normalisation: A reader for the nineties.* London: Routledge.

The Scottish Office. *Mental Health (Scotland) Act 1984. Notes on the Act.* The Scottish Office: Home and Health Department.

Wechsler, D. (1981). *Wechsler Adult Intelligence Scale – Revised* (British Supplement). Texas: Psychological Corporation.

Wechsler, D. (1999). *Wechsler Adult Intelligence Scale$^{UK}$* (3rd ed.). London: Psychological Corporation.

Williams, C. (1995). *Invisible victims: Crime and abuse against people with learning disabilities.* London: Jessica Kingsley Publishers.

Wong, J. (1997). Assessment of capacity to make treatment decisions in adults with learning disabilities. *Tizard Learning Disability Review, 2*(3), 35–39.

World Health Organisation (1992). *ICD-10 classification of mental and behavioural disorders: Clinical description and diagnostic guidelines.* Geneva: World Health Organisation.

# AFTERWORD

From the presented discussions on the definitions of learning disabilities – and of the rather formal contexts in which they may occur – it is important, as stated in the Introduction to this document, that the reader does not to infer that psychometric testing is sufficient, or always necessary, to produce a meaningful assessment of a person with learning disability. Indeed without a broader framework, any assessment based solely on psychometric assessment – and any resultant classification – would miss many important aspects of the person who is being assessed. This general view cannot, perhaps, be expressed more eloquently than by the sentiment expressed in the following:

---

**Rebecca**

'When I first saw her – clumsy, uncouth, all-of-a-fumble – I saw her merely, or wholly, as a casualty, a broken creature, whose neurological impairments I could pick out and dissect with precision: a multitude of apraxias and agnosias, a mass of sensorimotor impairments and breakdowns, limitations of intellectual schemata and concepts similar to those of a child of eight. A poor thing, I said to myself ...

'The next time I saw her, it was all very different. I didn't have her in a test situation, 'evaluating' her in a clinic. I wandered outside, it was a lovely spring day, with a few minutes in hand before the clinic started, and there I saw Rebecca sitting on a bench, gazing at the April foliage quietly, with obvious delight. Her posture had none of the clumsiness which had so impressed me before. Sitting there, in a light dress, her face calm and slightly smiling, she suddenly brought to mind one of Chekov's young women – seen against the backdrop of a Chekovian cherry orchard. She could have been any young woman enjoying a beautiful spring day. This was my human, as opposed to my neurological, vision ...

'As I approached, she heard my footsteps and turned, gave me a broad smile, and wordlessly gestured. 'Look at the world', she seemed to say. 'How beautiful it is' ...

'She had done appallingly in the testing – which, in a sense, was designed, like all neurological and psychological testing, not merely to uncover, to bring out deficits, but to decompose her into functions and deficits. She had come apart, horribly, in formal testing, but now she was mysteriously 'together' and composed.'

*Sacks, O. (1985)*

*Rebecca in The Man who Mistook his Wife for a Hat.*

# Appendix 9

# GOOD PRACTICE GUIDANCE ON WORKING WITH PARENTS WITH A LEARNING DISABILITY

**Department of Health, 2007**

**A.9**

## INTRODUCTION AND EXECUTIVE SUMMARY

### What is the purpose of this good practice guidance?

The purpose of this practice guidance is to:

- Help services to improve their support for parents with a learning disability and their children;
- Increase the chances of the children of parents with a learning disability continuing to live with them in a positive and supportive environment that meets the children's needs.

The guidance is for both adult and children's services. In particular, it is for commissioners of education and social care services, for all service providers and is for the information of Primary Care Trusts. A key aspect of good practice is multi-agency working and thus this guidance is concerned with social care, health and education services and with the role of both statutory and independent sector services.

Appendix A summarises the research evidence, while Appendix B sets out the policy and legislative framework relating to parents with learning disabilities and their children.

The guidance should be read in conjunction with the legislation and guidance referred to in Appendix B, in particular:

- Fair Access to Care Services: Guidance on eligibility criteria for adult social care. Department of Health, 2002.
- Framework for the Assessment of Children in Need and their Families, Department of Health et al, 2000.
- Statutory guidance on Inter-agency co-operation to improve the well-being of children: Children's Trusts. HM Government, 2005.

- Working Together to Safeguard Children: A guide to multi-agency working to safeguard and promote the welfare of children, HM Government, 2006.
- Statutory guidance on making arrangements to safeguard and promote the welfare of children under section 11 of the Children Act 2004, HM Government 2007.

## Why is this good practice guidance needed?

As the research summarised in Appendix A illustrates, practitioners often experience some difficulties supporting families are affected by parental learning disability:

- Children whose parents have learning disabilities and who are in contact with children's social care services have high levels of needs;
- There is little evidence of effective joint working between adult and children's services. Children's services practitioners, and adult learning disability workers, rarely have a good working knowledge of the policy and legislative framework within which each other are working. Appendix B therefore sets out the respective policy and legislative framework with the aim of increasing understanding of both the responsibilities of children's and adult social care, and of parents' entitlements.

Whilst the same values about safeguarding and promoting the welfare of children should be applied to the children of learning disabled parents as to the children of non-learning disabled parents, such families have specific needs which require particular knowledge and skills if the professionals working with them are to provide an equitable service to these children and their parents. A specialised response is often required when working with families where the parent(s) has a learning disability but many children and family social workers do not feel adequately equipped to work effectively with them. At the same time, many adult learning disability services struggle to effectively support parents with learning disabilities.

Section 1 of the guidance sets out the key features of good practice, for both children's and adult services, in working to support families affected by parental learning disability.

Section 2 covers good practice where safeguarding procedures are necessary, while Section 3 sets out some key guidelines for good practice in commissioning services.

The recommendations in this good practice guidance are underpinned by current legislation and statutory guidance for both children's and adult services, and by disability discrimination legislation. This guidance will assist local authorities to fulfil their disability equality duty to promote equality of opportunity for disabled people. It will do this by helping to ensure that people with learning disabilities have equal opportunities to be parents and bring up their children, and that parents with learning disabilities have equal access to family support services.

## SECTION 1 KEY FEATURES OF GOOD PRACTICE

This Section should be read in the context of the following guidance:

- Fair Access to Care Services: Guidance on eligibility criteria for adult social care. Department of Health, 2002.
- Framework for the Assessment of Children in Need and their Families, Department of Health et al, 2000.
- Statutory guidance on making arrangements to safeguard and promote the welfare of children under section 11 of the Children Act 2004. HM Government, 2007.

The following good practice guidance is also relevant:

- The Common Assessment Framework for Children and Young People: Practitioners' Guide, HM Government, 2006.
- What To Do If You're Worried A Child Is Being Abused. HM Government, 2006.

The general aims of good practice in supporting parents with learning disabilities and their families are to:

- Improve children's well being, in other words to enable them to:
  - Be healthy
  - Stay safe
  - Enjoy and achieve
  - Make a positive contribution
  - Achieve economic well-being.
- Enable children to live with their parents (as long as this is consistent with their welfare) by providing the support they and their families require.

Good practice is underpinned by the policy, legislation and guidance set out in Appendix B (which sets out the specific responsibilities of both children's and adult services). Legislation and associated guidance sets out that:

- Children have a right to be protected from harm
- In family court proceedings children's interests are paramount
- Children's needs are usually best met by supporting their parents to look after them
- Local authorities and all other agencies working or in contact with children have a responsibility to safeguard and promote children's welfare
- Parents with learning disabilities have the right to an assessment of their needs for support in their daily lives; such assessment should include any

assistance required with parenting roles and tasks; parents should have their assessed needs met where eligible and considering available resources in line with Fair Access to Care Services
- Parents with learning disabilities are entitled to equal access to services, including parenting support and information services
- Public bodies have a duty to actively promote equality of opportunity for people with learning disabilities.

Good practice is also underpinned by an approach to parenting and learning disability which addresses needs relating to both impairment and the disabling barriers of unequal access and negative attitudes. Such an approach recognises that:

- If the problem is seen as entirely related to impairment and personal limitations, it is difficult to understand how to bring about positive changes for parents and their children.
- If the focus is, instead, on things that can be changed (such as inadequate housing) and support needs that can be met (such as equipment to help a parent measure baby feeds), there are many more possibilities for bringing about positive improvements.

> "When problems are seen as rooted in people's personal deficits and limitations they may seem intractable and out of reach. Shifting the focus onto features of people's lives that can and should be changed challenges the negative stereotypes that inform such thinking and opens up possibilities for social action in support of families"
>
> *Booth and Booth, 1997, p. 38.*

There are five key features of good practice in working with parents with learning disabilities:

1. Accessible information and communication
2. Clear and co-ordinated referral and assessment procedures and processes, eligibility criteria and care pathways
3. Support designed to meet the needs of parents and children based on assessments of their needs and strengths
4. Long-term support where necessary
5. Access to independent advocacy.

This Section covers details of each of these features.

## 1.1 Accessible information and communication

Accessible information and communication is crucial to enabling parents with learning disabilities to engage with services and to therefore maximise the chances of children's needs being met.

# Good Practice Guidance on Working with Parents with a Learning Disability

**1.1.1** All services for parents and children should make information and communication accessible to parents with learning disabilities.

Information about universal services made available to parents and prospective parents should be in formats suitable for people with learning disabilities. This means:

- Easy Read versions of leaflets
- Information on tape and CD/DVD
- Fully accessible websites
- Creating opportunities to tell people with learning disabilities face-to-face about services for parents and parents-to-be.

Parents with learning disabilities need to hear the message that it is not unusual to require support with parenting, and that information and communication will be provided in ways accessible to people with learning disabilities.

Parents need accessible information and communication about relevant services at all the different stages of their children's lives: from midwives and health visitors all the way through to Connexions and youth services.

Communication with schools is particularly important: parents have a responsibility to ensure their children attend and are expected to be involved in their children's education. Parents with learning disabilities cannot fulfil such responsibilities unless information and communication is made accessible by teachers and schools. Unnecessary difficulties are created in parents' relationships with their children's schools if the school does not think carefully about how to communicate effectively with parents and how to involve them in their children's education.

> "The school put their letters on tape. And they gave me stickers to put in each of my children's homework book which I used to say when homework had been done, so I didn't need to sign it."[1]

**1.1.2** Adult learning disability services should take steps to ensure that people with learning disabilities who become parents know about the support available.

Adult learning disability services are well-placed to provide new parents and parents-to-be who have learning disabilities with accessible information about both universal and specialist services. Such information should be made available in all the places that people with learning disabilities are likely to be, including GP surgeries, day centres, colleges, employment projects, supported housing, etc.

---

[1] Quotations given are from parents with learning disabilities consulted during the course of writing this good practice guidance.

**1.1.3** Learning disability services should provide accessible information to parents with learning disabilities about their entitlements to an assessment of their need for support with parenting and about the ways in which this support could be provided.

Few parents with learning disabilities are aware of the support they may be entitled to from adult social care services. Attention should be given to providing information about their rights, as this may help to overcome the fear that an involvement with services as a parent with learning disabilities puts them at risk of losing their children into care.

**1.1.4** Children's social care should take steps to ensure that adults with learning disabilities who become parents know about the support available, and about their responsibilities as parents.

A key barrier faced by children's social care in carrying out their responsibilities is that parents with learning disabilities are often frightened of asking for support when they need it. Accessible, useful information provided by children's social care can go a long way to overcoming this fear. Independent sector organisations are a particularly important way of getting information to people with learning disabilities as there is less stigma and fear associated with them.

> "I thought that if social services got involved that would mean my children would be put on the child protection register".

**1.1.5** When children's and/or adult services carry out assessments, write plans, and provide services to parents with learning disabilities information should be provided in accessible formats. Communication should happen in ways which are accessible to individuals with learning disabilities.

---

**Key messages from parents**

Social workers who are good at communication:

- Are respectful
- Turn up on time
- Speak directly to parents with learning disabilities
- Don't use jargon
- Think before they talk to you
- Listen and 'hear' you
- Explain what is happening
- Do what they say they will do
- Be honest if they cannot help you
- Are patient
- Make enough time to communicate with you.

➡

*Good Practice Guidance on Working with Parents with a Learning Disability* 215

> Reproduced with permission from training materials developed by CHANGE and parents with learning disabilities (for more details see Resources section).

Assessments should only be done with informed consent (unless required by the Courts). Parents should therefore be given information – in the format suitable to them – about why an assessment is being carried out, what it will involve, and what might happen as a result.

People may misunderstand or misinterpret what a professional is telling them (this is true generally, not just for people with learning disabilities). This may be because they don't understand particular words, or because they have only understood or been told part of the information. People can also pick up messages from body language which may not be what the professional wants to convey. It is very important to check what someone understands, and to avoid blaming a person for not understanding or getting the wrong message.

Sometimes information is given and communication happens in meetings involving a number of professionals (such as child protection conferences: see also Section 4). It is important to make information and communication accessible in this context as well. Meetings can be very disempowering for parents. Jargon should be avoided and parents should have someone to support them prepare for the meeting and take part in it, if this is what they want.

> "We need people in meetings to have patience and take extra time. It also helps to have someone with you to help explain things. And also for there not to be too many people in the room".

**1.1.6** Information and communication should also be accessible to children.

Children also have entitlements to information about services that may help them and their families. They are entitled to be fully involved in any assessment of their needs, according to their age and understanding. They may have their own access needs relating to age and impairment/disability and good practice should ensure that these are addressed.

**1.1.7** Those involved in communicating with, and providing information to, parents and children should take advantage of the resources available to make information and communication accessible to people with learning disabilities.

Details are provided in the Resources section of this guidance.

## 1.2 Clear and co-ordinated referral and assessment procedures and processes, eligibility criteria and care pathways.

Referral and assessment procedures, eligibility criteria and care pathways should prevent avoidable difficulties arising by:

- Recognising low levels of need which, if unaddressed, are likely to lead to difficulties for parents and undermine children's welfare
- Recognising support needs at the early stages of the parenting experience
- Anticipating support needs which may arise at different stages in a family's life cycle.

> "The challenge for health and social services lies in ensuring that children whose parents are finding it difficult to care for them to (i) get enough help and support to assure their safety and well being, and (ii) receive help early enough to minimise the risk of children becoming looked after".
>
> Commission for Social Care Inspection, 2006, p.4.

**1.2.1** Adult and children's services, and health and social care, should jointly agree local protocols for referrals, assessments and care pathways in order to respond appropriately and promptly to the needs of both parents and children.

These protocols should take into account the processes set out in Working Together to Safeguard Children (2006) (see charts on pages 143–147). The Social Care Institute for Excellence has published guidance and a resource for the development of joint protocols to meet the needs of disabled parents in general (www.scie.org.uk).

The process of writing local protocols provides a valuable opportunity for the different services involved to get a better understanding of each other's roles and responsibilities. Some services have developed protocols to cover all parents with additional support needs, others just cover parents with learning disabilities. Some protocols only include adult and children's social care, others also include health and sometimes education and housing.

The following issues should be included, whatever form a local protocol takes and will need to be agreed by the services concerned:

- Referrals
- Sharing information between services
- Provision of accessible information to parents and children
- Assessment responsibilities, including criteria and arrangements for joint assessments
- Provision of assistance/information to parents and children to enable them to participate fully in the assessment
- Eligibility for different services
- Financial responsibilities, including provision for joint funding
- Charging
- Service provision, including joint working
- Service reviews
- Implementation of the protocol, including training.

*Good Practice Guidance on Working with Parents with a Learning Disability* 217

Protocols may also cover commissioning, or separate joint commissioning protocols may be required. Good practice in commissioning is covered in Section 3.

When considering which agencies and services need to agree joint protocols it is important to address the following issues:

- Young parents and parents-to-be with learning disabilities may be in transition between children's and adult services
- Parents with learning disabilities may experience a range of needs and difficulties, including a physical or sensory impairment and/or long-term health condition, mental health problems, domestic violence, substance abuse problems
- Some parents with learning disabilities experience significant housing problems, including; homelessness, harassment from neighbours, difficulties in maintaining a tenancy.

It will therefore be important that local protocols include all relevant agencies and professional roles involved in addressing these issues.

The Resources section of this guidance includes the contact details of some agencies that have agreed joint protocols and are willing to share these.

**1.2.2** Attention should be paid to promoting good communication between relevant agencies.

The process of writing and implementing joint protocols should promote good communication between the different agencies concerned. Some other initiatives (which may or may not be part of joint protocols) which have also been found to promote better communication between different services and professionals include;

- Liaison posts: e.g. a post within adult learning disability services with specific responsibility to liaise with children's services, or vice versa
- Joint training
- Practice development meetings or networks involving the range of services and practitioners supporting parents with learning disabilities
- Professional consultation services: e.g. designation of a particular children and families social worker to provide professional consultation to adult social care; designation of a community learning disability nurse to provide professional consultation to children's safeguarding teams. One protocol specifies that such consultation will be available within very short time frames in order to react to emergency referrals.

**Good practice example**

Following a steady increase in the numbers of parents with learning disabilities a Multi-Agency Consultation Group was set up covering

> South Norfolk. This meets monthly to offer support/advice to professionals/agencies that work with families where one or both parents may have learning difficulties. Professionals are offered a 'slot' at the meeting to present a case and the multi-agency team offer advice and, if necessary, appropriate referrals are made.
>
> From Thetford Sure Start – for more information contact: Bridgitte Shad, Health Care Co-ordinator, bridgitte.shad@norwich-pct.nhs.uk.

**1.2.3** Identification of needs should start when a pregnancy is confirmed.

Procedures, criteria and pathways therefore need to be agreed between maternity services and children's and adult social care. Such agreements could relate to parents with learning disabilities in particular or to all groups of parents and their children who may be identified as vulnerable. An important starting point will be to recognise:

- Pregnant women with learning disabilities are entitled to universal services
- Universal services are required to make "reasonable adjustments" to make their services accessible and suitable for people with learning disabilities
- Early assessments of support needed to look after a new baby will help to prevent avoidable difficulties arising.

**1.2.4** Adult and children's social care services should jointly agree referral procedures to prevent parents and children falling between the two services.

It is good practice that, as a general rule, referrals relating to the needs of parents with learning disabilities should be directed to Learning Disability services, unless there are concerns about children's welfare, in which case a referral should also be made to children's social care. If a referral is made directly to children's services, and it then becomes apparent that a parent has a learning disability, a referral should then also be made to adult Learning Disability services.

> **Good practice example**
>
> One local Practice Guidance document includes the following agreed referral procedures between adult and children's services:
>
> "Where there are no concerns for the child's welfare, but the parent is unable to provide the appropriate level of care due to disability, parenting support will be offered from the Adult Social Care Team, through a Community Care Plan.
>
> Where Adult Social Care teams are aware of concerns for a child's welfare, a referral should be made to the Children and Young People service for an assessment.  ➡

> Where children's teams become aware that a parent may have a learning disability, a referral to the Learning Disability Team should be made".
>
> Essex County Council, 2006. Practice Guidance: Referral and Joint Working Arrangements for working with parents and carers who have a learning disability, p.3. Further details from: Kate Evans, Service Manager, Family Centre and Family Group Conferences, kate.evans@essexcc.gov.uk.

**1.2.4** Eligibility criteria for children's and for adult social care services should enable consideration of each family's needs and circumstances. Eligibility criteria should also enable service responses at an early stage, to prevent avoidable difficulties arising.

Eligibility should not be determined by general exclusions or based on one type of criteria, such as IQ.

Developing joint protocols will give services the opportunity to consider the impact of their eligibility criteria on each other's services. For example, if a parent is deemed not eligible by adult services for support with parenting roles and responsibilities, this may mean that their children's welfare suffers and they become children in need and/or suffer significant harm. The development of joint protocols provides an opportunity to prevent this happening, by ensuring that support is provided at an early stage (as set out in Fair Access to Care Services, paragraph 65). This may mean recognising that a combination of learning disability and parenting responsibilities creates a higher level of need than if needs only relating to learning disability are considered.

> **Good practice example**
>
> One joint protocol agreed between children's and adult services recognises:
>
> "Services should be targeted at families who have additional need which means a different interpretation of the criteria relating to the threshold for service provision than that currently operated by specialist teams.
>
> The combination of impairment and parenting responsibilities within the overall context of the individual family's circumstances may generate a higher degree of need for support than a personal assessment of the disabled/ill adult alone.
>
> Disabled parents or children of disabled parents should automatically be entitled to an assessment". ➡

> Norfolk County Council, 2006. Enabling parents with a disability or long-term illness: Joint Policy and Protocol, p.7. Further details from: Joan Inglis, Project Manager, Support for Disabled Parents, joan.inglis@norfolk.gov.uk

**1.2.5** Local protocols should clearly specify responsibilities for assessment and care planning.

Good practice is promoted where there is clear agreement between adult and children's social care as to the circumstances in which single or joint assessments are required and who should take the lead. For example:

- Adult learning disability services have responsibilities for assessment and care planning when there are no child welfare concerns and where the parent needs assistance with the routine tasks of looking after children;
- Adult learning disability and children's services jointly co-ordinate assessment and care planning where parents need support in the medium to long-term to enable them to meet their children's developmental needs.
- Children's services lead assessment and planning (with specialist input from adult learning disability services) where intervention is required to prevent children suffering impairment to their health or development or significant harm and/or there is a disabled child in the family.

Whatever level of concern there is about children's welfare, practitioners need to be aware of parents with learning disabilities' entitlements to support under community care legislation, and to ensure that they receive the assessment and service response they are entitled to.

**1.2.6** Services in contact with parents with learning disabilities should promote good practice in assessment by using appropriate assessment materials and resources and/or access specialist expertise.

Needs relating to learning disability should be considered whatever the level of assessment, whether it is an assessment of additional needs being carried out by a universal service using the Common Assessment Framework, or a child in need assessment using the Framework for the Assessment of Children in Need and their Families, or a section 47 enquiry to establish whether a child may be suffering harm. This means that a range of professionals who are in contact with children may need to consider, using the Common Assessment Framework, the possibility of parental learning disability and its impact on children. Children's social care will also need to consider the impact and needs associated with learning disability when assessing children in need, and in safeguarding children.

Where a parent has a learning disability it will be important not to make assumptions about their parental capacity. Having a learning disability does not mean that a person cannot learn new skills. Learning disabled parents may need support to develop the understanding, resources, skills, experience and confidence to meet the needs of their children. Such support is particularly needed where they experience additional stressors such as having a disabled child, domestic violence, poor physical and mental health, substance misuse, social isolation, poor housing, poverty or a history of growing up in care.

The information gathered for any type of assessment should be no more than is necessary, and multiple assessments should be avoided. People with learning disabilities have often been subject to multiple assessments and may find these intrusive, particularly if they have not had a good experience of service responses to assessment.

Many parents with learning disabilities are understandably very worried that their children may be taken away from them. This fear can create real barriers in establishing the relationship necessary to carry out a good assessment. Consideration should be given as to who is the best person to carry out an assessment and/or what specialist expertise may need to be sought.

> "It can be worrying to admit to having problems with your child's behaviour, especially if they say he's fine at school and yet you're having problems with him at home."

Diagnostic psychometric assessments can provide information about whether a parent has a learning disability and about their skills and abilities. However, "Although such information is useful, it must be stressed that there is no direct correlation between the results of these tests and parental adequacy" (McGaw and Newman, 2005, p.27). A list of such assessment tools is given in the Resources section.

Assessments should cover family and environmental factors, as well as parental capacity. Research tells us that family and community support networks are particularly important for parents with learning disabilities and their children. We also know that parents with learning disabilities are particularly likely to experience difficult housing situations and poverty. Both the Common Assessment Framework and the Framework for the Assessment of Children in Need and their Families require that family and environmental factors are covered.

Adult learning disability services should ensure that Person Centred Planning is made available to parents with learning disabilities as part of both the assessment of their needs and the planned response to these needs. Person Centred Planning is a process of life planning which enables the identification of a person's strengths, needs, relationships and the barriers they face. It is a particularly appropriate method to use where people with learning disabilities are parents (see Resources).

**Good practice in assessment of parents with learning disabilities**

The Framework for the Assessment of Children in Need and their Families, and Person Centred Planning guidance lay down the foundations for good practice in assessing the needs of parents with learning disabilities. Whatever the type and level of assessment being carried out, the following are also key elements of good practice:

Assessors should be knowledgeable about both their statutory responsibilities, and about parents' legal rights, including their entitlements under community care legislation.

Where learning disability is suspected, an initial screening tool should be used in order to determine whether a specialist assessment is required (see Resources section).

Assessors should be sensitive to the stigma attached to a learning disability label. Every effort should be made to frame the issue as one of identifying particular support needs.

Psychometric assessments should not be relied on as the sole or primary measure of parenting capacity.

Out-of-home assessments should be avoided if at all possible, unless the home environment is disempowering to the parent.

Parents should be told, in plain language, what the assessment is, what it is for, what it will involve, and what will happen afterwards. They may need to be told more than once, for example, a parent may need to be reminded what happened at the last meeting.

Close attention should be paid to parents' access needs (this is a legal requirement). These may include:

- Putting written material into an accessible format
- Avoiding the use of jargon
- Taking more time to explain things
- Telling parents things more than once
- Beware, however, of the risk of sounding patronising.

Assessments should include the role of significant adults in the parent's life, to establish positive and/or negative contributions to the parenting role and effects on children's welfare.

Assessors should be aware that previous experiences may create significant fear about the role of children's social care services. Parents may be hostile and anxious, and considerable effort may be required to prevent this fear becoming a real barrier to a comprehensive assessment. ➡

> Assessors should generally be wary of misinterpreting the effects of cognitive impairment. Advice and specialist input should always be sought when parental learning disability is suspected.

## 1.3 Support is designed to meet the needs of parents and children and is based on assessments of their needs and strengths

**1.3.1** Support to develop and enhance parenting skills should be suited to the parent's learning needs and circumstances.

Support should be based on, and adapted to, the learning needs of parents. For example, if parents with learning disabilities are to benefit from parenting education programmes – whether run in a mainstream or specialist setting – such programmes will need to be adapted to meet the particular learning needs of the parents concerned (and this, indeed, is a requirement under the Disability Discrimination Act 1995).

> **Good practice example**
>
> "The Community Team for Parents with Learning Disabilities in Stockport wanted to support parents with learning difficulties, where children's social care had concerns about their ability to prepare adequate meals for their children. The team worked together with adult education to set up a course on cookery and child nutrition suited to the information needs and learning styles of parents with learning difficulties. Initially adult education said that the course could only be certificated if it was assessed through written means but the team negotiated and worked with them to devise more appropriate forms of assessment. The parents were then able to return to social services with certificates to show that they had learned the required skills".
> (Tarleton et al, 2006)

In the case of parent support services, an assessment of a parent's learning needs and circumstances should inform the support provided to develop parenting skills. Research indicates that – for parents with learning disabilities – the key elements of successful parenting skills support are:

> "Clear communication, and ensuring parents have understood what they are told
>
> Use of role play, modelling, and videoing parent and professional undertaking a task together, for discussion, comparison and reflection
>
> Step-by-step pictures showing how to undertake a task
>
> Repeating topics regularly and offering opportunities for frequent practice

Providing/developing personalised "props": for example, finding a container which will hold the right amount of milk for the child so that the parent does not have to measure out the milk".
(Tarleton et al, p.54)

**1.3.2** A family-centred approach should be taken to parenting support, responding to the needs of all family members (including fathers), rather than just the mother or just the child.

**1.3.3** A range of services are required. All families are different and at different stages of their life cycle families require different types of support.

Families affected by parental learning disability may benefit from some or all of the following types of services:

- Support to use universal ante- and post-natal services
- Parents' groups
- Courses in parenting skills and child development
- Croups and courses aimed specifically at fathers
- One-to-one support in parenting skills and child development
- Practical support in the home
- Assistance to use direct payments to purchase their own support
- Support with children's social and academic development
- Behaviour support services
- Counselling
- Advocacy services
- Family planning services
- Information and advice to children
- Support foster care/shared care
- Short breaks services.

Those with responsibility for putting together care plans, in response to assessments, need to be able to draw on a range of support services to suit each family's needs and circumstances. The implications of this for commissioning are covered in Section 3.

---

**Good practice example**

"All of the parents spoke warmly of the workers that supported them. They particularly appreciated workers who supported them to do things for themselves. Parents spoke about getting help with daily routines, cooking, budgeting and cleaning their homes. In these instances, workers often came to parents' houses early in the morning and again in the early evening when they particularly needed support. The majority of parents said that 'nothing could be better' about the support they received. In ➡

> most cases the amount of support given had been reduced as parents became more confident in their skills"
> (Tarleton et al, 2006, p.37)

> "The social worker helped me to get things done like painting and decorating – it made a big difference to how the house felt to live in".

**1.3.4** Support services should be available to help parents to promote their child's welfare at different ages and in a variety of situations.

It is against children's interests if support is provided to enable their parents to look after them while they are young but the necessary support is not then provided as children grow older and needs change.

For example, most parents need information, advice and support to help their children if they experience bullying at school or in their local communities. The children of parents of learning disabilities may be more likely to be bullied and their parents may have less personal and community resources on which to draw to help children resist bullying and its impact. Advocacy services for people with learning disabilities can be an important source of support, where these are available, but it is also necessary for schools and other services to think about how parents with learning disabilities can be helped in these circumstances.

Many parents need help with parenting adolescents and parents with learning disabilities may need access to support which recognises the impact of their learning disability. Parents with learning disabilities are entitled to expect that organisations that provide support with parenting teenagers make the necessary reasonable adjustments so that they can use such services. They and their adolescent children may also need access to specialist parenting support.

> "The child psychologist saw all of us, the whole family, first. Then he saw my son on his own. And then he told us how to do things to encourage good behaviour. It made a big difference, [my son] got a lot better and he's much happier."

**1.3.5** Where a number of different agencies are involved in supporting families affected by parental learning disability, a consistent and co-ordinated approach should be taken to the aims and objectives to be achieved.

Parents with learning disabilities are often in contact with a range of different organisations and professionals, and in these circumstances sometimes receive conflicting messages about what they should be aiming for. A lack of consistency and co-ordination confuses parents and places them at an unnecessary disadvantage.

**1.3.6** Children should be provided with support in their own right.

The children of parents with learning disabilities may need support in their own right. For example, their health or developmental needs may suffer while their parent is learning to better meet these needs and/or parent support services are being put in place. Children, particularly older children, may be at risk of taking on inappropriate caring roles within the family, or their welfare may be threatened by inadequate parental supervision. In such situations, children will meet the 'child in need' criteria and adult and children's services should work together to address children's needs, while at the same time work is done with parents to increase their capacity to meet their children's needs. Neither intervention is a substitute for the other but should be provided in tandem.

---

**Good practice example[2]**

Jake is 13 and lives with his mother and 2 siblings all of whom have learning disabilities (Jake does not). Jake's social worker felt that he didn't have sufficient opportunity at home to do his homework as his mother relied on him to help with his younger brother. She was also concerned that he didn't spend much time with friends his own age. She arranged for him to attend an after-school homework club on three days a week and to go to a football club every Saturday morning. The adult learning disability team re-assessed his mother's support needs and provided some additional help with preparing supper for the three children.

---

**1.3.7** Parents may need emotional support.

Parents with learning disabilities may have low self-esteem and lack confidence because of previous life experiences. They may therefore need support to build their confidence.

Parents may particularly need emotional support when children's social care become involved because of concerns about children's welfare. Fear that children are going to be taken away can make it harder for parents to respond positively to assessments and interventions. In such circumstances, parents need support from someone who they feel is "on their side" and who can help them positively engage with services. Such support is often provided by adult learning disability services, and by independent sector services and advocates.

---

**Messages from parents**

- Listen to children
- Help children to understand what a social worker is and what their job is
- Help the children say what they want to say    ➡

---

[2] Good practice examples concerning individual families are anonymised descriptions of cases provided by some of the services consulted with for this good practice guidance.

- Recognise positive changes, even if they're very small
- Put judgements in the background (we know you're judging us but don't behave like you are when you're talking to us)
- Help us to understand how the system works and who does what
- Put in support workers to help us get the children to school on time and things like that
- Build up trust so that we feel OK about letting you into our house and sharing information with you
- Don't patronise us
- Believe that we can change
- Acknowledge what we are doing, not just what we're struggling with.

Taken from a meeting with parents with learning disabilities in Bristol

## 1.4. Long-term support where needed

"You don't wake up and not have a learning difficulty. We have a mindset within learning disability services – we are generally there for life."
Social worker in a community learning difficulties team quoted in Tarleton et al, 2006, p.31

**1.4.1** A need for long-term support does not mean that parents cannot look after their children.

Some parents with learning disabilities will only need short-term support, such as help with looking after a new baby or learning about child development and childcare tasks. Others, however, will need on-going support. Most may need support at various different points of their family's life cycle for two main reasons. Firstly, although a parent with learning disabilities can learn how to do things, their cognitive impairment will not go away. Just as someone with a physical impairment may need personal assistance for the rest of their life so a person with learning disabilities may need assistance with daily living, particularly as new situations arise. Secondly, children and their needs change. A parent may have learnt to look after a baby and young child and be coping well. However, as the child enters adolescence other support needs may arise.

**Good practice example**

The Family Support Unit at the Home Office funded Home-Start and the Ann Craft Trust to run a three year project, providing volunteer supporters to parents with learning disabilities. Volunteers received specialist training. A total of 18 families were provided with the service, some over the three year period. Referring professionals were positive about the project, as were most of the parents. A number of large families were referred to the project, whereas it had initially been expected that most referrals would concern prospective parents and parents with babies and young children. These families would have benefited from support at

> an earlier stage. A common problem experienced by families was harassment and violence from neighbours, and a number of them had to move house because of this.
> (Cooke, 2005)

**1.4.2** Where a need for long-term support with parenting tasks is identified, it should form part of the community care and/or child in need plan.

Early identification of support needs will help prevent unnecessary difficulties arising but it should be recognised that some support needs may be on-going and this should be reflected in care planning.

> **Good practice example**
>
> A twenty one year old mother became pregnant. She lived on her own, her husband having left her. She had a learning disability and her previous child had been permanently removed from her care. She was alienated from her extended family. The initial plan was to apply for a court order to remove the child at birth but attempts were made to examine any other possible options.
>
> It was decided to explore the possibility of placing the mother with a carer on the Adult Placement scheme. The aim was to provide the woman with a supportive environment where she could improve her life skills and then provide a safe environment for the baby where the mother could be helped to provide adequate care. An adult carer was identified and the mother moved in prior to the baby's birth. The intention is that this is a long-term placement which will continue for as long as the mother and child require such support.

**1.4.3** Practitioners should aim to build a relationship with parents where they feel able to ask for support as needs change.

Children's welfare is more likely to be effectively promoted if parents feel that practitioners are seeking to work in partnership with them to improve outcomes for their children, and if they experience positive responses to their needs.

## 1.5 Access to independent advocacy and to support for self-advocacy

**1.5.1** Self-advocacy support should be made available to parents to help to build confidence and self-esteem.

Lack of confidence and low self-esteem can create parenting difficulties – poor hygiene can be associated with low self-esteem for example, or a parent may fail to attend a mother and baby group because of a lack of self-confidence. A self-advocacy group can help boost self-esteem and confidence, and thereby encourage the development of parenting skills. Such support can also help parents develop strategies for coping with harassment and bullying.

**1.5.2** Advocacy and self-advocacy should be made available to help parents access and engage with services.

Parents with learning disabilities may experience difficulties in getting access to housing which is suitable for them and their children. In such circumstances they may well need self-advocacy skills and/or advocacy support in their dealings with housing providers. They may also need assistance with ensuring they and their family receive the benefits to which they are entitled.

Parents with learning disabilities sometimes have a long history of difficult relationships with children's social care, particularly if they have had previous children removed from their care. These experiences can create hostility, a feeling of a lack of control, and a reluctance to engage with services. Advocacy and support for self-advocacy can help parents to understand professionals' concerns, while at the same time giving parents knowledge about their rights and confidence to state their needs. Advocacy may also be necessary if a parent is to give informed consent in respect of a service intervention.

**1.5.3** Independent advocacy should always be provided where children are the subject of a child protection plan and/or care proceedings instituted.

Any parent involved in a child protection conference and/or care proceedings should be informed about local and national sources of independent advocacy. It is particularly important that parents with learning disabilities have access to independent advocacy in these situations. Commissioning strategies should address the availability of local advocacy (see Section 3) as these are not always readily available.

It is very important that parents have access to independent advocacy at an early stage and also that advocates have appropriate skills and knowledge of both learning disability and child protection issues.

The next section of this guidance covers situations where safeguarding procedures are considered necessary.

## SECTION 2   GOOD PRACTICE WHERE SAFEGUARDING PROCEDURES ARE NECESSARY

This Section should be read in the context of the following guidance:

Working Together to Safeguard Children: A guide to inter-agency working to promote and safeguard the welfare of children.
http://www.everychildmatters.gov.uk/workingtogether/

Information Sharing: Practitioners' Guide.
http://www.everychildmatters.gov.uk/resources-and-practice/IG00065/

Protocol on Advice and Advocacy for Parents (Child Protection)
http://www.dh.gov.uk/assetRoot/04/01/89/00/04018900.pdf

National Standards on the Provision of Children's Advocacy Services.
http://www.dh.gov.uk/assetRoot/04/01/88/93/04018893.pdf

Where there are concerns that children of parents with learning disabilities are at risk of significant harm, good practice will be promoted by:

- Clarity about rights, roles and responsibilities, including the legislative basis for action and the entitlement of parents to support under both children's and community care legislation
- In depth assessments, including appropriate specialist input from both children's and adult services
- Information sharing between relevant agencies and professionals
- Involvement of parents and children, and the provision of independent advocacy.

## 2.1 Promoting children's best interests

Children have a right to be protected from harm, and for their interests to be paramount. They also have the right to receive the necessary support in order that, wherever possible, they remain living with their parents.

**2.1.1** Local authorities have a duty, under the Children Act 1989, as amended by section 53 of the Children Act 2004, to ascertain the wishes and feelings of children when carrying out assessments and making decisions about service responses.

Children also have the right to information at all stages of the safeguarding process, from the outcome of section 47 enquiries through to court proceedings. Consideration should always be given to how to make such information accessible to children, and to the need to provide the information more than once in order for children to make sense of it.

**2.1.2** Where section 47 enquiries conclude that a child is not at risk, or not at continuing risk, of significant harm, it will be important that, where appropriate, action is taken – under section 17 of the Children Act 1989 and community care legislation – to prevent future problems arising.

It is particularly important to avoid the situation where poor standards of parental care, which do not however meet the threshold of significant harm to a child, subsequently deteriorate because of a lack of support provided to the parent. A failure to provide support in this type of situation can undermine a child's right to remain with their family. It is also important to provide any necessary support when a child is no longer the subject of a child protection plan, in order to prevent a subsequent deterioration in parental care (see 2.2.5 and 2.2.9 below).

**2.1.3** Where a child protection conference is convened, a child should be invited and supported to participate, subject to their age and understanding.

The chair should meet the child beforehand to explain the process to them and an independent advocate should be provided where appropriate. Where it is not appropriate to involve a child in the conference, children's social care should ensure that the child's wishes and feelings are conveyed to the meeting. It is good practice to avoid the situation where one worker is representing the views of both parents and children.

**2.1.4** When a key worker is appointed for a child whose parent has a learning disability, it is important that the worker has some understanding of learning disability or, if not, that the worker has access to such expertise.

**2.1.5** Children who are provided with accommodation under Section 20 of the Children Act 1989 by a local authority are entitled to independent advocacy services.

This means they should have access to an advocate who works for them and no-one else and who helps to ensure that they:

- Understand what is happening to them
- Can make their views known
- Where possible, exercise choice when decisions are being made about their care.

Section 7 guidance sets out the standards for children's advocacy services (Department of Health 2002). It is important (and required under the Disability Discrimination Acts 1995 and 2005) to ensure that the children of parents of learning disabilities have equal access to independent advocacy services.

**2.1.6** Local authorities should promote contact with family members for children who are the subject of care orders, unless the court has given them permission to refuse contact.

Children's wishes and feelings about contact with their family should be taken into account, including the venue and timing of contact. In the majority of cases, it will be in a child's best interests for them to maintain links with their family, however occasional this contact may be and even where there is no prospect of the child returning to their family. It is in children's best interests if their parents are supported to avoid conveying negative and/or contradictory messages about substitute carers.

Continuing contact with siblings, grandparents and other family members is usually in a child's best interests, and should be promoted whenever it is in the child's best interests.

## 2.2 Ensuring equitable treatment for parents with learning disabilities

Parents have a right to a private and family life, but children have a right to protection from harm.

**2.2.1** Parents whose children are the subject of section 47 enquiries should always be given information about independent sources of advice and advocacy, both locally and nationally.

Where formal independent advocacy is not available, parents should be encouraged to involve a friend, relative or member of their local community to support them through the process.

**2.2.2** It will be important that every effort is made to ensure that independent advocates are those who have the necessary skills and expertise concerning both learning disability and child protection.

Informal supporters should be provided with advice and information, or referral to relevant organisations, to help them carry out their role effectively and constructively.

**2.2.3** Unless sharing information would place the child at risk of significant harm, parents should be fully informed about, and – as much as possible – involved in the whole process, from the outcome of section 47 enquiries through to court hearings.

They should be provided with whatever assistance may be required to enable them to understand what is happening and to express their views. Information should be provided in a format which is accessible to them. It should be recognised that information may well need to be provided more than once in order for parents to understand what is going on.

It is good practice to identify – at an early stage – someone or another agency who can help the parent understand what is happening and to contribute to assessments and, where possible, to care planning. Such support can be crucial to gaining parents' co-operation and can help to avoid, for example, having to go to court to obtain a Child Assessment Order.

**2.2.4** Core assessments involving families affected by parental learning disability should always include specialist input concerning the impact of learning disability.

Core assessments should also include seeking information from others who may know the parent(s) well, providing the parent gives their consent.

It should be recognised that, in many cases where there are risks of significant harm to children of learning disabled parents, parents usually face other difficulties in addition to learning disability. These may include mental health and/or physical health problems, domestic violence, substance abuse. Assessments should therefore also include, where appropriate, specialist input on these issues.

**2.2.5** Where it is a partner (who may or may not be learning disabled themselves) of a learning disabled parent who poses a risk of harm to the child it will be important to seek to support the non-abusing parent with learning disabilities to protect their child.

Assessments should also address the possible vulnerability of the learning disabled parent and their need to be protected from harm. Specialist input to assess and meet the needs of a vulnerable adult may be required.

**2.2.6** Where section 47 enquiries conclude that a child is not at risk, or not at continuing risk, of significant harm it will be important that action is taken to prevent future problems arising.

It is particularly important to avoid the situation where poor standards of parental care, which do not however meet the threshold of being of significant harm to a child, subsequently deteriorate because of a lack of support provided to the parent. A failure to provide support in this type of situation can undermine a parent's rights to a private and family life, and may also contravene an authority's disability equality duty. Families affected by parental learning disability are likely to have an on-going need for support, and where a child protection plan is not considered necessary, a child in need plan should be drawn up for each identified child in need, drawing on the good practice identified in Section 1 of this guidance.

**2.2.7** Parents should be invited to attend child protection conferences and support provided to enable them to fully participate.

Chairs of child protection conferences should meet with the parent beforehand to explain the process to them and there is an expectation that they will be provided with an independent advocate if this is what they wish. The extended family can often play an important role in supporting parents with learning disabilities and they should be invited if the parent so wishes.

Careful consideration should be given to ensuring that all communication associated with the child protection conference – from invitation through to the conduct of the meeting – is accessible to the parent with learning disabilities. Information should be sought, from the parent and/or their advocate, about what communication format is accessible to them.

> **Good practice example**
>
> "One child protection conference chair always asks for a parents' 'word bank'. This includes the words that parents can read and understand. All subsequent letters to parents and any papers they need to see, then have to be written using words in the 'bank'. The 'word bank' is drawn up by the parents and a trusted professional before the child protection meeting"
> (Tarleton et al, 2006, p.86)

**2.2.8** Where children are subject to a child protection plan, it is good practice to appoint a key worker for the parent(s) with learning disabilities (as well as a key worker for the child/ren).

Both key workers should be part of the core group and should have expertise, or access to expertise, in supporting families affected by parental learning disability.

**2.2.9** Extended family members should be part of the core group, if the parent wishes this and if they have a role to play in supporting the family.

> "Where friends or family members are helping to support a parent with learning disabilities in the context of child protection procedures it is good practice to provide information and advice to such supporters to enable them to fulfil this role effectively. They may be referred to specialist advice services, such as the Family Rights Group, or to relevant local independent organisations; and/or they may be given information about the child protection process and their potential role within it".
>
> See section on the involvement of supporters in Protocol on Advice and Advocacy for Parents (Child Protection), Department of Health, 2002, p.27.

**2.2.10** Where a child protection plan is drawn up and this involves action to be taken by parents, the chair should ensure that parents are fully supported to understand what is required of them and that support is provided to help achieve this.

This may well involve working with adult learning disability services and/or an independent sector agency. Parents should only be judged on whether they have complied with any requirements if it can be shown that:

- They were given clear information about what was required of them
- The necessary support has been made available to them.

---

**Good practice example**

A voluntary organisation, specialising in supporting people with learning disabilities, was asked to undertake a community-based assessment of a mother with a two year old son. Her previous experiences of services and the pending care proceedings meant "she was finding it impossible to engage with professionals she regarded as patronising, judgemental and unreliable". The organisation developed a "mutually respectful relationship" with her and "together we were able to identify several areas where appropriate support would significantly improve her parenting skills". The assessment resulted in 10 hours of support per week being provided for three months and the date of the final court hearing was put back to accommodate this. At the end of this period, parenting capacity was assessed as having improved sufficiently to mean that her child should remain with her. The voluntary organisation will continue to visit once a week.

Taken from Circles Network Annual Report 2003-2004

---

**2.2.11** When a child is no longer the subject of a child protection plan, it is important that support to parents is continued according to assessed need.

There is a danger that high eligibility thresholds in children's social care can mean that support is withdrawn. This may mean that parents struggle to maintain improvements in their parenting capacity and they enter a 'revolving door' of re-referrals which may their children being looked after by the local authority. The involvement of both children's and adult services in providing services to members of the family will help to prevent this happening.

**2.2.12** When children are placed in foster care, parents should receive practical support to maximise their chances of improving their parenting capacity.

Without this, parents will have little chance of reunification with children who have been removed from their care. Parents are likely to have strong reactions to separation from their children (particularly when it triggers feelings from previous experiences of loss). They will need help with these painful emotions in order that their reactions do not unnecessarily jeopardise their chances of reunification with their children.

> **Good practice example**
>
> Children's social care had been involved for some time with the Everett family. Ms Everett has learning disabilities, her partner does not. They have two children – a son aged 20 and a daughter aged 13, Rachel (who has learning disabilities). Ms Everett treated Rachel as confidante and best friend and wanted to have Rachel at home with her. Consequently, her school attendance was very poor. There were also significant concerns about a lack of hygiene, nutrition and general care. Rachel was placed on the child protection register, removed to temporary foster care and children's social care applied to the court for a Care Order. However, the judge felt that the family hadn't been given sufficient opportunity to see if things could improve with support.
>
> Children's social care then arranged for support to be provided by a local voluntary organisation.
>
> They:
>
> - Supported the family during Rachel's contact home visits by making sure everything was in place in preparation for the visit, such as food
> - Supported the family when contact visits were extended to include Sunday nights and ensured that Rachel then went to school the following morning
> - Helped with hygiene, routines and engaging with other services
> - Helped both parents to access Learn Direct in their village
> - Arranged, through the GP, for Ms Everett to see a counsellor with whom she explored her childhood experiences and their impact on her as a mother.
>
> Ms Everett was able to see that Rachel was a lot happier when she went to school regularly, seeing her friends and doing activities outside school such as horse-riding (which was arranged by the foster carer).
>
> Rachel has returned home, attends school regularly and has been taken off the child protection register. She still goes horse-riding and occasionally stays overnight with the foster carer. The voluntary organisation's support worker visits once a month to check whether Ms Everett needs any more support.

**2.2.13** As long as continuing parental involvement when children are placed in foster care is not considered detrimental to a child's welfare, it should be positively encouraged and promoted, and parents should be supported to be involved in their children's lives.

This involvement should encompass both contact between parents and children and the involvement of parents in the decisions affecting children's lives.

"Because foster care basically provides for shared parenting, birth parent involvement is beneficial to everyone involved – child, parents, foster carers and social worker".
*A Child's Journey through Placement*, Vera Fahlberg, 1994

**2.2.14** Placement with extended family members should always be considered.

Support from the extended family can work well and can take the form of 'shared care' or of permanent placement. On the other hand, there are some circumstances where extended family members would not provide suitable support, and there are other circumstances where extended family members attempt to 'take over' care of children without appropriate involvement of parents. Assessments which take into account the wider context of the parents' and children's circumstances and needs will ensure that care planning is fully informed by both the possibilities, and the limitations, of extended family involvement.

**2.2.15** Where possible, foster care placements should be made with carers who have experience and/or training in working in partnership with parents with learning disabilities.

**2.2.16** Parents should be informed of the complaints procedure and it will be important that such procedures are conducted in ways which ensure people with learning disabilities equal access to all stages of the complaints process. This should include information in easy to understand formats and any support required to use the complaints procedure.

**2.2.17** Local authorities should make reasonable adjustments to procedures in relation to care proceedings in order to avoid discrimination against parents with learning disabilities.

One key issue for parents with learning disabilities involved in court proceedings is their need for enough time to understand what is going on, to be fully involved in any assessments and care planning, and to have the chance to learn and demonstrate improved parenting capacity. Good practice for the courts (and for solicitors and Guardians Ad Litem) is outside the remit of this guidance. However, while children's interests must be paramount, it will be important that local authorities make whatever reasonable adjustments are required to their own practices and procedures in order to give parents with learning disabilities equality of opportunity to retain the care of their children.

Moreover, in order to fulfil their disability equality duty, anticipatory action should be taken to ensure this equality of opportunity, rather than just responding to individual cases as they arise. It will be important, for example, that monitoring of timescales for assessments, care plans and care proceedings looks at whether targets are creating obstacles to making reasonable adjustments for parents with learning disabilities.

**2.2.18** Parents should have access to both emotional and practical support when the child protection process concludes with children being removed.

Parents' grief should be recognised and responded to. Such bereavement is particularly hard to bear when parents have experienced other losses in their lives (including in their own childhoods) and services should be aware of parents' vulnerability and needs for considerable support in such a situation. Parents should be supported to avoid the situation where they conceive another child without their parenting support needs being addressed. Repeated removals of babies and young children into care can be avoided if the necessary support is provided to people with learning disabilities, under Fair Access to Care Services. It will also be important to work with health colleagues to enable people with learning disabilities to have access to family planning and other health services.

> "They were all coming round my house and then when he was adopted they stopped coming and no-one talked to me about it. It was very hard".

## SECTION 3 GOOD PRACTICE IN COMMISSIONING

Good practice in supporting parents with learning disabilities depends on a commissioning strategy jointly developed and agreed between adult and children's services, and encompassing health, education, housing and social care services in both the statutory and voluntary/independent sectors.

Arrangements for developing such a strategy will depend on local arrangements for commissioning adult learning disability services and local Children's and Young People's Plans. The principles for commissioning are set out in the National Service Framework for Children, Young People and Maternity Services (Department of Health/Department for Education and Skills, 2004a, pp. 112-3). A framework for joint planning and commissioning has also been published: Joint Planning and Commissioning Framework for Children, Young People and Maternity Services, 2006, www.everychildmatters. gov.uk/_files/312A353A9CB391262BAF14CC7C1592F8.pdf. The Department for Education and Skills has published a number of resources for commissioners
http://www.everychildmatters.gov.uk/strategy/planningandcommissioning/.

It is important that adult and children's services take joint responsibility for commissioning services to meet the needs of parents with learning disabilities and their children. This joint responsibility will need to be taken at all four stages of commissioning:

- Identifying needs and mapping existing service provision
- Allocating resources
- Developing services
- Monitoring and reviewing.

## 3.1 Identifying needs

**3.1.1** A commissioning strategy should be based on knowledge of current and likely future needs.

Adult learning disability services need to have an idea of the demand for support from parents with learning disabilities. An audit of the current numbers of parents with learning disabilities and an estimate of future numbers would provide an important starting point for a commissioning strategy.

Children's social care need to know the number of children in need, and the number within the child protection system, whose parents have learning disabilities. Again an audit of current numbers and an estimate of future numbers would provide a useful starting point for commissioning.

**3.1.2** A commissioning strategy needs to based on an audit of current service provision and an identification of the gaps in service provision.

An audit of current service provision is an opportunity to establish where in the statutory and independent sector, across health, social care, housing and education, parents with learning disabilities and their children currently receive support. Such an audit could cover not only specialist services but also mainstream universal settings, such as midwifery services, health visitors, after schools clubs, etc. A lot of this information will be available already as part of the Children and Young People's Plan, Supporting People strategies, and so on.

Housing is a major issue for many families affected by parental learning disability so it will be important to include housing in audits of needs and services. It is also helpful if commissioning strategies recognise both the role of schools and the support needed by parents if they are to promote their children's educational development. Parents have a key role to play in supporting their children's education, and there is evidence that they sometimes experience barriers to fulfilling this role.

One method which has proved useful to commissioners in a range of contexts is to select a sample of 'cases' or placements and analyse the needs (including unmet needs), service responses and costs. This method has proved particularly useful in identifying low incidence, high cost needs.

**3.1.3** Service user perspectives should inform the identification of need.

Families affected by parental learning disability, and those who work with them, can provide valuable perspectives on existing service provision (both specialist and mainstream), unmet need and ways of meeting such needs. It is helpful if commissioning strategies include proposals for consulting with these groups. Consideration will have to be given to the resources needed to enable such consultation to take place and the time-frame for drawing up the strategy in order to take account of what is required to consult effectively.

## 3.2 Allocating resources

**3.2.1** It is good practice to have formal joint commissioning arrangements which are underpinned by formal pooling of budgets. Informal arrangements are too vulnerable to changes in personnel or changes in priorities.

**3.2.2** Pooling budgets helps to promote a more integrated approach to commissioning, eligibility and care planning, and service provision.

Most importantly, pooling budgets should prevent the problem where parents with learning disabilities can fall between children's and adult services as each attempts to defend their respective scarce resources.

Section 31 of the Health Act 1999 makes possible the pooling of health and local authority resources to meet the needs of a particular population group. There are no restrictions on local authority adult and children's services pooling resources and local authorities may also pool resources with 'relevant partners' such as District Councils under Section 10 of the Children Act 2004.

> "The key advantage of pooled funding is that it opens up the prospect of original thinking about how better outcomes might be achieved. It permits thinking that is independent of any unhelpful traditions, vested interests, ways of working and constraints on the spending of funds that have hitherto existed."Everything you wanted to know about pooled budgets but were afraid to ask, www.everychildmatters.gov.uk/_files/1CB4E7D2B038F853D5523B49DD0E2693.doc p. 6. See also, www.everychildmatters.gov.uk/strategy/planningandcommissioning/poolingbudgets/

## 3.3 Developing services

**3.3.1** The development of services should be underpinned by the principles and aims of both Valuing People and Every Child Matters.

Valuing People committed Learning Disability Partnership Boards to "ensure that services are available to support parents with a learning disability" and set out four key principles for meeting the needs of people with learning disabilities generally. These are:

- Legal and civil rights: "People with learning disabilities have the right to ... marry and have a family, ... with help and support to do so where necessary"

- Independence: "... the starting presumption should be one of independence, rather than dependence, with public services providing the support needed to maximise this. Independence in this context does not mean doing everything unaided"
- Choice: "We believe that everyone should be able to make choices"
- Inclusion: "Inclusion means enabling people with learning disabilities to do ... ordinary things, make use of mainstream services and be fully included in the local community"
  (Department of Health, 2001, p.23)

The Children Act 2004 placed a statutory requirement on children's services authorities to improve 'well-being' for all children in their area by enabling children to:

- Be healthy
- Stay safe
- Enjoy and achieve
- Make a positive contribution
- Have economic well-being.

Children's services authorities also have a duty to reduce inequalities in well-being between young children in their area.

> **Good practice example**
>
> In one local authority, adult learning disability services and children's social care pooled resources to develop a 'shared care' service for families affected by parental learning disability. This matches families with experienced foster carers who share the care of children and make a long-term commitment to supporting the family.

**3.3.2** Good practice in commissioning considers both the role of mainstream services and the development of a range of specialist services.

Local services will know from their own experiences, and we also know from the research summarised in Appendix A, that a range of service responses are likely to be needed to meet the needs of families affected by parental learning disability. Some of these responses concern the development of particular expertise or provision within existing mainstream or social care services; others concern the development of specialist services. They include:

- Expertise in working with parents with learning disabilities amongst midwifery and health visiting services
- Liaison roles between different services, e.g. between adult and children's social care
- Expertise in assessments of parents with learning disabilities where there are concerns about children's welfare

- Parent support services – both specialist and mainstream services
- Parenting courses, parents' groups: both specialist and mainstream services
- Independent advocacy services
- Direct payments support services
- Adult placement services for parents with learning disabilities and their children
- Foster carers experienced and/or trained in working partnership with parents with learning disabilities
- Housing and housing related support
- Accessible information and availability of communication resources
- Counselling and therapeutic services, and self-advocacy/self-help groups.

> **Good practice example**
>
> A Local Safeguarding Children Board identified that resources were required to make child protection conferences and related documentation accessible to parents with learning disabilities, and to provide advocacy support. The Assistant Director for Social Services (Learning Disability) and the Director of Children's Services agreed to jointly fund such resources.

**3.3.3** Service user perspectives should inform the development of both mainstream and specialist services.

Both parents and children usually have clear ideas about what would meet their needs and it is important that these messages inform any commissioning strategy. Current service providers, including specialist services in the independent sector, also have a valuable perspective. Commissioning strategies should include proposals for consulting with these groups. Resources may need to be allocated to enable such consultation to take place and the time-frame for drawing up the strategy should take account of what is required to consult effectively.

"Children on the child protection register said their parents needed:

- Practical help
- Therapeutic help
- Clear communication [about what needed to change]; and
- Time to get 'back on track'."
    (Commission for Social Care Inspection, 2006, p.19)

**3.3.4** Training for both children's and adult services on working with parents with learning disabilities.

Both children's and adult workers will need specific training in order to respond appropriately to the needs of families affected by parental learning disability.

Child protection training strategies should include adult learning disability services. Those responsible for commissioning training will also need to ensure that specific training is available on assessing and meeting the needs of parents with learning disabilities for all workers who come into contact with them and their families. It is helpful if this includes mainstream services such as midwifery and health visiting.

It is often helpful if parents with learning disabilities are involved in delivering such training. The Resources section of this good practice guidance provides some information about both training materials and organisations that can provide training.

## 3.4. Monitoring and reviewing the effectiveness of service responses

**3.4.1** Services to parents with learning disabilities and their children should be monitored and reviewed using the frameworks and criteria operated by Learning Disability Partnership Boards and children's services.

However, it will be important to gather such data in a way which enables the outcomes for parents with learning disabilities and their children to be distinguished from other service user groups. This is the kind of exercise which will be required as part of the Disability Equality Duty, so that local authorities can assess whether they are fulfilling their duty to promote equal access and equal opportunities for disabled people.

**3.4.2** Statistical data on comparative outcomes can be supplemented by qualitative data in order to fully understand the reasons for any differences in outcomes.

For example, some organisations have expressed concern that the children of parents with learning disabilities, who enter the child protection process, are more likely to be permanently removed from their parents than the children of parents who do not have a learning disability. If monitoring of service provision in a locality reveals such a pattern, it is advisable to use qualitative methods such as case audits to understand why this is, and the implications for service provision.

**3.4.3** Monitoring and reviewing of services should include the perspectives of service users.

As in all stages of the commissioning process, the perspectives of parents with learning disabilities and their children will be key to any evaluation of how services are doing in meeting their needs. The involvement of parents with learning disabilities is also an important part of fulfilling the disability equality duty, as required in the Disability Discrimination Act 2005 (see Appendix B).

# APPENDIX A   WHAT DO WE KNOW ABOUT THE NEEDS AND CIRCUMSTANCES OF PARENTS WITH LEARNING DISABILITIES?

Research can tell us about the likely needs, or risk of negative outcomes, associated with a range of factors. It cannot tell us what is true for a particular parent, child or family.

Research can therefore be useful if it alerts workers to the factors that they should be looking out for. However, research should not be used to bolster an assumption that a particular family's characteristics and/or situation will inevitably lead to a negative outcome.

Similarly, research can tell us what type of intervention helps most parents and children who have a particular set of needs. It cannot tell us what will definitely help this particular parent or their children. There is, however, an increasing body of evidence about the types of support which help promote positive improvements for families affected by parental learning disability. Unfortunately, there is also evidence that many parents with learning disabilities do not receive such support.

## What do we mean by "learning disability"?

The White Paper, Valuing People, states that learning disability includes the presence of:

> "A significantly reduced ability to understand new or complex information, to learn new skills (impaired intelligence); with a reduced ability to cope independently (impaired social functioning); which started before adulthood, with a lasting effect on development".
> (Department of Health, 2001, p.14)

It is important to recognise that:

- A particular level of IQ cannot be taken as the only defining characteristic of learning disability
- Individuals can have different ability levels across the different components of IQ and other tests
- While 2.2% of the population is recognised as having a learning disability (varying from 'mild' to 'profound'), another 6.7% fall within an IQ range of 70-80 (Weschler Adult Intelligence Scale -Revised, 1997)
- It can therefore be difficult to clearly demarcate those parents who have learning disabilities and those who do not

(This is a summary of the useful discussion in McGaw and Newman, 2005, pp. 8-14)

In the context of parenting, it is more helpful to identify support needs associated with learning disability than to take a rigid approach to the definition of learning disability. Parents with learning disabilities may have support needs associated with impairment, but they may also have support needs associated with other factors such as poor health or inadequate housing.

## Learning disabilities or learning difficulties?

Many people who have the label 'learning disability' have said they prefer to be called 'people with learning difficulties'. They use this term to mean "people who since they were a child had a real difficulty in learning many things. We do not mean people who just have a specific difficulty in learning, for example, people who only have difficulty with reading which is sometimes called dyslexia" (Emerson et al, 2005). One of the objections that people have to the term 'learning disability' is that it can be taken to mean that they are not able to learn. Such an assumption has particular implications for parents who may be facing a situation of having to prove that they can look after their children.

On the other hand, the term 'learning disabilities' is used within the statutory framework for social care support while the term 'learning difficulties' is used within the special educational needs statutory framework, and the two definitions are not the same. Indeed, it is clear that when people self-define themselves as 'people with learning difficulties' they mean people who, within the statutory framework, would be referred to as 'people with learning disabilities'.

This practice guidance is about helping practitioners to promote good practice in fulfilling their statutory responsibilities in terms of both supporting parents and safeguarding and promoting children's welfare. Therefore it is more appropriate to use the term 'parents with learning disabilities' because this is the term that is used within the legislation and statutory guidance. However, practitioners will want to be sensitive to how people define and describe themselves and to use language that parents are comfortable with in their contact with them.

## What do we know about the needs and experiences of families, in contact with social care, where at least one parent has learning disabilities?

Almost all the information we have about parents with learning disabilities concerns those who are in contact with social care, and it mostly concerns mothers. We know very little about the needs and experiences of families where at least one parent has learning disabilities but who are not in contact with social care; and we know very little about the experiences of fathers with learning disabilities.

Estimates of the total number of parents with learning disabilities in the United Kingdom vary widely, from 23,000 to 250,000. What is clear, however, is that there are increasing numbers of parents with learning disabilities in contact with services. Over the last decade or so, clinical psychologists have reported an increase in request for assessments, and community learning disability teams have seen an increase in the number of parents with learning disabilities on their caseloads. Most children and family teams have at least one family affected by parental learning disability on their caseloads (see Booth and Booth, 2004) There are also varying estimates of the proportion of parents whose children are removed from their care. It would appear, from of a recent national survey of people with learning disabilities, that about 40% of parents are not living with their children.[3] They are more likely to be living with their children if they are living with other relatives (particularly in the case of mothers) and fathers are more likely to be living with their children than mothers. Six out of ten mothers, who live either on their own or with a partner, are not living with their children aged under 18.[4]

In one local authority area, about a sixth of family court care proceedings concerned children with at least one parent who has learning disabilities and in about 75% of cases children were permanently removed from their family (Booth et al, 2005). However, analysis of case files across 10 local authority areas found that in less than a fifth of cases involving parents with learning disabilities were their children removed, most were fostered rather than adopted, and there "was no evidence to suggest that parental learning disability in itself was the reason children were removed" (Cleaver and Nicholson, forthcoming). There is anecdotal evidence of local variations in social care practice and court decisions.

## Most parents with learning disabilities in contact with social care experience a range of difficulties.

Parents with learning disabilities, who are in contact with social care, often experience poverty and unemployment; poor housing and difficult neighbourhoods; and lack of information (Social Care Institute for Excellence, 2005). While these are factors experienced by most families in contact with children's social care, parents with learning disabilities have particularly high levels of need, often experiencing severe poverty and inadequate housing (Cleaver and Nicholson, forthcoming). Moreover, the lack of information experienced by poor families generally is compounded for parents with learning disabilities by the inaccessibility of most forms of information.

Research on parenting support generally, finds that it is very difficult for stressed families to benefit from such support when they face disadvantages such as poverty, poor health and difficult housing situations (Moran et al,

---

[3] Secondary analysis of data from Emerson et al, 2005.
[4] These figures were provided by Eric Emerson in a secondary analysis of data from Emerson et al, 2005.

2004). Social care services, therefore, often need to work with other agencies to attempt to, for example, improve a family's housing situation.

> "I want my children to have a nice house and a garden to play in, and a good education. I want the support to get these things."[5]

Families affected by parental learning disability are also particularly likely to experience negative attitudes, and worse, from those with whom they come into contact. For example, small scale studies (e.g. Cooke 2005) and messages from parents with learning disabilities themselves (e.g. CHANGE 2005) indicate that harassment and bullying, and sometimes violence and financial or sexual exploitation, can be a major problem for parents with learning disabilities and their children.

Most parents with learning disabilities who receive core assessments from children's social care also experience other difficulties such as "poor mental and physical health, domestic violence, growing up in care, or substance misuse" (Cleaver and Nicholson, forthcoming).

Parents with learning disabilities may also have low self-esteem and lack confidence, primarily because of previous experiences of discrimination, abuse and segregation. People with learning disabilities are more likely to have experienced physical, emotional or sexual abuse as children and young adults, and will carry the legacies of these experiences into their own parenting experiences.

Some professionals have raised concerns that parents with learning disabilities experience undiagnosed mental health problems, including post-natal depression, and argued that it is important to diagnose and respond to such needs (see discussion in Cotson et al, 2001, pp. 291-292).

Professionals consulted for this guidance raised their concerns that physical health problems experienced by parents with learning disabilities are also sometimes undiagnosed.

The presence or absence of social support would seem to be more important than the presence or absence of learning disability in terms of the implications for parenting capacity. Social support and stress are negatively correlated amongst mothers with learning disabilities, "suggesting that the former may buffer the adverse effects of the latter" (Feldman et al, 2002). The larger, more recent and more helpful the support network reported by mothers with learning disabilities, the better their psychological well-being and the greater likelihood of positive parenting experiences (Kroese, et al, 2002).

---

[5] This, and other quotes from parents with learning disabilities, come from meetings held with parents as part of putting together this good practice guidance.

## Learning disability may also mean that a parent has some specific support needs relating to their impairment.

There is no clear relationship between IQ and parenting, unless it is less than 60 (McGaw and Newman, 2005). However, although IQ is not a good indicator of parenting capacity, cognitive impairment may mean that a parent has difficulty with reading and writing, remembering and understanding, decision-making and problem-solving, and this will create particular support needs. Indeed, most parents with these difficulties recognise that they need practical support and help with learning about child care (Tarleton et al, 2006). Parents who came to a National Gathering of parents with learning disabilities emphasised, for example, that they need information in accessible formats: "The information given to parents in booklets like "Birth to 5'[6] isn't accessible to parents with learning disabilities. We need information in pictures, plain English, and on tape" (CHANGE, 2005, p 17).

Parents' learning disability can also impact on their children's development in that, for example, their own language difficulties may inhibit their ability to stimulate their children's language development. This may mean they need advice about verbal interaction with children and/or additional support to children to help with language development (Cotson et al, 2001, pp 290-291).

## Children's experiences

We know very little about the experiences of children of parents with learning disabilities, other than that which concerns their parents' experiences of children's social care and the child protection system. A recent study of assessments of families affected by parental learning disability found that half the children had severe developmental needs and two-thirds were experiencing family and environmental disadvantages (Cleaver and Nicholson, forthcoming).

One study interviewed 30 adult children of parents with learning disabilities about their experiences of childhood and adulthood. These were children who remained with their families and no comparison was made with children taken into alternative care. Four themes emerged from the interviews:

- More attention needs to be paid to the protective factors which promote resilience amongst children and which "shield them from the potentially harmful effects of parenting deficits";
- Parental "competence may more properly be seen as a feature of parents' social networks rather than as an individual attribute". Outcomes for children are not just a function of the skills or attributes of their parents but also of the presence and extent of the skills of their extended family,

---

[6] This booklet, published by the Department of Health in 2005, is given to all new parents. CHANGE have produced a series of accessible books for parents with learning disabilities; see Resources section for details.

neighbourhoods and communities. There is therefore a need to pay attention, not just to parent education and training, but also to promoting and nurturing other forms of support;
- For most of the adult children in the study, their relationship with their mother and/or father was extremely important to them;
- Experiences of social exclusion ran through the children's childhoods and, for those with learning disabilities in particular, continued into adulthood. These experiences included: bullying and harassment at school and in their local neighbourhoods; poverty and unemployment; experiences of not being listened to by people in authority.

(Booth and Booth, 1997, pp 37-38)

A group of children of parents with learning disabilities (aged between 13 and 18), were consulted as part of drawing up this practice guidance. They identified bullying – at school and in their neighbourhood – as a major issue for them. The bullying included physical violence.

> "The police said if they get so many warnings they would prosecute but they didn't prosecute them and I think they should have. I don't understand why the police didn't do anything about it."

> "What helps is other people helping you be strong."

> "I just ran away from the bullying. The school didn't do anything."

The young people were asked about the help their families received from social care. They said that having people coming into the home to help their parents can be good because they help with tidying up and with decorating, and they also help with forms to get benefits.

> "The house looks a lot better." Did that mean a lot to you? "Yes, because I can have my boyfriend to visit." Was it hard having a stranger coming in? "No not really, I accepted the fact that they came in".

However, they also said that having people coming into their home can feel like an invasion of their privacy, there are often too many different people coming in, and their parents find it stressful.

> "I used to go out when the helper came in. I just didn't want to be there. There were so many different ones. It just felt they were invading our privacy".

> "They don't explain things properly and so you don't understand what they want....My mum gets stressed because she feels she's being pushed".

When asked what could be done better, the young people said that their families needed more help with filling forms and claiming benefits, and help with reading instructions such as recipes for cooking. They also felt that it generally took too long to get help and that their parents found it stressful when they were pushed to do things too quickly. The young people felt very strongly that professionals should listen to children more.

> "They should listen to us, instead of just taking the adults' point of view."

> "They should pay more attention to children."

> "A child's voice can make a lot of difference."

The Commission for Social Care Inspection consulted with children on the child protection register and reported that they felt that "many parents get too little help, too late". The young people "had strong views about the importance of helping parents, both in their own right and in relation to children's needs. They recognised that parents need clear messages about what needs to change, and help to do so" (Commission for Social Care Inspection, 2006, p.44).

## The role of the extended family

The role of the extended family is particularly important for parents with learning disabilities (Tarleton et al, 2006). The recent survey of people with learning disabilities in England found that those who had children were more likely to still be living with them if they were also living with other relatives. This was particularly the case for mothers – nine out of ten of mothers living with other relatives still had their children with them, compared to only four out of ten who lived in their own households.[7] McGaw and Newman conclude, from their survey of what works with parents with learning disabilities, that: *"The importance of family ties should be recognised and no actions taken that damage such ties"* (McGaw and Newman, 2005, p.59).

Extended family members may also provide an alternative to formal foster care. While "kinship care' is associated with greater stability for the children concerned and better continuity in terms of family and cultural issues than foster care, there is also evidence that kinship carers are likely to experience greater economic difficulties and poorer accommodation than non-kin foster carers (see Broad 2005). Some grandparents have reported that they are not only incurring costs of looking after their grandchildren but are also providing continuing financial support to their adult children" (Social Care Institute for Excellence, 2006).

However, there are some situations where the behaviour of family members adds to the risk for children, or where they 'take over' the role and tasks of parenting in ways which are detrimental to the parent/child relationship (Tarleton et al, 2006, p.64).

---

[7] These figures were provided by Eric Emerson in a secondary analysis of data from Emerson et al, 2005.

## Risk and child protection issues

Learning disability is not correlated to deliberate abuse of children: "... IQ by itself, is not a predictor either of the occurrence or of the non-occurrence of purposeful child abuse ..." (Tymchuck, 1992, p.168). Most concerns about children's welfare where parents have learning disabilities relate to inadequate levels of childcare and, when children are recorded on the child protection register, it is usually under the neglect or emotional abuse categories. This is "neglect by omission [and] is a result of a lack of parental education combined with the unavailability of supportive services" (Cleaver and Nicolson, forthcoming).

Even then, however, it would appear that learning disability is not the decisive factor. Recent research, which looked at 101 parents in contact with a learning disability parenting service, found that IQ of the main parent-carer was not correlated with risk of child protection concerns. On the other hand, parental childhood trauma, parent's physical disability and having a child with special educational needs were associated with high risk of child protection concerns. In addition, having a partner with a higher IQ than the main parent-carer was also associated with a higher risk of significant harm or care proceedings (McGaw et al, forthcoming). Where children's social care remove children from the care of families affected by parental learning disability, there are usually other difficulties faced by parents, in addition to learning disability. These include mental health and/or physical health problems, domestic violence, substance abuse, isolation from family and friends, poverty and inadequate housing (Cleaver and Nicholson, forthcoming; see also Brophy, 2006).

## The experiences of adults' and children's social care when responding to families affected by parental learning disability

Recent research has highlighted the difficulties that both children's and adults' social care experience when responding to the needs of families affected by parental learning disability.

## Children's social care experience a number of barriers in their work with families affected by parental learning disability

Children whose parents have learning disabilities account for only a small proportion of all children referred to children's social care, and, as a recent study pointed out, "it would, therefore, be unrealistic to expect social workers from children and family teams to have the expertise and specialist skills needed to work with people with learning disabilities" (Cleaver and Nicholson, forthcoming). Nevertheless, this study of children of parents with learning disabilities, whose welfare was of concern to children's social care, found "little evidence of social workers in children and family teams making use of professionals with specialist skills in working with people with learning disabilities or taking advantage of relevant tool kits or questionnaires and scales aimed at assessing parenting skills" (Cleaver and Nicholson, forthcoming).

> "They explain things in words you don't understand and you think help I don't understand what she's saying and you ask her to say it again and she uses the same language and I feel really stupid because I still don't understand but I don't feel I can ask her to say it again".[8]

This study also found that parents with learning disabilities are less likely than other parents to approach children's social care for help. Those who come to the attention of children's social care exhibit higher levels of family, environmental and child development problems than families unaffected by parental learning disability. In most cases, families were also experiencing other difficulties, such as poor mental and physical health, domestic violence, substance abuse, or the impact of having grown up in care. Many of the parents were also bringing up a disabled child.

The study challenged the idea that children of parents with learning disabilities are removed precipitately by children's social care: only 17% of the sample was removed over the three year period of the study and removal only followed a range of service provision. However, the researchers also conclude that there was very little evidence of on-going support to parents: most support provided was time-limited and short-term; most of the cases were closed but were then re-referred; and half the children who continued to live with their parents had their names placed on the child protection register during the three year follow-up period (Cleaver and Nicholson, forthcoming).

The difficulties that children's social care experience in delivering effective support to families affected by parental learning disability are reflected in the dissatisfaction with such interventions expressed by parents themselves. Parents with learning disabilities involved in another recent research project felt that children and families services:

- Did not understand people with learning disabilities
- Did not listen to them
- Expected them to fail
- Did not give them clear messages regarding what was expected of them
- Treated them differently from other parents who needed support
- Used their need for support, or any difficulties with their child, against them as evidence that they could not parent
- Used their previous history of having children removed, when they had not had adequate support, against them
- Provided no support once their children had been taken from them.
 (Tarleton et al, 2006)

---

[8] Parent with learning disabilities participating in a group discussion carried out as part of preparing this guidance.

"Once my daughter went into foster care, I was told I couldn't carry on going to the Sure Start parenting group because she wasn't living with me. But nothing had been decided for definite then. I felt I wasn't being given a chance to do better."

## Adult learning disability services also sometimes have difficulty in meeting the needs of parents with learning disabilities

A survey of community learning disability nurses found they did not generally feel adequately prepared by their pre-or post-basic training to support parents with learning disabilities (Culley and Genders, 1999). Although there has been an increase in the numbers of parents with learning disabilities receiving a service from Community Learning Disability Teams, there continue to be gaps in training (Tarleton et al, 2006).

Eligibility criteria for adult learning disability services often mean that parents with learning disabilities do not receive this service. For example, a study of a community learning disability team in an East London borough found that parents with IQ scores of 70-85 comprised a significant proportion of referrals but following assessment none were offered support or intervention in the medium to long term. At the same time, generic family support services were reported as inadequate to meet their needs (O'Hara and Martin, 2003).

## There are considerable barriers to communication and collaboration between adult learning disability and children and family services

There is much evidence of a lack of communication, co-operation and joint-working across adult and children's services, and between health and social services, where a parent has a learning disability (e.g. Tarleton et al, 2006). There is also evidence of children and families social workers believing that adult learning disability services do not pay sufficient attention to children's welfare; and of adult learning disability services believing that children and families social workers have little understanding of the needs of parents with learning disabilities.

"The two sides don't talk to each other and we're stuck in the middle."

The problems arising from a lack of co-ordination between children's and adult services are exacerbated where parents with learning disabilities have additional mental health, substance abuse and domestic violence problems. Evidence from inspections indicates that those who come to the attention of children's social care were usually not known to adult learning disability services and, in any case "because the thresholds of these services were so high these parents were unlikely to receive support from them" (Department for Education and Skills, 2003, p27).

## What do we know about what helps parents with learning disabilities and their children?

A National Gathering of over 200 parents with learning difficulties and those supporting them said these are the things that help people with learning difficulties be good parents:

- Accessible information about you and your baby's health, and about how to look after your baby
- Self-advocacy groups; coming together with other parents
- Getting support before things go wrong and become a crisis
- Being assessed in your own home, not in an unfamiliar residential family centre
- Assessment and support by people who understand about learning disabilities
- Advocacy
- Making courts more accessible
- Support for fathers
- Support for women and men experiencing violent relationships.
(CHANGE, 2005, pp.6-7)

There is considerable evidence that – for most parents experiencing problems – better parenting can be achieved if particular types of support, interventions and teaching methods are made available (Lloyd, 1999; Moran et al 2004). This is just as true for parents with learning disabilities as it is for parents who do not have learning disabilities (McGaw and Newman, 2005).

However, support, interventions and teaching methods all need to be appropriate to parent's particular situation and learning requirements. Parenting support which is suitable for most parents is unlikely to be delivered in a way which is right for parents with learning disabilities: "Service providers need to be wary of the argument that all parents should be treated alike and offered the same services as the mainstream population. Empirical research and clinical practice indicate that the majority of services are as yet inadequate in meeting the needs of families that may need extra, specialised help" (McGaw and Newman, 2005, p.14).

It is also necessary to be wary of assuming that what is best for most parents with learning disabilities will be best for all. For example, while home-based interventions show the highest rates of improvement for most parents with learning disabilities, there are some parents for whom the home environment is not suitable, perhaps because they live with their parents or other family members who exert too much control over them to enable them to learn effectively (see the summary of research in SCIE, 2005).

## What type of support is known to have good outcomes?

The following research findings have important implications for those planning and delivering services:

### *Self-directed learning can bring about long-term improvement in parenting skills*

A Canadian learning disability service has been providing a parent education programme since 1981. Self-directed learning was developed to teach basic child care, health, and safety skills to parents with learning disabilities. *"Controlled field studies with 33 parents found that 96% of the self-trained skills rapidly reached the same level seen in competent parents and were maintained for as long as 3.5 years".* Most of the parents also received other support services. These were families facing considerable difficulties: child protection services were involved in 79% of families and all were living below the poverty line (Feldman, 2004).

### *Group education combined with home-based intervention is more effective than either home-based intervention or a group education programme on its own*

Parents with learning disabilities who received a group education programme, together with home-based intervention, experienced a statistically significant improvement in self-concept and awareness in comparison with a control group of parents with learning disabilities who received home-based intervention only (McGaw, Ball and Clark, 2002).

A further analysis, of the same programmes, indicated that group work on its own was less effective than programmes which also included concurrent home-based interventions (McGaw and Newman, 2005, pp.35-36).

### *Parents with learning disabilities value both advocacy services and those which support self-advocacy*

Advocates are particularly valued by parents with learning disabilities in helping them to address the environmental disadvantages they experience, such as inadequate housing; making information and communication accessible; and to develop self-esteem and self-confidence (CHANGE, 2005; Tarleton et al, 2006). An action research project found that both individual advocates and advocacy support groups were positively valued by parents and by professionals with whom they were in contact. The following roles were provided by advocates:

- a witness to parents' dealings with officials and practitioners
- a buffer by fielding or deflecting matters that might exacerbate stress
- a voice making sure parents' views were heard

- a go-between improving links between families and services
- an interpreter putting information into language that parents could understand
- a listener enabling parents to talk things over
- a scribe helping with letters and forms
- a problem-solver helping families think things through
- a fixer sorting out problems of service delivery
- a conduit channelling the lessons learned in supporting one family for the benefit of another
- a sounding-board encouraging families to have confidence in their own ability to cope by helping them to work things out for themselves
- a confidante with whom confidential information could be safely shared
- an ally unambiguously on the family's side
- a sleuth tracking down and searching out information
- a mentor sharing general knowledge and experience
- an observer looking out for early signs of stress
- a mover and shaker making things happen.

(From Booth and Booth, 1998)

## There would appear to be some key characteristics of successful interventions

A review of research on interventions with families affected by parental learning disability concluded that practitioners need to draw on a range of possible interventions in order to put together support needed by a particular family. It is also important that long-term support is available when needed (McGaw and Newman, 2005, p.47).

In addition:

- Interventions should build on parents' strengths as well as address their vulnerabilities
- Interventions should be based on performance rather than knowledge and should incorporate modelling, practice, feedback and praise
- Tangible rewards may promote attendance at programmes, rapid acquisition of skills and short-term commitment
- Other methods of engagement are needed long-term
- Intensive service engagement is more effective than intermittent service engagement
- Programmes should be adapted to the actual environment in which the skills are needed in order to enable parents to generalise their learning
- Teaching should be in the home if possible and if not, in as home-like an environment as possible
- Factors in the family's environment which promote children's resilience should be identified and enhance
- The importance of family ties (for most – though not all – parents and their children) should be recognised and no actions taken that damage such ties

- Interventions should increase the family's experience of social inclusion rather than cause or contribute to their social exclusion.
  (From McGaw and Newman, 2005, p.58).

## Good co-ordination and communication between children's and adult services is key to effective interventions

A survey of research literature and examination of good practice concerning parents who have additional support needs generally (including parents with learning disabilities) concluded that the following measures are required:

- Collective ownership (across adult and children's services, and across health, social care, housing and the non-statutory sector) of the need to provide early support
- Financial structures which make transparent the benefits of providing support in time to prevent higher levels of need arising
- Clear procedures for appropriate referrals at the point of first contact
- Positive action to overcome parents' potential distrust of, and disengagement with, services
- Recognition that adult services should have a lead role in responding to parental support needs
- Recognition that housing needs can be a significant barrier to parenting capacity, and that disabled parents may need assistance in supporting their children's education
- Recognition that adult services have a continuing role of supporting parents when children's services carry out their responsibilities under section 47 of the Children Act 1989.
  (Social Care Institute for Excellence, 2006)

## Preventative approaches are key to safeguarding and promoting children's welfare

Best practice surveyed (Social Care Institute for Excellence, 2006) recognised that there is a continuum of prevention:

- Preventing unnecessary problems from arising by addressing specialist low-level parent support needs for information, equipment and assistance
- Preventing harm to children and family crises, which could lead to children being accommodated
- Supporting parents whose children have been removed from home, with a view to reuniting families where possible
- Post-crisis support aimed at anticipating and preventing future difficulties.

Addressing needs at all stages of this continuum requires:

- Changing eligibility criteria to take parenting needs into account so that responses can be put in place at lower levels of need than currently recognised within adult services

- Recognition that if parenting needs are responded to within the adult social care framework then children are less likely to be in need
- Recognition that needs relating to impairment/illness and disabling barriers must be addressed before making judgements about parenting capacity
- Bringing in children's social work expertise at points where – working in partnership with adult social care – it is possible to prevent further problems arising
- Having clear policies and procedures for joint involvement in critical situations with the aim of building resilience and ability to cope in the future
- Joint commissioning and joint working in order to provide flexible, ongoing support where required and anticipating changes in needs in relation to both impairment/illness and family circumstances.

## Conclusion

While there is evidence that families affected by parental learning disability experience a range of difficulties, it is also clear that most parents with learning disabilities are not receiving the type of support which is known to bring about improved outcomes for children.

## APPENDIX B  POLICY AND LEGISLATIVE FRAMEWORK

This Appendix sets out the policy and legislative framework for both children's and adult services. This framework provides the foundation for the features of good practice identified in the good practice guidance. Policy documents, legislation and guidance are *highlighted*.

We first set out the policy framework for supporting parents with learning disabilities and their children, and this is then followed by summaries of the legislation and guidance.

### The policy framework for supporting parents with learning disabilities and their children

Government policy is set out in Green and White Papers and National Service Frameworks. Two key aspects of the current policy framework are that:

- Disabled people and their families should experience equality of opportunity
- Adult and children's services, across health, education and social care, should work together to improve outcomes for children and their families.

The White Paper *Improving Life Chances of Disabled People* set out the general policy aim that all disabled people (including people with learning disabilities) "should have full opportunities and choices to improve their quality of life and ... be respected and included as equal members of society" (Prime Minister's Strategy Unit, 2005, p.7). The earlier White Paper *Valuing People* included within its strategy for people with learning disabilities a specific policy aim of: "Supporting parents with learning disabilities in order to help them, wherever possible, ensure their children gain maximum life chance benefits" (Department of Health, 2001, Sub-objective 7.4).

For children and parents generally, the policy aim, set out in *Every Child Matters: Change for Children*, is that every child, whatever their background or their circumstances, should have the support they need to:

- Be healthy
- Stay safe
- Enjoy and achieve
- Make a positive contribution
- Achieve economic well-being.
    www.everychildmatters.gov.uk/aims/

Local authorities are required to take the lead in drawing up strategic Children and Young People's Plans to identify where these outcomes need to be improved and how to bring about these improvements. The *Childcare Act 2006* places a duty on local authorities to reduce inequalities in well-being between young children in their area.

A key aim of current policy is to shift the focus from dealing with the consequences of difficulties in children's lives, to preventing things from going wrong in the first place. Three initiatives are intended to help achieve this: The *Common Assessment Framework* (CAF) is to help people in contact with children (particularly those in universal services) identify any additional needs children may have if they are to achieve the five Every Child Matters outcomes (see www.everychildmatters.gov.uk/deliveringservices/caf/). It also aims to improve multi-agency working by providing a clear process for a holistic assessment of a child's needs, taking account of the individual, their family and their community. All local authority areas are expected to implement the CAF between April 2006 and the end of 2008.

The *Lead Professional* is the person responsible for co-ordinating actions identified in the assessment and will be a single point of contact for children with additional needs who are being supported by more than one service or practitioner (see www.everychildmatters.gov.uk/leadprofessional).

*Contact Point* will be the quick way to find out who else is working with a child or young person and allow services to contact one another more efficiently. This basic online directory will be available to authorized staff who need it to do their jobs. It will hold basic information on every child, including the name

and contact details for the general practice where they receive primary health care, the school they attend and contact details of practitioners working with the child. Contact Point will not contain any detailed information (such as case notes, assessments, clinical data or exam results). The legal framework for the operation of Contact Point will be provided by Regulations made under section 12 of the Children Act 2004. Currently, information sharing is supported by practice guidance for practitioners.
http://www.everychildmatters.gov.uk/deliveringservices/informationsharing/

The *Integrated Children's System* (ICS) is a framework for working to improve the outcomes for children in need. All local authorities are expected have an electronic system to support the use of the Integrated Children's System. This means that children's social care staff are using electronic case records routinely to help them in their work. This is intended to help managers and practitioners collect, use and share information systematically and effectively.
(see www.everychildmatters.gov.uk/ics/)

The *National Service Framework for Children, Young People and Maternity Services* recognises that some parents, including those with learning disabilities, require:

- An early identification of their support needs
- Specialised forms of support
- Collaborative arrangements between adult and children's social care
- Department of Health and Department for Education and Skills, 2004a, pp.44, 69.

---

**National Service Framework for Children, Young People and Maternity Services: Core Standards**

Markers of good practice:

1. Multi-agency working to support parenting is outlined in any local strategic and service plans.
2. Information and services to support parenting (by both mothers and fathers and carers) are available and coordinated through local multi-agency partnerships.
3. Support for all parents with pre-school children is available from early years settings including nurseries, Sure Start local programmes and Children's Centres.
4. Parents whose children are experiencing difficulties (for example, because of learning disabilities and/or difficulties or challenging behaviour) receive early support and evidence-based interventions; requirements for local provision are identified in strategic planning.
5. Collaborative arrangements are in place between services for adults and those for children and families to ensure effective joint ➡

> assessment and support/treatment to enhance parent's parenting capacity and protect and promote the well-being and welfare of children.
> 6. Adults caring for looked after children have early, accessible, multidisciplinary support.
> 7. Primary Care Trusts and Local Authorities ensure that local parents are involved in the planning and delivery of services, with representation from all local communities and groups.

Where children are at risk of experiencing significant harm, a key marker of good practice is that:

> "A broad range of integrated, evidence-based services are available to prevent children and young people from being harmed, safeguarding those who are likely to suffer significant harm, and address the needs of those children who have suffered harm, at the same time, providing support to their parents/carers."
> (Department of Health and Department for Education and Skills, 2004a, p.146)

***Supporting People*** is also an important part of the policy framework for services to people with learning disabilities as many (including those who are parents) are either living in, or require, supported housing in order to live independently in the community. Supporting People provides housing-related support services. Local authorities are required to analyse the need for such services in their area, and develop (with relevant partners) commissioning strategies to meet these needs. The policy is also intended to encourage the development of packages of care and support jointly between housing, health and social care (Department of the Environment, Transport and the Regions, 2001, p.13). In addition, the ***Homelessness Act 2002*** places a duty on housing authorities to work with other agencies to tackle and prevent homelessness.

## The legislative framework for supporting parents with learning disabilities and their children

Legislation and guidance set out the responsibilities of organisations and the rights of individuals. The legislation and guidance for supporting parents with learning disabilities and their children is described below under two main headings: the responsibilities of adult social care; the responsibilities of children's social care.

It is also important to recognise that all the services referred to below – from the provision of information, assessment, the putting in place of services to meet assessed need, to action taken to protect a child from significant harm – are covered by Part 3 of the ***Disability Discrimination Act 1995***. This requires service providers to make 'reasonable adjustments' to ensure that a disabled person receives the same level of service as a non-disabled person.

In addition, both adult services and children's services authorities have a duty to promote equality of opportunity for disabled people (including parents) in their local population (Disability Discrimination Act 2005). This means that they should take pro-active steps to ensure equal access and equal treatment. This applies to all their functions, from drawing up Children and Young People Plans, commissioning services, assessments through to service provision.

## 1. The responsibilities of adult social care

Adult social care have responsibilities laid down by both community care legislation and children's legislation.

### 1.1 Information

The **Chronically Sick and Disabled Persons Act 1970**, Section 1(2) requires local authorities to make available information about the services they provide for disabled people; and to ensure that disabled people know about both local authority services and any other relevant services provided by other organisations. Whether or not someone is eligible for help from adult social care, they must provide information about other sources of support and advice.

The **Disability Discrimination Act 1995**, Part 3 gives disabled individuals the right to 'reasonable adjustments' to be made in the way information is provided, so that it is accessible to them. The **Disability Discrimination Act 2005** places a responsibility on public bodies to ensure that disabled people generally have equal access to their services (including the provision of information).

### 1.2 Assistance with daily living

Adult community care legislation and guidance lays down a framework for the assessment and meeting of needs for assistance with daily living.

Adults who come within the definition of disabled person within community care legislation, or who "appear to be in need of community care services" are entitled to an assessment of their needs (**Disabled Persons Act 1986**, Section 4; **NHS and Community Care Act 1990**, Section 47(1)).

**LAC(93)10** set out clearly that, when assessing whether someone is eligible for community care services, councils have a general duty not to 'fetter their discretion' and to consider each individual's circumstances (Department of Health 1993) This has been confirmed by subsequent case law. Operating blanket policies in community care services would breach the duty to assess an individual's need for services. General exclusions using a particular level of IQ, for example, are unlawful.

Policy guidance, **Fair Access to Care Services**, on how assessments should be carried out states that they should be "rounded and person-centred" and take into account housing, health and other needs (Department of Health, 2002a, Paragraph 35). The assessment should include what support is required in order to fulfil family roles and responsibilities. The assessor should recognise that "individuals are the experts on their own situation and encourage a partnership approach to assessment" (Ibid). During the assessment process, the person being assessed should be given every opportunity to express their views and, if necessary, assistance (such as an advocate) should be provided to enable them to do this (Ibid).

**Fair Access to Care Services** also sets out the framework for determining eligibility. Family roles and responsibilities must be taken into account in all four eligibility levels set out in the guidance. In determining eligibility, for example, 'critical' level includes: "vital family and other social roles and responsibilities cannot or will not be undertaken"; while 'substantial' level includes: "the majority of family and other social roles and responsibilities cannot or will not be undertaken" (Department of Health, 2002a, Paragraph16).

When determining eligibility, social care should take into account any risks in both the short and the long-term to the ability to carry out family roles and responsibilities. This consideration should cover not only risks to a parent not being able to fulfil their parenting roles, but also risks to children and other family members and carers. Adult social care are therefore required to take into account the possible effects of not meeting levels of need which currently do not qualify (as 'critical' or 'substantial' for example): "The council should have satisfied itself that needs would not significantly worsen or increase in the foreseeable future for the lack of help, and thereby compromise key aspects of independence, including involvement in ... parenting responsibilities" (Ibid. Paragraph 65).

If adult social care decide that someone is eligible for help a care plan must be written showing how any eligible needs will be met. Services/direct payments should be provided in good time to prevent problems arising.

**Fairer Charging Policies Guidance** requires that assessments of whether someone should pay anything towards the cost of a service/direct payment should be accompanied by welfare benefits advice, and should include help with completion of benefit claims and follow-up action (Department of Health, 2003b).

*1.3  Adult social care responsibilities concerning children*

When responding to a referral for community care services, adult social care have a statutory responsibility to check whether the person has parenting responsibilities for a child under 18 and if so to explore any parenting and child related issues in accordance with the **Framework for the Assessment of Children in Need and their Families** (Department of Health et al, 2000, Paragraph 5.11).

The ***Children Act 1989*** places a general duty on local authorities to safeguard and promote the welfare of children. ***Fair Access to Care Services*** affirms this by requiring adult social care to address their duty to safeguard and promote the welfare of children when determining eligibility for adult community care services. "Where appropriate, councils should consider the use of the ***Framework for the Assessment of Children in Need and their Families*** to explore whether there are any issues relating to children in need and their parenting. The Assessment Framework should be used if it appears that there are children in need. On occasions, within one family, it may be necessary to concurrently assess the needs of an adult parent using the appropriate format for adult assessment, and the needs of the children and related parenting issues using the Assessment Framework" (Department of Health, 2002a, Paragraph 9).

*1.4 Direct payments*

***Direct payments guidance*** states that, where someone has been assessed as having eligible needs for support, direct payments must be offered as an alternative to services to anyone "who appears to the council to be able to manage them (either alone or with help)" (Department of Health, 2003a, paragraph 47). Payments can be made directly to the person who needs the assistance, or to someone who will manage the payments on their behalf (paragraph 42).

The guidance also states that "Councils should not make blanket assumptions that whole groups of people will or will not be capable of managing direct payments" and that any judgements about whether someone is capable of using a direct payment should "be made on an individual basis, taking into account the views of the individual and the help that may be available to him or her. Where an individual does not agree with the council's judgement, they should have access to advocacy and, if available, arbitration, to ensure that their arguments are properly considered, or access to the council's complaints procedure" (paragraph 48).

The guidance stresses that "Councils should ensure that needs assessments for disabled adults include parenting responsibilities" (paragraph 113) and that direct payments can also be given in lieu of services provided under the Children Act 1989: "In the interest of the family and to avoid duplication, local councils should ensure the assessment process is streamlined and coordinated between adult and children's services and other relevant departments such as education" (paragraph 114). ***Fair Access to Care Services Practice Guidance*** states that "It will be important for children and family teams to have agreed policies and protocols with adult teams" on how to respond to the needs of families where the parent is disabled (Department of Health, 2002d, p.10).

Advice and support services should be available to assist a person to decide whether they want direct payments and to provide any help they may need in using them (Ibid., paragraphs 24-35). These support services should be accessible, taking into account particular needs of people with learning disabilities (paragraph 31) and advocacy services should also be available for those who need them in order to use direct payments (paragraph 36).

If a person is receiving at least £200 week (or the equivalent in services) from their local council, and they receive the higher rate of Disability Living Allowance care component, they can apply to the Independent Living Fund for a grant to meet any additional needs that they have for personal assistance. However, this cannot include assistance with parenting tasks.

### 1.5 Housing

Housing needs should be covered in a community care assessment and, if appropriate, adult social care should involve the housing authority in the assessment and care plan (***NHS and Community Care Act 1990***, Section 47(3)). Parents and children may have entitlements to help with accommodation if they cannot stay where they are living because of violence, or they are staying with family/friends, or they cannot live with all members of their normal households in their current accommodation, or their current housing conditions are damaging their health (***Homelessness Act, 2002***).

Households with a disabled adult or a disabled child may be entitled to assistance with adaptations to their property, through both the ***Disabled Facilities Grant*** system and the ***Chronically Sick and Disabled Persons Act 1970***. A guide on housing adaptations sets out the relevant legislation and guidance, and recommends good practice (Office of the Deputy Prime Minister, 2004).

## 2 The responsibilities of children's services

### 2.1 Information

The ***Children Act 1989***, Schedule 2, Paragraph 1 (2) requires local authorities to publish information about services available to children in need and their families and take steps to ensure that such families know about services (including those provided by the voluntary sector). The ***Disability Discrimination Act 1995***, Part 3 gives disabled individuals the right to 'reasonable adjustments' to be made in the way information is provided, so that it is accessible to them. The ***Disability Discrimination Act 2005*** places a responsibility on public bodies to take action to ensure that disabled people have equal access to their services (including the provision of information).

### 2.2 Services to children in need and their families

The ***Children Act 1989*** places a general duty on local authorities:

"To safeguard and promote the welfare of children within their area who are in need; and so far as is consistent with that duty, to promote the upbringing of

such children by their families, by providing a range and level of services appropriate to those children's needs"
(Children Act 1989, Section 17).

A child is 'in need' if they are unlikely to experience a reasonable standard of health or development without assistance, or if their health or development is likely to be significantly impaired without assistance, or if they are disabled.

When a child is, or may be, 'in need' an assessment should be carried out using the *Framework for Assessment of Children in Need and their Families*. Assessments should cover the following three domains:

- The child's developmental needs
- The capacities of parents/carers to respond to these needs
- The impact of wider family and environmental factors on parenting capacity and on children.
    (Department of Health et al, 2000)

This policy guidance recognises that there are some families where children do not meet the 'children in need' criteria, and parents do not reach adult social care eligibility criteria, and yet support is necessary in order to prevent problems arising:

> "For example, a mother with a mild learning disability may not reach the criteria for help from an adult services team and her child's standard of care may not be sufficiently poor to meet the criteria for children's services intervention. However, the failure to recognise the need for early intervention to provide support to the child and family on a planned basis from both children's and adult services may result in the child's current and future development being impaired".
> (Department of Health et al, 2000, Paragraph 3.58)

In these kinds of situations, the statutory guidance says children's social care should:

- "Recognise the cumulative effect of lower levels of needs;
- Ensure a high degree of co-operation and co-ordination between staff in different agencies;
- Take extra care to ensure that "there is an holistic view of the child and that the child does not become lost between the agencies involved and their different systems and procedures."
    (Department of Health et al, 2000, Paragraph 3.59)

The guidance also stresses that children "should not be expected to carry inappropriate levels of caring which have an adverse impact on their development and life chances" and where there is a danger of this happening, "services should be provided to parents to enhance their ability to fulfil their parenting responsibilities" (paragraph 3.62). Children and young people who are taking on a caring role are entitled to an assessment under section 1(1) of the *Carers (Recognition and Services) Act 1995* and this assessment must be taken into account when a decision is made about what services to provide to the parent. Children's social care should consider whether a child's welfare or development might suffer if support is not provided to the child or family. "Services should be provided to promote the health and development of young carers while not undermining the parent" (Department of Health et al, 2000, paragraph 3.63).

Where parents have particular needs relating to learning disability (and/or mental health or other specific needs), a specialist assessment may need to be commissioned while carrying out an assessment using the **Framework for the Assessment of Children in Need and their Families** (Department of Health et al, 2000, paragraphs 5.36, 6.18-6.22)

Where a child is assessed as being in need of services in order to attain a reasonable standard of health and development, a Child in Need plan should be drawn up, with the agreement of the child and key family members, detailing the services to be put in place and the aims to be achieved (Ibid., paragraphs. 4.32-4.37). The objectives should be "reasonable and timescales not too short or unachievable"; and the plan should not "be dependent on resources which are known to be scarce or unavailable" (Paragraph 4.34).

Direct payments can be made to parents and to 16 and 17 year olds, in lieu of services provided under Section 17 of the Children Act 1989 (as amended by the **Health and Social Care Act 2001**, Section 58).

*2.3 Protection of children from significant harm*

Where a local authority has cause to suspect that a child in their area is suffering, or is at risk of suffering significant harm, they have a duty to make enquiries to establish whether action is required to safeguard or promote the child's welfare and a right to compulsorily intervene if such concerns are substantiated (Children Act 1989, section 47).

Detailed statutory guidance about managing individual cases is set out in Chapter 5 of **Working Together to Safeguard Children** (HM Government, 2006). Children may be provided with alternative accommodation, with their parents' consent, in order to safeguard their welfare; or where considered necessary, the local authority may apply to the court for an Emergency Protection Order so that a child can be removed to a place of safety (HM Government, 2006, Paragraph 5.51). Where parents/caregivers are unwilling to co-operate with an assessment, the court can be asked to grant a Child Assessment Order (HM Government, 2006, Paragraph 5.68).

An initial assessment should be carried out using the guidance in the **Framework for the Assessment of Children in Need and their Families**. If there is reasonable cause to assume that a child is suffering, or at risk of, significant harm and section 47 enquiries are initiated, a strategy discussion must be held to decide if section 47 enquiries should be undertaken. A core assessment is the means by which the section 47 enquiry will be carried out, involving all relevant agencies.

Core assessments under section 47 of the Children Act 1989 should:

- "Build a picture of the child's situation using information from a range of sources
- Always involve separate interviews with the child (as long as their age/understanding allows this)
- Usually involve interviews with parents/caregivers, and observation of the interactions between parents and child(ren)
- Include interviews with those who are personally or professionally connected with the child and parents/caregivers
- Draw on assessments by other professionals"
  (HM Government, 2006, paragraph 5.62).

The guidance also makes clear that "Individuals should always be enabled to participate fully in the enquiry process. Where a child or parent is disabled, it may be necessary to provide help with communication to enable the child or parent to express him/herself to the best of his or her ability"; and "If the child is unable to take part in an interview because of age or understanding, alternative means of understanding the child's wishes or feelings should be used, including observation where children are very young or where they have communication impairments" (HM Government, 2006, paragraph 5.63).

Where it is decided that the child is not at risk, or is not at continuing risk, of significant harm, children's social care and other relevant agencies should always consider whether services are required to prevent problems arising in the future (HM Government, 2006, paragraph 5.73)

Where enquiries confirm that a child is suffering, or at risk of significant harm, an initial child protection conference should be convened, involving the child, parents and all relevant agencies. If the conference decides that the child is at continuing risk of significant harm, an outline child protection plan should be drawn up. A key worker, who is a qualified experienced social worker, should be designated to co-ordinate inter-agency responses. S/he also has responsibility for ascertaining the child's wishes and feelings. A core group of professionals should be identified who will develop the detailed child protection plan and ensure that it is implemented.

The overall aim of a child protection plan is to:

- "Ensure the child is safe and prevent him or her from suffering further harm
- Promote the child's health and development i.e. his or her welfare

- Provided it is in the best interests of the child, to support the family and wider family members to safeguard and promote the welfare of their child"
 (HM Government, 2006, paragraph 5.124).

The guidance sets out the procedures and responsibilities for reviewing the impact of service interventions. Where it is considered necessary, a local authority may apply to the court for a care order (committing the child to the care of the local authority) or supervision order (putting the child under the supervision of a social worker, or a probation officer).

## APPENDIX C   RESOURCES

### 1. Making information accessible

#### *CHANGE*

The Words to Pictures Team: a team of people with learning disabilities who work with an illustrator to produce information in an easy read format using easy words and pictures. The Team produces CD Roms (picture banks) of hundreds of pictures for organisations working with people with learning disabilities. Illustrators in CHANGE can also draw additional pictures as and when necessary.

CHANGE turns other organisations' documents, posters, flyers, leaflets, Annual Reports into an accessible format and people with learning disabilities provide training around how to make information accessible and how to use the Picture Bank CD Roms.

For more information contact:
CHANGE, Units 19/20, Unity Business Centre, 26 Roundhay Road, Leeds LS7 1AB. info@changepeople.co.uk Tel. 0113 243 0202; Fax. 0113 242 0220.
www.changepeople.co.uk

#### *Mencap*

Mencap's Accessibility Unit publishes a guide on writing accessible documents: 'Am I making myself clear?' www.mencap.org.uk/download/making_myself_clear.pdf

Mencap can edit documents or write accessible documents. This involves writing in plain language, adding pictures and images to support the text and looking at layout and design. They also produce scripts, record audio tapes and offer training on producing accessible documents.
Tel. 020 7696 5551
accessibility@mencap.org.uk
www.mencap.org.uk/html/accessibility/accessibility_services.asp

## Making websites accessible

Since October 1999 website owners have had a legal duty under the Disability Discrimination Act to ensure that services provided via the web are accessible to disabled people.

The British Standards Institution (BSI) has developed guidance on commissioning accessible websites. Publicly Available Specification (PAS) 78 is available from BSI Customer Services on 020 8996 9001 and by email at orders@bsi-global.com. It costs £30.00 plus VAT and is available in the following alternative formats: braille, easy read, accessible PDF, large print, audio, DAISY and Welsh.

Mencap publishes a guide on making websites accessible to people with learning disability. www.mencap.org.uk/download/webaccess.pdf

## 2. Joint protocols and care pathways: good practice examples

In 2007 the Social Care Institute for Excellence will be publishing a Resource for developing protocols for joint working across adult and children's health and social care to support disabled parents and their children. This will include a protocol template. www.scie.org.uk

An increasing number of agencies are developing joint protocols. Three are referred to in the guidance. Contact details to find out more are as follows:

**Stockport** Primary Care Trust, Stockport Social Services and Stockport NHS Foundation Trust: Care Pathway for Pregnant Women with Learning Disabilities.
For information, contact:
Denise Monks
denise.monks@stockport.gov.uk

**Essex** County Council Practice Guidance: Referral and Joint Working Arrangements for working with parents and carers who have a learning disability.
For information contact: Kate Evans, Service Manager, Family Centre and Family Group Conferences,
kate.evans@essexcc.gov.uk

See also, Commissioning Strategy for Parents with a Learning Disabilities.
For information contact: Steve Bailey, Participation Development Manager,
Steve.Bailey@essexcc.gov.uk

**Norfolk** County Council
Enabling parents with a disability or long-term illness: Joint Policy and

Protocol.
The protocol is on the Valuing People Support Team website: http://valuingpeople.gov.uk/dynamic/valuingpeople115.jsp
For information contact:
Joan Inglis, Project Manager, Support for Disabled Parents, joan.inglis@norfolk.gov.uk

## 3. Resources for working with parents with learning disabilities

The **Working Together with Parents Network** is a network of:

- Parents and carers with learning disabilities
- Professionals working with people with learning disabilities
- Statutory and voluntary organisations
- Other individuals or organisations with an interest in the area.

The Network aims to spread positive practice and to promote policy change, so that parents with learning disabilities and their children can get better support. http://www.bris.ac.uk/norahfry/right-support/

The **Valuing People** website has a section on parents with learning disabilities and contains a number of resources and useful links: http://valuingpeople.gov.uk/dynamic/valuingpeople115.jsp

## 4. Assessment Tools

*Parent Assessment Manual* by Sue McGaw, Kerry Keckley, Nicola Connolly and Katherine Ball. www.cornwall.nhs.uk/specialparentingservices/patientassessmentmanual.asp

*Learning Curves: The assessment of parents with a learning disability – A Manual for practitioners*, by Penny Morgan and Andy Goff. Norfolk Area Child Protection Committee.

*Learning Curves* can be downloaded from the Norfolk LSCB website, free of charge, www.acpc.norfolk.gov.uk. A4 wirebound paper copies are available from: Paul Shreeve (Norfolk LSCB Administrator), The Pineapple, 63 Bracondale, Norwich NR1 2EE (The cost is £8 including postage- cheques made payable to Norfolk County Council.)

## 5. Person Centred Planning

The **Valuing People Support Team** has a website devoted to person centred planning: http://www.valuingpeople.gov.uk/pcp.htm

**Circles Network** also provides a number of resources related to person centred planning: http://www.circlesnetwork.org.uk/what_is_person_centred_planning.htm

## 6. Parenting Skills Resources

**CHANGE publications:**

Planning a Baby booklet
You and Your Baby 0-1: a practical handbook for parents with learning disabilities to have at home for them to read.

For more information contact Frances Affleck or Philipa Bragman at CHANGE (contact details above)

**BILD publications:**

I want to be a good parent. Illustrated cards to help parents carry out a range of essential child care tasks. For use with support from health or child care workers.

I want to be a good parent
Five illustrated booklets giving practical advice for parents with learning disabilities:

> What's it like to be a parent?
> Children need healthy food
> Children need to be clean health and warm
> Children need to be safe
> Children need love

Both available from: BILD Publications, BookSource, 32 Finlas Street, Cowlairs Estate, Glasgow G22 5DU 08702 402 182 http://www.bild.org.uk/03books.htm

## APPENDIX D  BIBLIOGRAPHY

Booth, T and Booth, W. 1997. *Exceptional childhoods, unexceptional children*, London: Family Policy Studies Centre.

Booth, W. and Booth, T. 1998. *Advocacy for parents with learning difficulties*, Brighton: Pavilion Publishing.

Booth, T. and Booth, W. 2004. *Parents with learning difficulties, child protection and the courts*, www.supported-parenting.com/projects/NuffieldReport.pdf

Booth, T, Booth, W. and McConnell, D. 2005a. 'Care proceedings and parents with learning difficulties: comparative prevalence and outcomes in an English and Australian court sample, *Child and Family Social Work*, 10 (4), pp.353-360.

Broad, B. 2005. *Kinship Care: CareKnowledge Briefing 14,* www.careknowledge.com

Brophy, J. 2006. *Research Review: Child care proceedings under the Children Act 1989*, Department for Constitutional Affairs.

Care Services Improvement Partnership, 2006, *Who's holding the baby? Integrated health and social care child protection project*, www.bedsandhertswdc.nhs.uk/workforce_development/downloads/whb_final_report.pdf

CHANGE, 2005. *Report of National Gathering of Parents with Learning Disabilities*, Leeds: CHANGE.

Cleaver, H, Unell, I. And Aldgate, J. 1999. *Children's Needs – Parenting Capacity: The impact of parental mental illness, problem alcohol and drug use, and domestic violence on children's development*, London: The Stationery Office.

Cleaver, H. and Nicholson, D. 2003. *Learning disabled parents and the Framework for the Assessment of Children in Need and their Families*, Unpublished interim report to the Department for Education and Skills.

Cleaver, H. and Nicholson, D. forthcoming. *Children living with learning disabled parents,* Report for the Department for Education and Skills.

Commission for Social Care Inspection, 2006. *Supporting Parents, Safeguarding Children: Meeting the needs of parents with children on the child protection register*, London: Commission for Social Care Inspection.

Cooke, P. 2005. *ACTing to Support Parents with Learning Disabilities*, Nottingham: Ann Craft Trust.

Culley, L. and Genders, N. 1999. 'Parenting by people with learning disabilities: the educational needs of the community nurse' *Nurse Education Today*, 19(6), pp 502-508.

Department for Education and Skills, 2005. *Everything you wanted to know about pooled budgets but were afraid to ask*, www.everychildmatters.gov.uk/_files/1CB4E7D2B038F853D5523B49DD0E2693.doc

Department for Education and Skills, 2003. *The Children Act Report 2002*, London: Department for Education and Skills.

Department for Education and Skills, 2004 *Commissioning Checklist: A step by step guide to better planning and commissioning of placements and services for looked after children and children with special educational needs and disabilities in residential schools*, www.everychildmatters.gov.uk/_files/ 690C3686F70CD128BE1BBEF340B64CA2.pdf )

Department for Education and Skills and Department of Health, 2004a. *National Service Framework for Children, Young People and Maternity Services: Core Standards,* London: Department of Health. www.dh.gov.uk/assetRoot/04/ 09/05/66/04090566.pdf

Department for Education and Skills and Department of Health, 2004b. *The National Service Framework for Children, Young People and Maternity Services: Maternity Services,* London: Department of Health. www.dh.gov.uk/ assetRoot/04/09/05/23/04090523.pdf

Department of Health, 1993. *Approvals and directions for arrangements from 1 April 1993 made under schedule 8 to the National Health Service Act 1977 and sections 21 and 29 of the National Assistance Act 1948, LAC(93)10,* London: Department of Health.

Department of Health, 2001. *Valuing People: A national strategy for learning disability in the 21st century,* London: The Stationery Office. www.archive. official-documents.co.uk/document/cm50/5086/5086.htm

Department of Health, 2002a. *Fair Access to Care Services: Policy Guidance,* London: Department of Health. www.dh.gov.uk/assetRoot/04/01/96/41/ 04019641.pdf

Department of Health, 2002b. *Fair Access to Care Services: Practice Guidance,* London: Department of Health. www.dh.gov.uk/assetRoot/04/01/97/34/ 04019734.pdf

Department of Health, 2002c. *National Standards on the Provision of Children's Advocacy Services,* www.dh.gov.uk/assetRoot/04/01/88/93/04018893.pdf

Department of Health, 2002d. *Protocol on Advice and Advocacy for Parents (Child Protection),* www.dh.gov.uk/assetRoot/04/01/89/00/04018900.pdf

Department of Health, 2003a. *Direct Payments Guidance: Community care, services for carers and children's services (direct payments) guidance,* England, London: Department of Health. http://195.33.102.76/assetRoot/04/06/92/62/ 04069262.pdf

Department of Health, 2003b. *Fairer Charging Policies for Home Care and other Non-Residential Social Services,* London: Department of Health. www.dh.gov.uk/PolicyAndGuidance/HealthAndSocialCareTopics/SocialCare/ FairerChargingPolicies/fs/en

Department of Health, Department for Education and Employment and Home Office, 2000. *Framework for the Assessment of Children in Need and their Families*, London: Department of Health. www.archive.official-documents.co.uk/document/doh/facn/facn.htm

Department of the Environment, Transport and the Regions, 2001. *Supporting People: Policy into Practice*, London: Department of the Environment, Transport and the Regions. www.supporting-people.org.uk/policyguidance.asp

Emerson, E, Malam, S, Davies, I and Spencer, K. 2005. *Adults with Learning Difficulties in England 2003/4*, www.ic.nhs.uk/pubs/learndiff2004

Feldman, M.A., Varghese, J, Ramsay, J. and Rajska, D. 2002. 'Relationships between social support, stress and mother-child interactions in mothers with intellectual disabilities' *Journal of Applied Research in Intellectual Disabilities*, 15, pp.314-323.

H M Government, 2005. *Statutory guidance on Inter-agency co-operation to improve the well-being of children: Children's Trusts*, www.everychildmatters.gov.uk/strategy/guidance/

H M Government, 2006. *Working Together to Safeguard Children: A guide to inter-agency working to safeguard the welfare of children*, http://www.everychildmatters.gov.uk/workingtogether/

H M Government, 2006. *Common Assessment Framework for Children and Young People: Practitioners' Guide*, www.ecm.gov.uk/caf

H M Government, 2006. *Information sharing; Practitioners' Guide*, www.ecm.gov.uk/deliveringservices/informationsharing/

HM Government, 2007. *Statutory guidance on making arrangements to safeguard and promote the welfare of children under section 11 of the Children Act 2004*, www.everychildmatters.gov.uk/safeguarding/

Kroese, B.S, Hussein, H, Clifford, C. and Ahmed, N. 2002. 'Social support networks and psychological well-being of mothers with intellectual disabilities' *Journal of Applied Research in Intellectual Disabilities,* 15 (4), 324-340.

Lloyd, E, ed. 1999. *What works in parenting education?* Ilford: Barnardo's.

McGaw, S. and Newman, T. 2005. *What works for parents with learning disabilities?* Ilford: Barnardo's.

McGaw, S. Shaw, T, Scully, T. and Pritchard, C. forthcoming. 'Predicting the Unpredictable? Identifying high risk versus low risk parents with intellectual disabilities'.

Moran, P, Ghate, D, and van de Merwe, A. 2004. *What works in parenting support? A review of the international evidence*, London: Department for Education and Skills. www.prb.org.uk/wwiparenting/RR574.pdf

Morgan, P and Goff, A. 2004. *Learning Curves: The Assessment of Parents with a Learning Disability*, Norfolk Area Child Protection Committee.

Office of the Deputy Prime Minister, 2004. *Delivering Housing Adaptations for Disabled People: A good practice guide*, ODPM. http://www.odpm.gov.uk/index.asp?id=1152861

O'Hara, J and Martin, H. 2003. 'Parents with learning disabilities: a study of gender and cultural perspectives in East London' *British Journal of Learning Disabilities*, 31, pp.18-24.

Prime Minister's Strategy Unit, 2005. *Improving the Life Chances of Disabled People*, London: Cabinet Office. www.strategy.gov.uk/work_areas/disability/

Social Care Institute for Excellence, 2005. *Helping parents with learning disabilities in their role as parents*, www.scie.org.uk

Social Services Inspectorate, *A Jigsaw of Services: Supporting disabled adults in their parenting role*, London: Department of Health.

Tarleton, B, Ward, L. and Howard, J. 2006. *Finding the Right Support: A review of issues and positive practice in supporting parents with learning difficulties and their children*, Bristol: University of Bristol. www.baringfoundation.org.uk/FRSupportSummary.pdf

Tymchuck, A. 1992. 'Predicting adequacy of parenting by people with mental retardation' *Child Abuse and Neglect*, 16, pp. 165-178.

# INDEX

*References are to paragraph numbers.*

| | |
|---|---|
| ***A Jigsaw of Services*** | 2.5 |
| shortcomings highlighted | 2.5 |
| **Adoption proceedings** | 5.28 |
| litigation capacity, and | 5.28 |
| **Adult social care** *see also* Community | |
| care legislation | 2.7 |
| assessment of needs | 2.7 |
| current guidance | 2.7 |
| Direct Payments Guidance | 2.8–2.10 |
| ongoing areas of concern | 2.24 |
| *Putting People First* | 2.7 |
| supported parenting within | 2.7 |
| Wales | 2.22 |
| **Appropriate assessments** | 6.9 |
| | |
| **Bar Council** | |
| litigation capacity, approach to | 5.16 |
| | |
| **Care proceedings** | |
| expert psychiatric evidence | 3.14 |
| expert psychological evidence | 6.3 |
| **Case summaries** | 6.1 |
| **Children Acts 1989 and 2004** | 2.11–2.14 |
| children at risk of significant harm | 2.12 |
| ideology | 2.11 |
| minimum intervention | 2.11 |
| 'partner services' | 2.15 |
| personal factors, and | 2.13 |
| structural factors, and | 2.13 |
| supportive measures | 2.11 |
| **Choice of partner** | 3.4, 3.5 |
| **Community care legislation** | 4.15 |
| assessment | 4.16 |
| Chronically Sick and Disabled Persons Act 1970, s 2(1) | 4.20 |
| criticism of | 4.21 |
| discretion of local authority | 4.24 |
| eligibility | 4.22 |
| Health Services and Public Health Act 1968, s 45 | 4.19 |
| human rights, and | 4.15 |
| judicial review | 4.27, 4.28 |
| National Assistance Act 1948, Part III | 4.17, 4.18 |
| resources | 4.25 |
| substantial needs | 4.27 |
| support under | 4.15 |
| trigger for assessment | 4.21 |
| trigger for duty to provide services | 4.22 |

| | |
|---|---|
| **Community care legislation**—*continued* | |
| unmet needs | 4.27 |
| **Community care services** | |
| meaning | 4.16 |
| **Contraception** | |
| capacity to make decision | 6.5 |
| | |
| **Developmental delay** | 3.11–3.13 |
| parental learning disability, and | 3.12 |
| raising child with special needs | 3.13 |
| research statistics | 3.11 |
| **Direct Payments Guidance** | 2.8–2.10 |
| **Discrimination** | |
| social engineering, and | 6.1–6.5 |
| threshold test, and | 4.12 |
| | |
| ***Every Child Matters*** | 2.13, 2.14 |
| support needs of disabled parents | 2.14 |
| | |
| **Family Procedure Rules 2010** | A.7 |
| representation of protected parties | A.7 |
| | |
| ***Good Practice Guidance on Working with Parents with a Learning Disability*** | 2.15, A.9 |
| ensuring equitable treatment for parents with learning disabilities | 2.19–2.21 |
| failure of local authorities to act on recommendations | 2.20 |
| good practice in commissioning | A.9 |
| importance of | 2.24 |
| Joint Committee on Human Rights, and | 2.20 |
| key features of good practice | 2.17, A.9 |
| legislative framework | A.9 |
| policy | A.9 |
| policy shift | 2.16 |
| promoting children's best interests | 2.18 |
| purpose | A.9 |
| resources | A.9 |
| text | A.9 |
| | |
| **Harm** | |
| meaning | 4.5 |
| significant harm, and | 4.7–4.9 |

**Independent expert**
  letter to   A.6

**Judicial review**
  community care, and   4.27, 4.28

**Learning disabilities**
  access to services   A.8
  age of onset   A.8
  assessment of impairment of
    intellectual functioning   A.8
  assistance for survival   1.13
  benefits legislation   A.8
  British Psychological Society
    definitions   1.16
    guidance   1.10
  categories   1.11
  clinical definitions   A.8
  cognitive limitation arising during
    developmental period   1.15
  confidence limits in psychometric
    assessment   A.8
  core criteria   1.11
  criminal justice system   A.8
  defining   1.9
  Equality Act 2010   1.17
  gate-keeping   A.8
  'hidden majority'   1.8
  impairment of adaptive/social
    functioning   A.8
  initial assessment   1.9
  local government   A.8
  Mental Capacity Act 2005   1.18
  mental health legislation   A.8
  principles applicable in cases   6.4
  psychometric assessment   1.12
  related definitions   A.8
  social model   1.8
  statistics   1.19, 1.20
  systems   A.8
  use of term   1.7
  Vineland Adaptive Behaviour
    Scales   1.14

**Learning disabled mother**
  negative stereotype   3.2

**Learning disabled parenting**   1.1
  Baring Foundation research   1.31
  Booth and Booth research   1.22
  care orders   1.4
  case-law   1.2
  child protection   1.3
  Cleaver and Nicholson research   1.27
  contextual background to legal
    issues   1.32
  expectations   1.31
  government policy   1.2
  human rights, and   1.4, 1.5
  indirect discrimination in
    assessment process   1.25, 1.26
  law   2.1
  neglect, and   1.23

**Learning disabled parenting**—*continued*
  over-representation in care
    proceedings   1.2
  policy   2.1, 2.2
  reference to children's social care
    services   1.27–1.30
  research studies   1.22, 3.17
  social services, and   1.31
  statistics   1.19, 1.20
  UN Convention on Rights of
    Persons with Disabilities   1.6
  UN Standard Rules on
    Equalization of
    Opportunities for Persons
    with Disabilities   1.6

**Litigation capacity**   5.1
  adoption proceedings, and   5.28
  Bar Council approach   5.16
  common law test   5.5–5.7
  criminal proceedings, and   6.11
  determination at earliest possible
    opportunity   5.14
  fluctuating nature of   6.6
  issue-specific   5.8, 5.9
  Mental Capacity Act 2005   5.10
    enabling principles   5.10
    impairment or disturbance   5.11
    two-stage test   5.13
    understanding   5.12
  procedure   5.14, 5.16–5.18
  referring client to appropriate
    expert   5.17, 5.18

**Litigation friend**   5.1
  action for benefit of protected
    party   5.26
  application for order appointing   5.20
  appointment   5.19
  certificate of suitability   5.20
  departure from client's wishes   5.27
  FPR 2010, r 15.2   5.3
  lay person   5.23
  Official Solicitor   5.19, 5.24, A.4
  practical issues   5.26
  preventing step in proceedings
    without   5.4
  protected party as client   5.26
  role   5.26

**Maternal stress**   3.7
**Mental Capacity Act 2005**   A.2
  capacity, assessment   A.3
  capacity, definition   A.3
  Code of Practice   A.3
  helping people to make their own
    decisions   A.3
  nature of   A.3
  persons who lack capacity   A.2
  scope   A.3
  statutory principles   A.3
**Mental health**   3.8–3.10
  children, of   3.10
  learning disabled parents   3.9

## Index

**Multi-agency coordination and support**
    need for     3.14
**Multi-disciplinary research base**     3.3

**National Health Service and**
    **Community Care Act 1990**     A.1
    community care services     A.1

**Official Solicitor**     5.19, 5.24
    application for release of papers     6.7
    application to instruct further
        expert     6.7, 6.8
    Appointment in family proceedings     A.4
    guidance where invited to act as
        guardian ad litem or
        litigation friend     A.5
    role of     6.6
    seeking report from child and
        family psychiatrist     6.8
    severe budgetary constraints     5.25
**Operation to sterilise**
    best interests, and     6.5

**Parental childhood history**     3.6
**Parenting assessments**     3.15
**Parenting support**
    need for     4.1
**Procedural fairness**     6.9
**Protected parties**     5.1
    client, as     5.26
    meaning     5.3
**Psychological assessment**
    application for     6.10

**Research base**     3.1, 3.17
    implications     3.14
    statistical significance of different
        background variables     3.15
**Research findings**
    consideration by court     6.4
**Residential assessments**     3.15
**Right to respect for family life**
    interference with     6.9

**Risk factors**     3.4

**Significant harm**
    concept, effect of     4.10
    establishing     4.1
    harm, and     4.7–4.9
    lack of definition     4.6
    significant, meaning     6.1
**Social engineering**
    discrimination, and     6.1–6.5

**Threshold test**     4.1
    application     4.1, 4.2
    Children Act 1989     4.5
    criteria     4.3
    discrimination, and     4.12
    jurisdictional basis     4.4
    objectivity     4.11
    parents' religious and cultural
        beliefs     4.12
    reasonable support     4.14
    significant harm     4.6
    subjectivity     4.11
    unreasonable level of care     4.13

*Valuing People 2001*     2.3
    key principles     2.3
    needs of learning disabled adults as
        parents     2.4
    objectives for public services     2.4
    support needs     2.6
**Valuing People Now**
    A New Three-Year Strategy for
        People with Learning
        Disabilities     2.21

**Wales**
    Being a Family
        Parents with Learning
            Disabilities in Wales     2.23
    Statement of Policy and Practice
        for Adults with a Learning
        Disability     2.22